1. Pinacoteca Nazionale, Siena's art museum
2. Museo dell'Opera del Duomo
3. Accademia dei Fisiocritici
4. San Pietro in Castelvecchio
5. Palazzo Pubblico
6. Palazzo Salimbeni (Monte dei Paschi)
7. Palazzo Chigi Saracini and Accademia Chigiana
8. Palazzo Tolomei (Banca Toscana)
9. Logge del Papa
10. University of Siena: Palazzo del Rettore
11. Loggia della Mercanzia
12. Fortezza Medicea
13. Duomo and crypt
14. San Domenico

19. Battistero
20. Santa Maria di Provenzano
21. Sant'Andrea
22. Fonte Nuova
23. Fonti di Follonica
24. San Giorgio
25. Santuario di Santa Caterina
26. Fontebranda
27. San Sebastiano
28. Santa Maria del Carmine

A. Fonte di Pescaia
B. Antiporta di Camollia
C. Fonte d'Ovile
D. San Pietro alla Magione
E. Biblioteca Comunale
F. Costone
G. Vicolo delle Carrozze
H. Spedale di Santa Maria della Scala
I. Piazza Postierla ("Quattro Cantoni")
J. Orto Botanico
K. Cimitero Monumentale della Misericordia
L. Giardino dei Pecci
M. Porta di Giustizia
N. Arciconfraternità della Misericordia (Oratorio di S. Antonio Abate)
O. Vicolo degli Orefici
P. Synagogue
Q. Palazzo Piccolomini (and Archivio di Stato)
R. Oratorio di San Bernardino
S. Basilica dell'Osservanza
T. Oratorio di Santissima Trinità
U. Santa Maria in Portico a Fontegiusta

Siena

Jane Tylus

City of Secrets

SIENA

THE UNIVERSITY OF CHICAGO PRESS / CHICAGO AND LONDON

Jane Tylus is professor of Italian studies and comparative literature at New York University, where she is also faculty director of the Humanities Initiative. Her recent publications include *Reclaiming Catherine of Siena: Literacy, Literature, and the Signs of Others*, also published by the University of Chicago Press, and *The Poetics of Masculinity in Early Modern Italy*, coedited with Gerry Milligan.

The University of Chicago Press, Chicago 60637
The University of Chicago Press, Ltd., London
© 2015 by The University of Chicago
All rights reserved. Published 2015.
Printed in the United States of America

24 23 22 21 20 19 18 17 16 15   1 2 3 4 5

ISBN-13: 978-0-226-20782-7 (cloth)
ISBN-13: 978-0-226-20796-4 (e-book)
DOI: 10.7208/chicago/9780226207964.001.0001

The University of Chicago Press gratefully acknowledges the generous support of New York University toward the publication of this book.

Endpapers: Map 1. Siena's Contrade and Key Sites. Courtesy of Dick Gilbreath, Gyula Pauer Center for Cartography and GIS, University of Kentucky.

Library of Congress Cataloging-in-Publication Data

Tylus, Jane, 1956– author.
    Siena : city of secrets / Jane Tylus.
        pages   cm
    Includes bibliographical references and index.
    ISBN 978-0-226-20782-7 (hardcover : alk. paper) —
    ISBN 978-0-226-20796 (e-book)   1. Siena (Italy)—History.
    2. Siena (Italy)—Description and travel.   I. Title.
    DG975.S5T95   2015
    945'.581—dc23
                          2014023742

♾ This book has been printed on acid-free paper.

In memorium
Doris Anne Tylus
12/28/1929–12/2/2014

Contents

Illustrations

Ah, Florence, Florence. Dazed, the wayfarers
doze off during their stop.
Better set off again,
take the road to Siena, right away.
MARIO LUZI, *EARTHLY AND HEAVENLY JOURNEY OF SIMONE MARTINI*,
TRANSLATED BY LUIGI BONAFFINI

CITY OF SECRETS
INTRODUCTION

One of the few rare books I possess is an early guidebook to Siena by Giovacchino Faluschi. It was written in 1784 expressly for foreigners like myself, and by the late eighteenth century quite a few visitors had been coming to Siena on the Grand Tour. Faluschi mentions the "stupor" and "admiration" that visitors and citizens alike share on seeing the Campo, Siena's distinctive piazza; the Palazzo Pubblico; the Duomo or cathedral. His times dictated his tastes. He spends pages on the Renaissance and the baroque period but is dismissive of the fifteenth-century imitators of the fourteenth-century artists Ambrogio Lorenzetti and Simone Martini (for whom he also has little patience). But there is one painting of Lorenzetti's for which he shows particular fascination, despite—or perhaps because of—its execrable state after four hundred years. After a detailed discussion of the spaces of the Palazzo Pubblico—the public armory, the customs house, the prison—Faluschi turns to a room that once was called the Sala del Mappamondo, the room of the map of the world. This is, ostensibly, because you "can still make out there the tattered remains of a topographical map, on which once appeared in detail the entire Sienese

1

Fig. 1 ◆ Duccio di Buoninsegna (?), *Rendition of a Castle to the Republic* (1328). Sala del Mappamondo, Palazzo Pubblico, Siena. Photograph: Scala/Art Resource, New York.

state." The map was attached to the wall on a wheel that could be rotated by hand "so that whoever was standing near it could see whatever he wanted to see." This was the inspired invention of Lorenzetti, a disk just shy of five meters in diameter. Its skid marks can still be seen, etched into a painting only recently rediscovered in the 1980s of a lord turning a castle over to another man, presumably in the Sienese countryside.

I bought Faluschi's guide in a little antiquarian bookshop in Siena called Itinera, aptly named given that it's on Via dei Pellegrini. This is the road pilgrims took from the Campo to the Duomo, now replicated in their numbers if not necessarily their religious spirit by tourists from Spain,

Japan, Sicily, Texas. The owner tried to talk me into buying a more expensive version that came with foldout maps and pictures. I now wonder if those inserts might have included Faluschi's rendition of Lorenzetti's rotating disk, flapping around on the wall of the big room where Siena's elected officials met to discuss how much to charge for the wine or the chickens that came into the city from the countryside, or which roads needed repairing, or whether to go to war with Florence. Such were major concerns in fourteenth-century Siena. There has been much discussion about what Lorenzetti's map actually showed. All agree, however, that Siena would have been at the center, with the pivot directly behind (the pivot is still there where the map attached to the wall). But the center of what? "Lo stato senese"—the Sienese state—as Faluschi maintains? Or as the name of the room itself suggests, the *mondo*, the entire world, or at least the world as Lorenzetti knew it in the fourteenth century?

Sienese megalomania being what it is—dating back at least to 1260, when the Sienese unexpectedly defeated a large Florentine army in the now godforsaken town of Monteaperti—it's possible that Lorenzetti would have painted on his map not just Siena's then ample territory but the whole world. Elsewhere in the Palazzo Pubblico, and even in the same room, there are allusions to that world, still visible long after the map was pulled off the wall and unceremoniously discarded. When you walk into the corridor leading to the Sala and immediately turn around, you see a baby Jesus perched on the shoulder of an enormous Saint Christopher, holding in his little fist a tiny globe: such is the weight that the giant Christopher has unknowingly taken on in ferrying the holy family across a swollen river. And in the Sala della Pace next door, Lorenzetti's much more famous painting *Buon Governo*, "good government," though not a map, asserts Siena's importance in the world by way of form and image. A wedding procession winds through a city that is recognizably Siena, busy with teachers, craftsmen, and merchants, while a well-ordered countryside lies at its gate, full of farmers, travelers, and productive fields. This is the Sienese state as the model for good government, center of the civilized world, as long as it played by the rules explicitly laid out in the painting's iconography.

Which it did not and, especially lately, does not. The victory of Monteaperti was short-lived, and so was the stable government for which

Lorenzetti produced, some eighty years later, both his *Mappamondo* and his *Buon Governo*. Plague intervened, and so, eventually, did Florence, starving the city into submission in 1555. Florence quickly insisted that Siena be seen on Florence's terms. Giorgio Vasari chose the victorious siege of Siena (which led to Cosimo de' Medici's appointment as grand duke of Tuscany) for one of the monumental paintings in the Sala dei Cinquecento in Florence's Palazzo Vecchio. And in 1603 the Florentines rebuilt Siena's Porta Camollia, the northernmost gate, destroyed in the siege, with the Latin inscription "Siena's heart expands to let you in": supposedly directed to Ferdinand I de' Medici, son of Cosimo, who was visiting the town. The Sienese were insulted by the slogan, and they still find offensive what in other circumstances would be a gracious gesture of hospitality.

Florence has become the more hospitable city in the centuries since then. It is Florence, for example, that mobilizes tour buses and tourists and offers a multitude of hotels around the city as well as within it. Florence is easily accessible by the autostrada (with four exits) and by train; the Frecciarossa, "fast train," connects the city to Rome, to Venice, to the world. Siena has none of these things. Even if the train line from Siena to Empoli, built in the 1840s by a Sienese engineer, was triumphant evidence of the town's move into modernity, today it is much lamented as slow and inefficient. For reaching Siena there is nothing better than the express bus that originates in Florence—although, as if one wouldn't want to stay in Siena for dinner, let alone a concert or a play, the last bus heads back to Florence at 8:30 p.m., even on weekends.

Like the casual visitors of Faluschi's Grand Tour, I too had been dropping in on Siena over the years, as a day-tripper reliant on Florence's bus. Three years ago I began staying more regularly, weeks, a month at a time, always in one of several apartments of a genial landlord named Maurizio, whose building lies off Vicolo delle Carrozze. More aptly, it's *on* the *vicolo*, or alley. Going through the double doors into the dark lobby, one has the distinct impression of still being on the path—a lane enveloped by masonry and turned several centuries ago into a dwelling. A faint sign that you can still dimly read as you approach the little entrance to the *vicolo* from Via Diacceto (where ice—*ghiaccio*, or *diaccio* in Sienese dialect—used to be stored) intimates the previous use of my humble apartment: as stabling for horses or carriages behind a grand hotel that would have rivaled any lodging one would find in Siena now, save the five-star Continental on Banchi di Sopra. (There are no hotels in the neighborhood any more; you have to go across the valley to either the comfortable Hotel Campo Regio or the spartan Alma Domus run by the Dominicans, where each room has a balcony where dyed cloth once was hung out to dry in the sun.) The narrow alley continues past a single stall very much in use today, for the racehorse representing the *contrada* of the Selva, the neighborhood where Maurizio's apartment is located. Cared for and groomed like a prince in the days before the Palio, the city's famous horse race, the *barbero*, as he—or she—is called, occupies the stall only a few days a year. Just past the stall is a garden where the Selva's residents, the Selvaioli, sometimes have small parties; over the last year they've done much to make this untidy patch of grass more appealing. Our *vicolo* then bends around to the left, tunneling narrowly between buildings—it was no surprise to learn that this was once a place where assassins waited for their victims—then out onto Via dei Pellegrini.

Once this dark little alley would have gone straight, ending up in Maurizio's living room and the hallway in the building where our studio is, behind a great door that has, in fact, no address. When I arrived the first time to rent the apartment and was waiting for someone to let me in, an elderly passerby insisted for a good five minutes that no one lived behind those big doors that conceal a former street, shrugging as he went off to the Tuberosa, a club where retirees pass the time playing bocce and cards. But on the other side of those doors the lane continues onto a ledge that looks out over a valley—hence the name of the road it's on, Via Vallepiatta, "street of the flat valley." It once housed a convent and a leprosarium, and before that the estates of a feudal lord. Francesco di Giorgio Martini, a Sienese Leonardo da Vinci who like Da Vinci was a painter, architect, sculptor, and engineer, once lived down the street, at number seventy-eight. His house backed onto the *vicolo*, and he asked Siena's Comune for permission to build a small bridge to connect this house to an adjoining one; the bridge is still visible. Francesco is said to have designed the little church of San Sebastiano, once the oratory for the weavers' guild and now the chapel for the Selva, at

the end of Vallepiatta. The Selva's headquarters—its *società*—is housed
in the former convent. With a population that is the smallest of Siena's
seventeen neighborhoods, the Selva includes the Baptistery behind the
Duomo; part of the massive hospital of Santa Maria della Scala; Andrea's
newspaper stand; Alberto's fruit stand; the excellent restaurant Il Divo;
my friend Elena's house; the best *pasticceria* in all of Siena, called Il Magnifico; the bookshop where I bought Faluschi's guidebook; Caffè Diacceto;
and the Costone—the precipitous slope down to the fountain of Fontebranda where Saint Catherine had a vision of Christ. The Selva also once
contained an orchard that helped feed the orphans of the hospital and
the urban poor. Possibly this was the impetus for the neighborhood's
name—the "forest"—even as its emblem features a rhinoceros, an animal surely foreign to the zone, standing in the shade of an oak tree.

All writing is local: you must always begin someplace. On and off,
the Selva was my center of the world for three summers and occasional
weeks in between—a period when Siena was in the international news
far more than it had been since the Middle Ages, had there been newspapers or the Internet then. A town that keeps to itself and welcomes in
tourists with relative indifference—there are few hotels and its website
is poor—was suddenly, frequently, in the press, with several articles
in the *New York Times* alone in January 2013. These were not good reasons for being in the news. In the fall of 2012 it was disclosed that Siena's
Monte dei Paschi, the oldest bank in the world and Italy's third largest,
had lost almost a billion euros because of risky speculation. The bank
employs a large number of Sienese, and its Foundation had for centuries funded the town's museums, its university, the Palio, its champion
basketball team, and its Series A soccer team. (At barely sixty thousand
people, Siena was by far the smallest town in Italy at the time to boast a
first-rate soccer club, now at a lowly level D.)

The Italian government brokered a loan to save the bank, but only
if the Monte would pay a whopping 9 percent interest, scheduled to increase each year. The crisis prompted one suicide, the closure of one-
third of the bank's branches throughout Italy, and the layoff of all Sienese
employees over fifty. The mayor was subsequently chased out of office in
protest and the chair of the bank's board was put on trial. The university,
one of the best in Italy, had already been in crisis, since a mysterious hole

in its budget had been discovered in 2008. Scholarships disappeared, staff was let go, faculty were forced into early retirement; as with the directors of the bank, administrators are being questioned for possible coverups. All this was going on while Siena was a contender to become Italy's next "cultural capital of Europe," an honor to be bestowed in 2014. "Siena Cambia" is the political party founded by Siena's recently elected mayor: "Siena Is Changing," suggesting that the city can move beyond this moment; indeed, that it is already moving beyond it. More sinisterly, it's a command: Siena, Change!

The slogan is intended to counter not only the Sanesi's five-hundred-year dependence on a bank that has failed them—thus jeopardizing every aspect of Siena's cultural and political life—but the impression that for some time Siena has been a city remote from the rest of the world. When you look at Siena from a distance, it can seem immobilized upon the hill, clay buildings baked into the land. This is what most guidebooks, if not Faluschi's, now tell you: it is unchanged since Lorenzetti painted his *mappamondo*, before the Black Death, before the decline of Siena's international influence, before the fall to Florence; before the dull centuries of Medici and then Hapsburg oversight shut down its creativity and its energy; before the railroad and the autostrada abandoned it to a proud isolation in the center of Tuscany. This is part of its charm, one is told; this is why one must contrast it with livelier cities like Florence, or Rome, an inevitable comparison from which Siena inevitably suffers. It takes several days to see living cities, only half a day to see a dead one, mummified like the animals in the museum of the Fisiocritici, eighteenth-century academicians who prided themselves on capturing every species that flew or crawled in the Sienese countryside and embalming them forever in their haunt on Via Tufi. Thus you can prowl about on foot, fantasizing about the days of Duccio and Saint Catherine as you tour the thirteenth-century Gothic cathedral and the fourteenth-century Palazzo Pubblico, perhaps climbing its tower to stare down at the Campo with its arc of buildings capped by homogeneous brown roofs and colored in consistent earth tones. From there you might notice the sweep of the Sienese horizon south to Mount Amiata, sitting like a luckless ship on the borders of what were once the papal states.

But this stasis appears only in the bird's-eye view. Siena has long been on the cutting edge of innovation: first city to pave its streets and its main piazza, saving residents and horses from continual onslaughts of mud and worse (1298); first to have a constitution in the vernacular (1309); first to have a publicly funded university (1321); first to use the *cambiale* or promissory note (1720s); first to bar traffic from its center (1965)—much to the surprise of cousins of ours who on their honeymoon plowed into the Campo in their rental car and were escorted out by understanding policemen. Siena is central now to discussions about urban environments, and architects are fond of seeing in the city's strong sense of place a model for sustainable communities. These innovations are all based on movement: of people, of water, of animals, of things, of money, of sound, through Siena and around it and out beyond its enclaves, driving it to change in small ways and large, sometimes imperceptibly, sometimes dramatically. The Palio—won once by the Selva during our three summers there—is the most obvious example of this dance, as the 1930s painter and poet Corrado Forlin recognized in his explosive painting of the race, publicly exhibited for the first time in Siena only in 2009.

Forlin was a futurist, and futurism was all about speed, the love of energy and progress. Cynically one might observe that the Palio is a cyclical movement, with horses starting out and ending in the same place, in a race that has been run the same way year after year for centuries (technically only since the seventeenth). Less pedantically, one might note that the horse race run twice a year is only the culmination of drumbeats that galvanize the neighborhoods or *contrade* a month before, the dinners that bring the Sienese out into the streets, the processions afterward as the winning neighborhood's denizens carry the prize: the *palio*, a thin silk banner with an image of the Madonna. And there is all that goes on unseen throughout winter and spring: delivering food to shut-ins, shoveling the dirt of a *contrada* onto the floor of the maternity ward so that babies can be "born" into their neighborhood, organizing classes for young boys eager to be drummers. The Palio is not just about horses running in a circle. Forlin's image with its dashing horses and its spiked towers is a Palio on fire, and he himself commented on the gasoline or *benzina* of continuing ritual—bringing with it energy, and danger, and life.

A less obvious example of movement is the catalyst for this book. The Selva's neighborhood can lay claim to a part—but only a part—of

Fig. 2 ◆ Corrado Forlin, *Splendore simultaneo del Palio di Siena* (1937). Oil on canvas. Private collection, Venice. Photograph: Matteo Chinellato.

the institution that defines in many ways the paradoxes that lie behind Siena's survival and its life, the hospital or Spedale della Scala: the unassuming brick building across from the far more colorful Duomo. The Spedale was an orphanage, a place for assisting the poor, and a hospital, and it remained a hospital long after the final pilgrim had left, closing its doors only in 1985, shortly after the writer Italo Calvino, suffering a sudden stroke, was cared for and died within its walls. Walking up to it now

from the Selva's territory—either by way of the staircase that comes up
from Francesco di Giorgio's church and past the homes where wet nurses
for the orphans once lived, or on the less steep Via Franciosa—you can
see the two little tiles on the hospital's faded wall that mark the border
between two neighborhoods: the black and yellow eagle of Aquila to the
left, the Selva's green and orange rhinoceros to the right.

But if the outside isn't colorful (and in fact it once was: Lorenzetti
covered its exterior with images from Mary's life, but they suffered the
same fate as his *mappamondo*), there's at least one interior room that is
one of the most vibrant in Siena, for many years accessible only to the
sick and those who cared for them. Called the Pellegrinaio—the pilgrims'
quarters—it's a long cavernous space with windows opening on the hills
just west of Siena. Here the infirm lay under the watchful eyes not only of
lay doctors and nurses but of the dozens of historical and fictional char-
acters who cover its two main walls. Half of the paintings concern themselves with the hospital's legendary founding in the ninth century and
its at times tendentious history, the efforts of its founders and directors
to separate themselves from the stranglehold of the Duomo that towers
directly to its east. The other wall colorfully illustrates the many activities that would have taken place within the hospital's 350,000 cubic meters on a normal day in the fifteenth century. Much more than what we
would associate with a typical hospital today, this was a community,
even a small city, and the paintings on the Pellegrinaio's walls reflect
it: teaching orphans to write and sending them out to work and be married; feeding the poor a weekly meal; distributing bread to pilgrims and
widows; and, of course, tending to the sick. A particularly gory image
shows two physicians cleansing a gaping wound on a man's thigh, while
behind them another patient is being carried in on a stretcher.

Sienese are still alive who lay beneath these magisterial paintings.
Now one can wander into this hall, empty of beds, patients, and caretak-
ers, and see the startlingly clear images of doctors, matrons, and teachers at work. But after several visits to the Pellegrinaio, I noticed something that doesn't quite belong in this carefully planned affirmation of
what once went on in Siena's most crowded building. Squeezed between
two massive paintings dedicated to the early years of the Spedale—to the

left we see the building of its walls, to the right the investiture of the rector—a youth with fancy boots is just disappearing behind a decorative
pillar, while a dog at his feet is either crouching or jumping up toward
his master. Given the fragmentary nature of the painting that is not quite
or is no longer a painting, it's hard to tell. Behind them both, considerably faded, is what looks to be a mountain with trees and greenery. The
lad seems to be at the beginning of a journey rather than at the end, and
he's not particularly invested in his departure: he cranes his neck to look
behind him even as his boots are pointed resolutely forward. He has a
knapsack on his back, and behind it sails out something that looks like
a kite. That only part of his body is visible from behind the column—
other such columns throughout the room serve as boundaries between
the paintings—suggests that he was there first, that the scene is a par-
tial one, and that this is a hidden story overtaken by the more important
story of the hospital itself.

Who is he, where is he going, and why is he here in this room that me-
morializes an institution that—more than the Palazzo Pubblico with its
Lorenzetti frescoes of good (and bad) government, more than the Campo
with its famed Palio races of midsummer, more than the Duomo with its
miraculous icon of the Madonna—is at the heart of what Siena is about
and what it might continue to be in this era of change and transformation? All the other painted occupants of the Pellegrinaio are at home
here, in the welcoming rooms of Siena's Spedale della Scala. Why does
he alone set off on a journey?

Finding out who he is was the easy part. Why he matters is less clear.
Before the rector of the Spedale in the early 1440s commissioned the imposing, monumental cycle dedicated to the hospital's history and daily
life, there had been another commission, less monumental: the story of
Tobias. Deemed an apocryphal book by Jewish elders and reformers beginning with Luther, who found it a "charming fable," the story is nonetheless still found in Roman Catholic Bibles, and in any case it would
have been in Old Testaments of the 1440s. Written during the Jewish di-
aspora of the late second or third century BCE, the tale survives in two
versions, in Hebrew and in Greek. It captures the quality of life in those
centuries for Jews in exile who lacked a center, needing to make lives

Fig. 3 ◆ Vecchietta (?) (Lorenzo di Pietro), fragment from the "Cycle of Tobias" (?) (1440s). Pellegrinaio, Spedale della Scala di Santa Maria, Siena. With the permission of the Comune di Siena.

for themselves in inhospitable places or, when that failed, doing what needed to be done by going elsewhere.

The story goes like this: A devout Jew—the eponymous Tobias—performs works of charity among his fellow Jews, including lending a large sum of money to Gabael, a distant relative. When hardship falls on Tobias—he becomes blind and can no longer work—he asks his son, "little" Tobias or Tobiolo, to claim the money for him in the far-off city where Gabael now lives. The boy goes off on the voyage accompanied by a guide who only at the end reveals himself as the angel Raphael. En route they experience great adventures: they slay a giant fish, exorcise a demon, find a wealthy wife for Tobiolo, retrieve the money from a grateful Gabael, then safely return home to Tobiolo's anxious parents, where Tobiolo applies the entrails of the fish to his father's sightless eyes and cures his blindness. (In a touching detail, the dog runs ahead so the aging Tobias will know his son has returned safely.) The Pellegrinaio's fragment lets us only imagine the presence of the angel urging Tobiolo on, a ghostly figure now consigned to oblivion, vanished behind the new story of the hospital's founding by painters who came in to do something different. That one of those painters, Lorenzo di Pietro, nicknamed Vecchietta, had also been involved in the Tobias commission makes me wonder if he purposely left us this single trace between imposing testaments to the hospital's earthly success, a remainder of an ancient Hebrew fable supplanted by the concrete existence of this Christian institution itself.

Yet perhaps Vecchietta preserved this allusion to a story about two Tobiases not only because of its direct relation to the Spedale—it is a tale about healing—but because of its relevance for Siena. (Florence's Bigallo, which also sits in the piazza of its Duomo and served as a charitable organization, features a decaying Tobias fresco from the 1360s—perhaps one reason Siena's rector decided to change course.) Tobiolo goes out to get back what his charitable father lent a relative, and he returns with sevenfold—a bride, horses, camels, money, and a cure for his father's blindness. This unabashed interaction of the worldly and divine revisits and rewrites some of the great stories of the Old Testament—Jonah, Jacob, Job—to wind up with a happy ending, but only because the young Tobias and his guardian angel dare to traverse worlds and thresholds, wrestling with demons and leviathans outside the walls of the city and returning in triumph. Far from being a city isolated unto itself, Siena has ensured its survival over the centuries by giving to the outside and also ferociously depending on it. Could these journeys and otherworldly interactions help make sense of what Siena has long been about?

This book charts a movement from the earthly to the divine as I return to my own wanderings under, across, and outside Siena and back again over the past three years: from its tunnels supervised in the 1470s by the Selvaiolo Francesco di Giorgio Martini, to its streets, churches, and Spedale filled by the crush of pilgrims, to the meandering network of roads taken by its merchants and bankers out into the fairs and capitals of Europe, to the circling route the horses run for the Palio, to the paths to heaven sought by its saints. Siena the provisional center, marked by highways and byways boring thirty meters deep into the soil, out into the *stato senese*, and up into heaven like the spokes of a wheel. Here where nothing happens, everything happens: daily life, the stuff of novelists and journalists. Starlings swarm around the Torre del Mangia, high-school students buy two slices of pizza for a euro on the Via delle Terme on their way home from school, workers pour asphalt on the ring road outside Fontebranda, grandmothers intone the 5:30 rosary at the church of San Giorgio. If it seems this is a place where time has stopped, one simply has to look deeper: the ice cream shop that closed, to our dismay, reopened two doors down; our fruit seller had to sell her store to a man from Staggia after her father died and she left to take over his shop near the Pinacoteca. A new escalator pops up from the train station (derided by one taxi driver as a waste of public funds, since it brings you not into the heart of the city but far from Porta Camollia, and in any case reduces tourists' reliance on taxis). The Teatro dei Rinnovati reopens in the Palazzo Pubblico. A mayor is ousted and the town is provisionally placed in the hands of a prefect from Perugia, who then loses the election for mayor to a man from Monteriggioni. And the Monte dei Paschi, which had always seemed like an eternal source of financial support even for those who weren't careful enough about their budgets—"Babbo [Daddy] dei Paschi"—teeters toward collapse.

Siena swings into view at the last minute as the bus from Florence rounds the final corner from the Medici's Fortezza and you see before you San Domenico with its bare facade like so many other Sienese churches and behind it, high on its hill, the Duomo with its gaily striped tower, its white-and-black stripes looking as though they've been painted on. And between Duomo and San Domenico lies the gaping valley of the Selva, from which I've tried to know a city that, like Tobias, is good at keeping secrets.

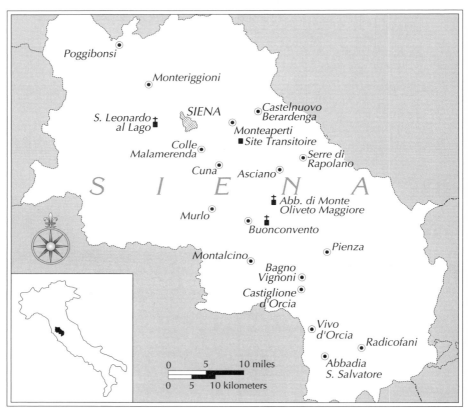

Map 2 ◆ The Province of Siena. Courtesy of Dick Gilbreath, Gyula
Pauer Center for Cartography and GIS, University of Kentucky.

TERRA AND ACQUA

1 The day before I left Siena in the summer of 2012 there was an earthquake, though not in the city proper. The town of Castelnuovo Berardenga, some thirty kilometers away, was at the epicenter, and the tremors measured only 2.7 on the Richter scale. When they came at roughly 10:00 p.m., some friends and I had just left the subterranean quarters of the restaurant Il Divo, beneath the base of the Duomo, where the waitress showed us an early medieval wall and, farther below, what she claimed were Etruscan tombs. We went on to get ice cream with the rest of Siena and paused briefly in the Campo in this period between Palios. It was newly bereft of the *terra*— the dirt—packed down ten days earlier for the first race. Brought in from warehouses outside the city where it is mixed to a special blend, the earth is dumped along the Campo's perimeter and bulldozed to an even layer. Throughout the week before the Palio it is lovingly watered, as though the workers were hoping flowers might burst forth from the bricks beneath. But now only the white-and-black colors of Siena's flag, the *balzana*, waved in a night breeze from the top of the Palazzo Pubblico. It was a cool evening. No one noticed, or thought to notice, tremors coming from the Chianti region.

For more than two centuries, the city has been spared the destruction wrought by powerful earthquakes. Small ones come with surprising regularity. Two weeks earlier, at almost the identical hour, and with the same magnitude, tremors had struck not far from Castelnuovo. But May saw the tragic earthquakes of Emilia Romagna—Mirandola, Mantua, Bologna—and L'Aquila and Assisi are still in recent memory. It could happen here again as it did on May 26, 1798, when Siena was left in a "chaos of debris," as one contemporary observer put it. It was a miracle, he and others surely thought, that only four people died. The earthquake drove Pope Pius VI from the monastery of Sant'Agostino, where he'd been in hiding for several months from the Jacobin forces attacking Rome, forcing him northward to Florence. It tore off the facade of San Cristoforo, a now unassuming church on Banchi di Sopra that had served as Siena's first town hall. It crushed Fonte Oliva, the town's easternmost fountain, with its three defensive arches built in 1246. And it halved the belltower of the Dominicans' church on the other side of town, although thanks to quick-thinking friars the head of Saint Catherine, still venerated in a side chapel, was saved.

The response of Ferdinand III, grand duke of Tuscany, was reassuringly swift. Not only were subsidies made available to the poor and tents and temporary shelters erected outside Siena's walls for the newly homeless, but a far-reaching architectural plan was put in place. The irregularities of Siena's buildings—many of them hundreds of years old—would be corrected. Unstable towers came down, upper floors were demolished and porches pulled apart; windows were all made to similar scale and arches constructed across roads to stabilize leaning buildings. Thus the arch in the sloping Via della galluzza under which many a tourist poses for a picture is not medieval at all. It's modern, an early nineteenth-century support funded by Austrians.

The earthquake became the precipitating event for much of what is perceived today as the at times monotonous regularity of Siena's buildings, a regularity that contributes to a sensation shared by all visitors to Siena: how easy it is to get lost. Perhaps more than in most places, Siena's distinctive topography has contributed to its destiny as a town where, as my son once remarked, you almost always know where you're going, but you don't always know where you are. This is the feeling of Siena's streets, almost all of them. Especially once you have left the main artery on the city's easternmost ridge, you encounter a complex and intertwined series of passageways. You can't see in front of you because the streets curve, working their way around a hill or one of the city's old walls; you can't see behind you, so you succumb to a constant sense of suspense that pushes you on. Nor is there vertical visibility. The streets can seem like galleries or tunnels as the facades of palaces and shops arch over you, blocking your view, so you welcome the sudden break to see down a side alley or sometimes, as in Via Giovanni Duprè, to catch a stunning view of the countryside that slopes below you when you'd forgotten it was there at all. There are improbable exits and entrances. Houses begin centimeters from the path your feet take, and suddenly a door swings open into a kitchen or living room, then just as suddenly swings closed before you can get a look inside. The less-traveled roads offer the most surprises: the descent and then the climb behind the Spedale, the neighborhood of San Francesco, the narrow Via del Sole that opens into the gentle hill toward Santa Maria dei Servi, and you turn from the steps in front of the church to see a breathtaking vision of Siena to your north.

"Se siete camminatori," "If you're hikers," a Sienese woman from the Selva once told two elderly tourists, rather sternly, "you can take this route": one with ups and downs, precipitous rises and falls, streets that careen downward to commit suicide near Fontebranda (the lugubrious description used by the lugubrious writer Federigo Tozzi early in the previous century). And the contemporary artist Antonio Possenti has illustrated these slippery streets that land you in the valley of the fountain with its butchers and tanners.

That Fontebranda was one of the centers of Siena's economic and social life when Tozzi left its "noxious air" for Rome in 1916 is testament to another feature of Sienese geology. There is no river running through Siena, with reliable crossings that might punctuate your visit, no neighborhoods that might be easily discernible like the Oltrarno in Florence or Trastevere in Rome. Unlike these towns that originated and grew up around their rivers, Siena with its curving, misaligned streets does not

Fig. 4 ◆ Antonio Possenti, *Maiale* (2006). Oil on panel. Courtesy of the artist.

bear the stamp of a Roman *castrum*, with a prominent grid of roads at right angles. But if the strange experience of Siena's streets is partly a product of nature, it's also due to Siena's curious history: the centuries of human efforts put into urbanizing such a difficult landscape and a passionate attachment to those efforts.

Siena's tenacious fidelity to its attempts to reconcile life with the hills and their lack of water is another reason for one's constant disorientation. "*Inglobare*," awkwardly translated as "inglobing," is heard frequently in reference to town planning and architecture, referring to the Sienese habit of literally encapsulating an old structure within a new one, incorporating the extraneous without canceling it from the face of the earth. Eight circuits of walls have enclosed the city over the past millennium, and the original ones can still be found, as in Il Divo. Most cities have torn down their old walls, as Florence did on the eve of becoming the capital of the new nation of Italy in 1865. But the Sienese are dogged about preserving the past rather than destroying it, except for the exceptional instance of the 1798 earthquake and its aftermath. Their archives, for example, are among the richest in Italy. They contain, among other documents, the earliest example of writing in an Italian vernacular; there are records from the eighth century of real-estate transactions and from the eleventh of trades at fairs. These administrative capabilities, arguably obsessions, try to control the controllable, which in this harsh landscape was not very much. Maintaining the old walls means maintaining another kind of archive, a record of the city's erratic formation and concessions to nature, testimony of the sheer difficulty of constructing a ring of walls over a jumble of hills.

Or as the Renaissance painter and mapmaker Francesco Vanni put it, *strane colline*, "strange hills." Three, to be precise. They rise slightly over three hundred meters, just high enough to capture the breezes that never reach the Florentine valley during its humid summers, ensuring few mosquitoes. Vanni was not using this term idly. In the years after Siena fell to Florence, Sienese had the choice of retreating into a pouting defense of their superiority or attempting to work out a modus operandi with their conquerors. Vanni, born in 1564, less than a decade after the defeat, did both. Florence had just been the subject of one of the first examples of axonometric perspective ever created: an urban plan based on an exact correspondence in scale between reality and design. The mapmaker was an Olivetan monk named Stefano Bonsignori, who had patiently drafted his detailed map of Florence for Francesco de' Medici, oldest son of Cosimo, the man who defeated Siena. His map first appeared in 1584 and was reprinted in Siena ten years later—prompting Vanni to petition the Medici to undertake a similar project for his own city.

The comparison is instructive. Bonsignori's map shows a rationally ordered city, modeled on the Roman grid and with all buildings neatly labeled and explained. In Bonsignori's "New Topography"—and it was indeed new—the Arno bisects the rectangular Roman *castrum*, inhabiting the dead center of the grid where Florence had its earliest walls, long ago dismantled. And within that grid, carefully delineated—*accuratissime delineata*, as Bonsignori promises—block after block of houses and courtyards stretch across the city, punctuated at regular intervals by recognizably Florentine structures: the Piazza della Signoria (with an off-scale statue of Cosimo de' Medici astride a horse, just as tall as the tower), the churches of San Lorenzo and Santa Croce, the Duomo dwarfing the Baptistery alongside it. It is a world of clarity and order and, one must imagine, to the viewer—particularly Francesco de' Medici—of deep satisfaction. Not a single person disrupts this exercise in architectural rationality that makes us Gullivers looming over miniature buildings, bridges, and farms, with one exception: Bonsignori himself. Holding an enormous quadrant, he sits poised above Florence in the hills southeast of the city, having found near San Miniato an appropriate perch from which to measure his town.

But for Siena, itself on hills, there could be no such perch. Thus Vanni appealed to Francesco's brother Ferdinando, who had taken over as grand duke when Francesco and his mistress/wife suddenly died in 1589, some say of poison though, as recent DNA tests suggest, it was probably malaria. Vanni deliberately compares his project with that of the monk Bonsignori, reminding Ferdinando that the mapmaker of Florence received two hundred scudi for his efforts, along with "vittles." But he is mainly interested in impressing Ferdinando with the difficulties of his enterprise. Whereas Bonsignori had a flat city to map, Vanni has a mountainous or at least a hilly one. The scholar Letizia Galli would have us imagine Vanni "constrained to climb up on a bewildering array of towers and other high points throughout the city to draw and measure houses, streets, churches and palaces, even to calculate the 570 *braccia* [arm's length, roughly a meter] of the Piazza del Campo."

Evidently Ferdinando was won over, or perhaps Vanni simply plunged ahead without the assurance of the grand duke's cash. His map, like Bonsignori's, gives us palaces, *piazze*, homes, and gardens. But in contrast to Florence's straight roads, the Sienese roads flow and curve, bending down and around to bottoms of hills where a gibbet awaits. The walls seem to come and go, disappearing into fields or ridges of trees; Siena's boundaries are more porous than Florence's, even as Vanni carefully marks out all eight exterior gates, barriers by night, entryways by day.

There are no inhabitants in Vanni's city either—and no representation of Vanni. But the map is crowded in a way Bonsignori's is not. Above Siena floats not a lone cartographer, but an entire choir of Sienese saints, *beati*, bishops, and hermits, with Mary at their center, beckoning down to Catherine on her left, San Bernardino on her right, and the city that called itself Sena Vetus Civitas Virginis—Siena, Ancient City of the Virgin—below. Beneath the saints, who occupy a full quarter of the map and thus present their own typography of Siena's sacred history, the city unfurls like a rose slowly opening its petals. Its one main artery loops down the center to end amid a swirl of lesser roads, its upper half bisected by other ribbons that form concentric circles around the Duomo or the Campo to vanish in the rural spaces beyond as countryside and orchards merge with the city.

Whereas the map of Florence is resolutely horizontal—one can easily take in all of the city by climbing above it—Vanni's map is emphatically vertical, with the campanile of the Duomo arching up toward Porta Tufi and the Porta in turn arching up to touch heaven, or at least the toe of S. Iohannes Mart., martyr for the church. Unlike Florence, flattened by a monk who holds a quadrant at a right angle to bind the city securely to terrestrial affairs, Siena rises improbably upward. Its three hills are all shifted to the southern side of the city. We become spectators at its northern base, gazing up from the (then battered) Porta Camollia near a gibbet and the oversized Medici fort, to San Domenico and San Francesco on opposing sides of the city, to the Duomo and the Campo—a dark smudge not quite in the map's center—and then to the several southern gates that lead us not so much outward toward Rome as up to the panoply of saintly people. Most of them are otherwise engaged, but a few— Saint Peter Martyr, Mary—cast an affectionate, perhaps anxious eye below. As it introduces a coherent street plan if not scientifically correct perspective, Vanni's map perpetuates the Sienese legacy that Florence could never claim. In providing a southern orientation, Vanni does not so much cater to his would-be Florentine patron, a Medici looking south from Florence, as suggest how Siena itself looks south: toward Rome.

Rome was in fact where Vanni and other painters of his generation—
the first generation to be born into a Siena that was no longer free—
spent their years in training, rather than in Florence, where Giorgio Vasari had recently painted Siena's defeat for the Palazzo Vecchio. But the
geological legacy is even more suggestive. Rome is Siena's topographical twin, and Jerusalem is too. These are sacred cities, cities on a hill, or
more precisely, hills—*queste strane colline*, as Vanni refers to them in his
letter. The hills, and Siena's disposition to save everything built on them,
turned the town into an essentially unmappable space. In the absence
of a master planner, with the conglomeration of buildings and arch-
ways and walls and the "inglobing" of old walls and old streets, the town
emerged as something appealingly random, a living organism that grew
in endearing and unpredictable ways. But the hills also gave the Sienese
a sense of purpose, allowing them to imagine a sacred dimension to their
chosen site, removed from the ordinary and profane. They are closer to
God, like a Babylonian ziggurat or the Tower of Babel (a fabulous painting of which, by an unknown Flemish artist, is in the Pinacoteca, Siena's
main art museum, its peak disappearing into striated mists) or Mount
Sinai, where Moses received the Ten Commandments. You can find
Mount Sinai in Siena too. The sixteenth-century artist Domenico Beccafumi, beloved by Faluschi, designed scenes from the life of Moses for
the pavement of the cathedral, directly beneath the dome, featuring the
mountain as both protagonist and looming backdrop as Moses descends
to his faithless people.

We don't know if Vanni was ever adequately paid for his labors, but
his map was printed innumerable times over the next several centuries,
usually without the reassuring saints at the top. (Most recently I spotted it in the stairway of the Osteria dell'Eremita, the Hermit's Restaurant across from Sant'Agostino, since—regrettably—closed. Someone
had scribbled on the map, "Siena trionfa ancora immortale": "Siena still
triumphs, immortal.") But most later versions of Vanni's map omit an
inset map of Siena's province that functioned as a clear reminder to Ferdinando and the Sienese themselves that Siena was not just a city but a

Fig. 5 ◆ (*Facing*) Francesco Vanni, *Sena Vetus Civitas Virginis* (1595).
Print. Courtesy of Harvard Map Collection, Harvard College Library.

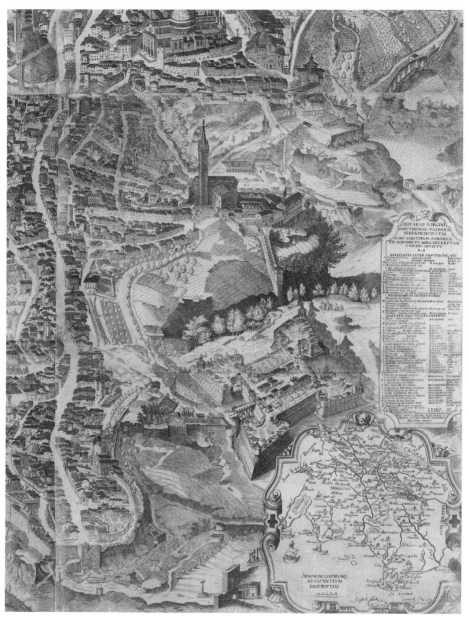

Fig. 6 ◆ Francesco Vanni, *Sena Vetus Civitas Virginis* (detail of figure 5) (1595). Print. Courtesy of Harvard Map Collection, Harvard College Library.

territory. Perhaps Vanni's miniature map is not unlike what he was still likely to have seen on Lorenzetti's *Mappamondo* in the Palazzo Pubblico. Siena sits almost at the top of a territory—Florentine lands are immediately above—that stretches west to the sea and the Sienese ports of Talamone and Porto Ercole, east to papal lands, and south to Mount Amiata and the island of Giglio (most lately in the news for the tragic sinking of a cruise ship that sailed too close to its shore. We ate lunch one day in an outdoor restaurant on the mainland, overlooking the site where twenty-eight people died. The ship was still beached on its side.) The rivers etched onto the map of this corner of Italy known for the swamps of the Maremma and the yellow hills of the Crete Senesi suggestively copy the routes of Siena's winding roads, and the shape of the landmass resembles that of the city itself—a torso without arms or legs. Or, as has often been suggested, it looks like a heart.

This similarity of shapes and design makes city and *stato*—Siena and its countryside—into mirror images of one another, even as Vanni distinguishes between them in a brief description written at the top of the map: this *antichissima* or most ancient city has walls encompassing five miles and possesses beyond those walls "120 castles, 800 towns, ports with access to the sea, famous thermal baths, and mines full of gold, silver, and other metals." The *terra* of the countryside—other than furnishing the dirt for the Palio twice a year—also provides minerals and sea access and water, in all of which Siena itself is deficient. It thus explains why Siena has been for centuries so dependent on the lands outside it. Such dependence was once ritually enforced on the feast day of Mary's assumption, August 15. Representatives from all eight hundred towns had to parade into the cathedral and give in tribute a huge quantity of wax—a valuable resource, since candles were the only source of light. Even today the city itself is not a major center of production. Only by leaving it, for Staggia Senese and other towns, will you find thriving artisanal industries: ceramics, wine, furniture making.

Compared with the riches of the countryside, such deficits explain why Siena never rose to become a great center of anything much in antiquity. As strange as the hills are, they are also not very high. The side that faces Siena's harshest, cruelest enemy, Florence, is virtually flat, and it may have been the difficulties of defending such a site that prevented the Etruscans from turning Siena into a center like nearby Chiusi or Volterra, considered impenetrable. (When today's buses arrive from Florence, they begin to descend at Porta Camollia, then swing up again on arriving at its westernmost point of access near San Domenico. Only there, as well as on the eastern side, does the city rise up sharply from the road, and it is no coincidence that two of the three escalators that take you into town were built where the climb is steepest. Even the imposing Porta Romana to the south oversees a road that declines only gradually, an easy and pleasant day's walk out of the gates and into the countryside.) In fact, for some time Siena was thought not to have had Etruscan settlers at all, although recent archaeological work suggests there were Etruscan encampments in the area of the Duomo and Spedale, where limited excavations continue.

The excellent archaeological museum of largely Etruscan lore is housed, appropriately, in the dark lower levels of the Spedale. One morning Debora Barbagli, the museum's director, takes us on a long and leisurely tour. We see shards of pottery, fragments of a wall that may go back to the sixth century before Christ, and evidence of man-made terraces in the area behind the Spedale, where there may have been an aristocratic residence. But, she tells us, most of the museum's wonderful works collected by eighteenth- and nineteenth-century aristocrats and the twentieth-century Fascist mayor Fabio Bargagli Petrucci (he was an aristocrat too) are from other regions, like Volterra and the area near Murlo, en route to the sea, which has an Etruscan museum of its own.

Records about Siena disappear until the first century BCE, when a town called Saena Julia became a military colony the year Augustus became emperor. It would have been a tiny colony, and it's not clear that it would have been in the same spot as modern-day Siena, although ruins of a chimney have been found alongside the Spedale, in Via dei Fusari. There's a sacrificial well with the remains of three dogs near the same spot, and bits of a Roman pavement have been found in Via del Porrione, perhaps then, as through the Middle Ages, the commercial area of the city; Porrione means "emporium." And the highest part of town, Castelvecchio, has walls that may date back to Roman times, while the crossroads now referred to as Quattro Cantoni—where roads to the Duomo and the Campo converge with the road to Porta Stalloreggi and

Via San Pietro—may have been the meeting point of the *cardo maximus* and *decumanus maximus*. But assumptions that the Campo was once a grand Roman forum, or the site of the Duomo a place for a temple, have long since been dismissed. If Siena's hills were not high enough to offer solace to great numbers of Etruscan settlers, they were too high and too uneven for a thriving Roman encampment.

These modest beginnings are a far cry from the story invented in the late Middle Ages to accommodate a more august one: how the twin sons of Remus, Romulus's unlucky brother, fled Rome on horseback and arrived in the area that is now Siena, improbably lugging a statue of the wolf that had nurtured their father and fratricidal uncle. One twin, Senius, lingered near the banks of the Tressa—then more of a river than it is now—and founded Siena, building the castle that would come to be known as Castelvecchio at the area's highest point. The other twin, Ascius, drawn to the river Ombrone, founded Asciano some twenty kilometers to the southeast. It is to these stories that Siena also owes the colors of its ubiquitous *balzana*, or flag. The simple white and black refer to the colors of the horses that transported the boys to Tuscany, or perhaps to the two plumes of smoke that rose when they offered thanks to Apollo and Diana for protection. These stories are also the reason for Siena's many statues of a wolf, in some cases shown with twin boys: in front of the Palazzo Pubblico and the Duomo, at the site of the Quattro Cantoni.

An equally powerful and improbable myth dominates the story of Christianity's origins in the city a millennium later. A young Roman nobleman, Ansano, was invited by an angel to preach the gospel in Siena and so, like the twins, he came north. The skeptical Sienese imprisoned him in a tower thought to adjoin the church known simply as the Prison of Sant'Ansano, open only one day a year—December 1—for his feast day. His thrilling voice emanating from the tower won over so many that he became known as the "Baptist of the Sienese." One trial by fire and another by boiling oil, both carried out in Selva territory, in the ditch behind what is now the looming hospital (called, appropriately, the Ditch of Saint Ansano) failed to silence him. He was smuggled out of his tower in the middle of the night and taken to the town of Dofana, where martyrdom by decapitation put an end to his preaching.

But one does not travel to Siena to find its classical roots, despite the riches of the archaeological museum in the basement of the Spedale, or even its early Christian roots. The evidence of those origins probably lies somewhere beneath Siena's holy center, which no one is very eager to dig up. And in the meantime the owner of Il Divo on the northern slope of the Duomo's hill is free to show patrons what he thinks is an Etruscan necropolis in the restaurant's lowest level, where the smell of must clings to the walls and the uniform gray cavities undeniably suggest tombs. (Almost every restaurant in Siena keeps its wine in cantinas that call up similar specters—from the bar Il Palio in the Campo, where we have a pizza late one June evening, to the ever crowded Osteria di San Giuseppe up the steep hill from the Campo in Via Giovanni Duprè.) But not in dispute are the origins of the embedded stones and wood in the rooms on the next level up of Il Divo, part of the fortifications that wreathed the still tiny city in the Middle Ages. This is a second ring of walls constructed in the early twelfth century. On returning to Il Divo one chilly January night, we have ample occasion to contemplate them over a meal of *involtini*, rollups with asparagus and fresh pecorino, and tagliatelle spiced with *tartufo*—it's the season for truffles, another treasure of Siena's countryside.

Much more than fleeting finds from seventh- or first-century wells, a stray bit of mosaic in Via del Porrione, or a fantastic story about twins hightailing it out of Rome, the walls provide the material and historical continuity that defines Siena's idea of itself and what is has offered to others for at least a thousand years. There's a toughness, a solidness to the rocks at the base of the room in Il Divo and to the wooden beams that no doubt have been repaired and replaced many times over the centuries. These constructions have lasted, delimiting and protecting the city that sprang up, waterless, on sandstone and impermeable clay. These were the years when the small cluster of buildings on Siena's highest hills—where the Duomo now sits, Castelvecchio to its south—was dominated by a bishop, aided by a group of advisers who represented the first vestiges of civil government. As in other Tuscan and Umbrian towns, the citizens' declaration of loyalty to an emperor from the north in the mid-twelfth century began a lengthy period of withdrawal from the clutches of the church. For over a hundred years Siena's increasingly autonomous government sided with distant emperors who essentially left the

Sienese alone, grand men who couldn't be bothered with the daily up-keep of one unimportant and far-off little town: Frederick Barbarossa, who gave Italian communes judicial status in 1183, the Sicilian Frederick II, and his unlucky son Manfredi, who died an excommunicate like his father and so many Sienese in those years who were subjected to a pope's vengeance. Thus defiant—of bishops, of popes, of the elements, and ultimately of negligent emperors—these hardy medieval Sienese built their city to last. If there are doubts about the scale of an Etruscan village or the existence of a Roman *castrum*, there can be none about the walled city of Christians that started to take shape some eight hundred years after the Magi visited Christ.

◆

Among the ingredients missing in Siena but plentiful in its country-side are mineral springs, the best ones an hour or so drive from Siena. The cascading waters from Bagni San Filippo start from 524 meters high, named for a priest who hid here, afraid he'd be elected pope if he emerged. The calmer piazza in the little town of Bagno Vignoni—full of water like a Venetian canal—is where a young and excessively modest Saint Catherine took the baths, much against her will. The Russian film-maker Andrei Tarkovsky chose the town as the site for his famous but enigmatic *Nostalghia*, and the mists rising from the baths next to what is called the Loggia of Santa Caterina set the stage for the movie's nebu-lous events that slowly unfolded in an era—the 1970s—when the piazza was still open to bathing. Now those seeking the water's wonders have to content themselves with private thermal baths. But it's much more entertaining (and free) to climb onto the rocks just outside the town for a shower beneath the warm waters that spill down the mountain next to the spot where a mill once dominated the countryside. The basin is at the bottom of the hill the town sits on, the cliff polished to iridescence from centuries of water now rushing, now trickling down its slopes. It looks more dangerous than it is. The rocks are surprisingly unslippery, as I discover to my relief when my sons finally persuade me to make the climb, holding my outstretched hand. We have gone back many times. During an outing one particular summer, after a winter and spring heavy with rain—bad for the olives, we're continually told, but good for the mudbaths—a multigenerational French family claims the pool. After a bit of raucous shouting and splashing, the stern patriarch—steel-gray hair, aquiline nose—gives the grandchildren (seven in all, ranging from about four to twelve) a tongue-lashing. The youngest bursts into tears. Later one of the two fathers pleads with the children less assertively—*doucement, doucement*—as the older ones charge up the path to explore. With the children gone, we can make out the strangled cries of frogs mating deep in the mud. We peel off our mud masks, the drying clay grayish green in the setting sun; it's the same clay that hardens into the small hills and caves of the Crete Senesi, that creates the hills of Siena.

This is in the Val d'Orcia, some forty kilometers from the city but still part of the ridge that was once, as Michael Kucher calls it, a "vast Pliocene sea bottom deposited three million years ago." Erosion carved out the river valleys that sit north and south of Siena, and the softer sandstone settled on top of the harder clay. Sandstone absorbs rainwater, but the impermeable clay does not, so forcing the water to change course, as in the Val d'Orcia, and form a spring. Fontebranda, for centuries Siena's most copious source of water, gathers the rain that seeps out of the steep hillside below the massively imposing church of San Domenico—sometimes referred to as Il Sasso or the Rock. But Fontebranda, whose arches we can just make out from our window, was hardly enough: the trick was to find water within the city. Dante quips in the *Divine Comedy* about Sienese vainly searching for an underground river called Diana beneath the road that descends from Castelvecchio toward Porta San Marco. And there is evidence of many citizens' excavating for wells in this part of the city, for which they were charged a hundred *soldi* (roughly twenty dollars in today's money). When the friars from the church of Santa Maria dei Servi wanted to dig a particularly deep well in 1326, they couldn't come up with the requisite fee. Two years later the Comune agreed to pay half. The river was never found, although the Tressa, "discovered" by Remus's son, is a kilometer or two southwest of the city. When we go out to find it, leaving by Porta San Marco and taking the windy Via Chiocciola—the street of the snail, again aptly named—we have a hard time. It is, in fact, little more than a stream that dries up over the summer, but you can still find the basin of a fountain where locals once gathered, and there's water in the bottom.

The land's unusual formation—sandstone on top of clay—enabled the Sienese even from remote times to excavate *bottini*. The word may derive from *botte*, or strikes, referring to the millions of impacts made by picks and crowbars against the subterranean layers of Siena to fashion tunnels for gathering the water that dripped slowly, inexorably, through gaps in the clay and carrying it into town. In fact, the stairways in Il Divo or in the now-closed restaurant of the Eremita are in many cases vestiges of the paths that go down to these tunnels, most of them gracelessly walled up with slapdash brick after World War II and after dozens of Sienese Jews had taken refuge there. The shop Maurizio used to rent out next to our apartment has such a bricked-up entrance, and we shine a flashlight over the top, trying to catch a glimpse of these centuries-old feats of engineering that gained the admiration of an emperor: Charles V, having just brought Rome to its knees in the famous sack of 1527, is said to have proclaimed that the "city below was even more beautiful than the one above." This was in large part because among the *bottini*'s civil engineers and planners were talented men who were constantly hired away from the city to work for dukes and princes. Francesco di Giorgio Martini was one of them, going on from supervising Siena's *bottini* to designing Naples's vast underwater networks and Milan's canals a generation before Leonardo da Vinci. But before masters like Francesco appeared, the process was more democratic. Three citizens were selected by lottery each year to supervise the increasingly elaborate network of tunnels and fountains. Thus did the *bottini* allow Siena to grow, and survive, as long as the city wasn't under attack. (During the siege by Florence in 1554, spies stole the closely guarded maps of Siena's tunnels and burrowed into the earth themselves to poison the water.) The mosaic pavement in the Duomo includes among its many biblical scenes the story of Judith, like that of Tobias part of the Old Testament Apocrypha. The pavement shows her triumphant return to her town of Bethulia carrying the head of the Assyrian Holofernes, the fearful general who had cut off the water supply of this little hill town in the desert in the hopes of forcing a proud people to submit. An eerie model for Siena, this fantasy of survival against all odds occupies a prominent place near the altar, not far from Beccafumi's *Mount Sinai*.

We inquire at the offices in the Palazzo Pubblico whether we can explore the *bottini*, and after a wait of several weeks we're told we can.

On a wretchedly hot day we enter a little metal door to the side of the
Fonte Nuova, northeast of the Campo, constructed in the last decade of
the thirteenth century and finished as Dante went into exile. Once the
Fonte Nuova was a fountain for slaughterers and butchers; by the middle
of the fifteenth century leather workers gathered there instead. In these
long, gloomy tunnels, dimly lit by our flashlights, we come upon fossils,
as well as signs of earthquakes and avalanches (one so severe that a new
bottino had to be dug around the detritus). There are also four plaques
left by an enterprising worker in the early nineteenth century who recorded his progress every hundred meters or so. About halfway through
our kilometer-long journey, the *bottino* takes a sudden curve, following
the *dorsale della terra*, "the spine of the earth," having now descended
some forty meters beneath the streets where pilgrims once walked and
where tourists now ready themselves for the first official day of summer
sales in shops. We pass beneath orchards, beneath the *casa di riposo*, or
retirement home, beneath the abandoned convent where in 1724 nuns
asked permission to dig a well to access this *bottino*. (We see the well;
some 355 wells are connected to the *bottini*, supplemented by the cisterns
dug in courtyards of private homes to catch the rain.)

Our guide, Ferdinando Capecchi, volunteers for a group called Associazione La Diana, after the mythical subterranean river that was never
found (although Ferdinando says there is a rich spring in the vicinity).
Many of the members are retirees. They lovingly tend to their tunnels
and have constructed a museum of water above the Fonte di Pescaia, just
beyond the western side of town. Today the *bottini* are a place of calm,
where we see what seems to be the peaceful conglomeration not just of
the centuries but of millennia: spaces of geological rather than human
time, even as the tunnels themselves are products of intensive human
labor. Just as Michelangelo left the marks of his chisel on his statues in
Florence's Accademia—and perhaps on his two small statues in Siena's
Duomo, although they are too high up to see well—so here his forebears
left signs of the thousands of blows they delivered while burrowing
into the earth. In a city where water was gold, one can imagine how
vexed was the tunnels' maintenance and how problematic their jurisdiction. Thus the owner of the hotel "della Campana," run by one Pas-
quino di Nanni da Prato, went to court in 1432 against the dyer Matteo

Fig. 7 ◆ Bottino di Fonte Gaia, Siena. Courtesy of Associazione La Diana, Siena. Photograph: Mauro Agnesoni.

di Francesco del Guercio and his son Francesco because the runoff from the dyes was getting into the water his guests used. The city regularly hired guards to protect the major fountains during times of political crisis and drought.

Over time the *bottini* slowly dried up, requiring constant maintenance and expansion even as they made for a spectacular underground city. Eventually the incrustations became "so entrenched that the city does not have the wherewithal to remove them," in the words of one Professor C. Toscani. He wrote in 1862, half a century before the city seriously began looking elsewhere for its water, to the slopes of that old volcano, Mount Amiata, near whose top there was a precious spring called Ermicciolo, prized since antiquity. Would there be a way to channel these abundant waters into Siena? Their chief source was discovered to be on lands belonging to the Cervini, an aristocratic family originally from Montepulciano; their town—more hamlet than town—is called Vivo d'Orcia, some nine hundred meters high and surrounded by an enchanting forest of silver firs and the ubiquitous chestnuts. The aging Countess Cervini still lives there, presiding over a striking palace easily visible from roads all around, designed by the Sienese Baldassare Peruzzi in the sixteenth century. Pressed by the city, after a long legal battle the Cervini sold their rights to the land and the building of the aqueduct began. On May 15, 1914, the water was brought sixty kilometers to Siena. Today every few meters along Siena's main roads, one sees a metal plaque inscribed "Acquedotti di Siena." Within, beneath, water gushes from an extinct volcano.

One of the guidebooks in the tourist shop in the Campo offers a hike into the mountain to find what used to be the Cervini's water. Vivo is as far from Siena as Siena is from Florence, but there is no fast way to get there. Roads bend and curve through the Valley of the Orcia, passing by Bagno Vignoni. Only after two hours do we make it to the slope, to ascend hills on well-marked paths past an old tannery, over gorges, and to the faceless modern building where the aqueduct begins, not far from the tiny Benedictine chapel marking the place where hermits once lived and guarded the spring. More intriguing is the path that takes you into the village itself—a handful of homes, some of them joined like roadside motels. Around the corner is a wood with imposing trees, a little church that is locked, and Peruzzi's palace, out of place in this corner of the world that has the rural feel of a Jane Austen novel. A man walking his dog turns out to be the contessa's son-in-law, and he invites us into the gardens behind the homes and then into his own cozy and beautifully furnished house, converted from former stables and recently written up in W magazine. Once Vivo was the center of thriving industries that exploited the waterpower: a mill, the tannery we've already spotted on the hill, and perhaps most impressively, a glass-blowing company and a paper mill that made some of the most elegant stationery in Italy. Over the centuries the Cervini family was behind all economic activity in this fertile place, but these pockets of production have given way to genteel ruins. Paper was once soaked in yawning basins overflowing with water, then hung out to dry on long poles; the basins are still there, empty except for dry leaves. Behind the cottages is a stunning view of the Tuscan landscape. Mountains arch above green fields soaking up this late June sun, the hay rolled into golden bales, the woods defining the edges of the long, low farmlands. As we stroll toward Peruzzi's palace, I envy the *fattore* or farm manager who pulls up beside the contessa's daughter in his red pickup and asks after her day. They exchange a few brief items of business, then he's off to a barn that is slowly collapsing into a hillside, its red sides aglow in the setting sun.

As monumental a feat as the aqueduct was, perhaps the greatest accomplishment over the centuries was the tunnel that allowed the Sienese to build a fountain in the very heart of town, changing a landscape where the fountains were found only at Siena's base and periphery, in valleys beneath the city's high, stony walls. This Maestro Bottino, into which schoolchildren annually descend, arrived in the Campo in 1346. To celebrate, the Sienese enlisted their great sculptor Jacopo della Quercia to build a monument for what they decided to call the Fonte Gaia—the joyful fountain. It was to have a far more elegant design than the other fountains; unlike Fontebranda, where horses drank, women did their laundry, and tanners rinsed out their stinking leather, the water from Fonte Gaia was reserved for human drinking—and it still is, with signs above the two spigots saying *acqua potabile*. Jacopo carved a series featuring Mary and the virtues, flanked by Adam and Eve in paradise and then their expulsion: thirteen statues gaily ring the blue basin, over which several Sienese wolves preside, almost always decked out with a live pigeon or two. But these sculptures were made of the soft, porous marble from the *montagnola senese*, the hills west of the city, that lets water filter through even as—in some geologists' reckoning—it cushions Siena from the most dangerous earthquakes. Four centuries later Jacopo's original work had disintegrated so much that a new fountain had to be sculpted by Tito Sarrocchi. In the Spedale, one level up from the archaeological museum, in an area once reserved for storing hay, we see Jacopo's originals next to the plaster casts Sarrocchi used for his nineteenth-century replacements. They are dishearteningly raw, the earth ravaged by water from the fountain itself as well as by rain. Only a face remains of Prudence, an arm and a lap from the statue of Mary.

Possibly the most moving of Jacopo's sculptures is the banishment of Adam and Eve from the Garden of Eden. After more than four hundred years of exposure to the Campo's wind and rain, Adam's twisted torso is all that survives, and the angel who bars Eden's gate has lost his arm. But the angel's authoritative hand is still clamped on Adam's hunched shoulder, enforcing God's command as Adam desperately tries to cover his shame and return to the garden. He and Eve are the original pilgrims, exiled forever from their homeland, even as the water that spilled into the basin below them was meant to symbolize a paradise regained in the Campo.

◆

Although he trained in Rome, the mapmaker Francesco Vanni spent most of his life in Siena, where he fathered a large brood of children, managing to marry one of them off to an aristocrat. Vanni's stepfather was the painter Arcangelo Salimbeni, who taught the boy his craft. Vanni must have been fascinated with his native town from an early age. His first extant effort to put Siena on a map is a painting dedicated to the Blessed Ambrogio Sansedoni, who successfully intervened with the pope in 1266 to release the Sienese from embargo and excommunication after they sided with the heretic emperor Frederick II and his son Manfredi, killed while fighting papal forces in Benevento. The painting is in the little Renaissance church of Fontegiusta—a name that sounds like it should mean the "just" fountain, but which is simply a place "near the fountain." We go there one Saturday morning while a maid is cleaning.

Fig. 8 ◆ Jacopo della Quercia, *Expulsion from Paradise* (1419). Marble.
With the permission of the Comune di Siena.

She offers to let us into the church's museum, where there supposedly is
a sword owned by Columbus, but I stupidly decline because I'm intent on
seeing the Vanni.

And there it is, to the right of the altar, past some life-size and surprisingly lifelike wooden statues of Mary and an angel—not Tobias's
guardian Raphael but Gabriel, more girl than boy. Vanni's painting
shows Sansedoni, a Dominican preacher and friend of Thomas Aquinas,
the Holy Spirit perched next to his ear, appealing to a stern Jesus and less
stern Mary above him. Sansedoni had appealed to a more earthly entity,
the pope, while visiting Orvieto, where Urban II was staying, but Vanni
chose to make the scene heavenly and hence more dramatic. Below the
pleading Ambrogio is the city. The hems of his black-and-white robes

lightly graze the campanile of the Duomo and what was once the high
tower of San Domenico, graced here in Vanni's depiction with a statue
of Saint Catherine on top. Parts of the city beneath him are covered by a
cloud; others—like the field between the Antiporta and Porta Camollia—
are bathed in full sunlight, including an extraordinary structure that at
first seems like a church facade (the church of Fontegiusta is dark inside; it's always best to consult a reproduction). But on second and third
glance it reveals itself as the cascading back walls of the Spedale della
Scala, positioned across from the Duomo's darkened cupola and almost
blackened tower, while its gothic facade presents as a muted gray. The
Palazzo Pubblico's tower reaches into the sky, competing with another
tower in the Campo: that of the Sansedoni palace. It might seem that this
is homage to the man who saved Siena from papal interdiction, but in
fact the tower of the Sansedoni household vied with that of Siena's civic
center until well into the 1750s, when it was finally dismantled and the
palace enlarged; today it is the seat of the troubled Foundation of the
Monte dei Paschi.

Yet, the Duomo and the darkness of the church aside, what the Fontegiusta painting gives us, more than anything else, is color. And so in this
bright version of what in the larger map is only black-and-white you're
surprised to see some colorful facades long lost, such as Simone Martini's *Glory of the Virgin* on the Antiporta outside the Porta Camollia.
Sienese buildings have an especially stark look, particularly in the winter or between Palios, when you miss the bright banners that decorate
each *contrada* in the days leading up to the race. Yet we must imagine a
city five hundred years ago covered with paintings ablaze with color: Lorenzetti's stories about the Madonna on the walls of the Spedale, Gentile
da Fabriano's Madonna of the Notaries in the Campo, Simone's Madonna
crowned in Porta Romana to balance the Virgin in glory in the Antiporta. Everywhere you looked there were colorful images, "doorways
to heaven," in Hayden Maginnis's phrase, and one should call to mind
these phantom paintings when bemoaning the severity of Siena's bricks.
The somberness of this city on a hill—the wood and stones of the walls,
the tunnels of the *bottini* below, manifesting the will to survive—was
brightened considerably by paint. If Mary McCarthy calls Florence a city
of stone, the Bargello its most representative museum with its Michelan-

gelo and Cellini, Siena was once a city of color, when gates and facades teemed with life. The Sienese chose this temporary veneer of beauty, the delicate shades of a Lorenzetti or a Simone Martini, knowing well that they couldn't last in their battle with the earth.

Still, of course, paint is of the earth, and it comes especially from the hills, described in geological detail in a volume published in 1862, *Siena e il suo territorio*, the proud product of a Siena newly released from others' domination thanks to the miracle of Italy's unification. A year earlier a newly elected Italian parliament proclaimed the first king, and for the first time in three centuries Siena had its own "territory," notwithstanding Vanni's efforts to include it on his map. The first section of the book is devoted to topography, and after perfunctory citations of the city's latitude and longitude the author, the same Professor Toscani cited earlier, launches into this: "The city of Siena is spread out on one of many *colline deliziosi* [literally, delicious or inviting hills] found in the area of the Chianti." Siena's are far from the only low hills in this region. The highest ones—such as Mount Amiata—are old volcanoes, within which much of the silver Vanni mentioned is buried. Smaller hills, of Siena's height, harbor other metals such as copper as well as the minerals that produced the colors of Vanni's work and many other Sienese paintings.

Thus on a visit to the Museum of Natural History run by the Accademia dei Fisiocritici, we encounter a little exhibit on what the poster calls "natural colors that originate in the south of Tuscany": the so-called *terre di Siena*. These are various earth tones: the burnt red sienna, the "cenobar" of the volcanoes, the bright orange and yellows burnished by the rich minerals of the hills. The ores contain much more than the (limited) gold and (far more ample) silver alluded to in Vanni's account: they also contain alum, a mineral salt used to make dyes adhere to cloth, ferociously sought throughout the Renaissance. The Fisiocritici were founded in 1691 with the intention of "scrutinizing and studying the secrets of nature, and as though we were judges, to refute with the aid of the natural sciences whatever's false so as to better understand what is true." This process of sifting and winnowing could explain why the Fisiocritici's emblem is the *lapis lidius*, the touchstone or "rock of comparisons" that merchants and moneylenders of old used to distinguish false gold and silver from true; you can see a sample of the rock in a glass case. As "nature's judges," these amateur scientists and archaeologists were not averse to letting their eyes overrule their religious sentiments, following in the footsteps of Galileo who, denied housing elsewhere in Italy after his trial, was the guest of Siena's Cardinal Ascanio Piccolomini for several months in 1633. Hence Father Ambrogio Soldani, an academy member who studied microscopic fossils, especially shells, wrote a controversial pamphlet four years before the big earthquake of 1798. In it he claimed that the bizarre metallic shower that fell on Lucignano d'Asso to Siena's south on June 16, 1794, did not come from the earth's atmosphere, as was thought, but resulted from the condensation of vapors from *bolide*—large unearthly bodies that crisscrossed the skies according to their own designs. His polemic started a dispute that eventually led to recognizing the extraterrestrial origins of meteorites.

Here in their spacious quarters—an old church given to them by the "king of the Etruscans" in 1816 when Italy was divided into temporary states after Napoleon's defeat—the Fisiocritici's findings are preserved, along with the colors from their mountains, carefully labeled. From the *terre bolari* of Mount Amiata alone there are dark pea green, a cinnamon yellow, clear red, dark red, calcinite black (the names sound more poetic in Italian: *verde pisello scuro*; *giallo cannella*; *rosso chiaro*; *rosso cupo*; *nera calcinata*). Some are powders, some chunks, some flat, gleaming bars, like the "cinnabar" or red *minium*, found only in Spain and on the slopes of Siena's extinct volcano, used to make the bright initials in medieval manuscripts, and the reason the Abbey of San Salvatore for centuries housed one of the biggest scriptoria in Tuscany. It is, in fact, from *minium* that we get our word "miniaturist," referring to the patient work of the medieval scribe. This is not because he worked in "miniature" illustrations (although he sometimes did), but because he used the bright colors that came from beneath the earth of Siena's countryside to point out phrases and words especially worthy of readers' attention.

◆

The yellows that came from the hills—"cinnamon yellow" but also lighter shades—were used for garments as well as for the soft and rolling hills in painted landscapes. But they were mostly deployed for the Virgin's hair in the images of Mary that once ornamented the exterior walls of the city's buildings and its gates. At every juncture, she is the one who greets the passerby and citizen and protects the entrances to the city, providing another layer of fortification and defense. All of Siena is in many ways a tribute to Mary, savior of the Sienese against the Florentines at Monteaperti six years before Sansedoni pleaded with a pope. The Duomo is a tribute to her assumption, the Spedale across the piazza a tribute to her annunciation. And the Campo is said to be designed in the shape of her mantle that protects the Sienese beneath it (although I prefer Faluschi's analogy: he likens the Campo of this water-starved inland town to a seashell). But it is in the realm of painting that the Sienese rendered special homage to Mary and produced their most remarkable works, rather than in sculptures carved out of *la montagnola senese*—or in architectural masterpieces, the Duomo not withstanding (and that in any case largely the handiwork of Pisan sculptors and designed by the monks of nearby San Galgano, who originated in France). It is in these colors, ground from the stones of the nearby hills, that Mary takes on what Machtelt Israëls calls her apotropaic role.

But these vanished colors survive only indoors, in paintings like Vanni's. For the work that brings all these threads together—the land, a bright palette of paint, and Mary as protector and defender—one can go to the Palazzo Pubblico to see a Mary who is herself protected, unlike Lorenzetti's frescoes once on the exterior walls of the Spedale or Jacopo della Quercia's sculptures once across the Campo. In the enormous room originally called the Sala del Consiglio, where Siena's leaders gathered to discuss affairs of state, locked in for a month or two at a time to ensure that they accomplished all they needed to do during their brief term in office, Mary looks out serenely over all, seated on a dais beneath an expansive and intricate canopy, Christ on her lap. Angels and a contingent of about thirty saints—some recognizable, some not—complete the scene. Lorenzetti's *Mappamondo* on the opposite wall would have reminded those gathered here that their decisions would affect the entire Sienese state, or perhaps the entire world; just below Simone's painting the officials who oversaw the meetings sat on their own dias. But the Virgin and her cohort were there first, several decades before Lorenzetti's map, and they remain long after the whirling disk is gone.

Simone is one of the only painters the great humanist Petrarch mentions in his fourteenth-century writings. It seems the two had known

Fig. 9 ◆ Simone Martini, *Maestà* (detail) (1315–21). Fresco. Palazzo
Pubblico, Siena. Photograph: Scala/Art Resource, New York.

each other in Avignon, where they worked for popes during the seventy years when the papacy removed itself to France. And perhaps it was even a close friendship. In Sonnet 72, Petrarch thanks Simone for a small painting of his beloved Laura, ending with the lament, "If only she knew to respond to my words!" Petrarch wishes he could be like Pygmalion, whose statue of a woman was turned to flesh by Venus, and who received "a thousand times what I yearn to have just once!" But some thirty years earlier, as Petrarch may well have known, Simone had painted his *Maestà*, in which a beautiful woman *does* answer those who beseech her. In this magnificent work, in the room that was the center of Siena's communal and civic life, and in lines that have captured the imaginations of viewers for centuries—but particularly since the painting's complete restoration in the late 1990s—Mary indeed "speaks" to the holy people who crowd around her while she sits beneath a rich and ornate canopy. In this crowded but not chaotic scene, Ansano and the other three patron saints of Siena extend toward the Virgin scrolls that once had inscribed on them their prayers, now lost. But we still have Mary's response, along the edge of one of the lower steps, in answer to their vanished petition for the protection and health of their city. In the Italian that was then a young language, and in the poetic form that Dante had invented for his *Divine Comedy*—the terza rima, with its aba/bcb/cdc rhyme—Mary promises to fulfill the "honest petitions" of those before her. But she is no pushover. She admonishes the "powerful" against harming the weak. And she notes that some "despise me and deceive my land / And are most praised when they speak the worst," closing with the threatening line, "Whoever is condemned by this speech, take heed."

"Terra mia": my land. The *terra* is, of course, Siena, brought together in the bodies of the men gathered to discuss laws, court cases, and petitions. Mary's lines are both a promise and a threat to those who don't govern with justice and mercy. But *terra* is also the land lovingly portrayed in Vanni's map (and once in Lorenzetti's). And while Mary invokes that land with its strange hills, the *terra* is expressed even more concretely in the painting itself. What is easily missed at first glance is that the *Maestà* is studded—"throbbing" or "pulsating" in Chiara Frugoni's phrase— with "real *things*." The scroll Jesus holds is actual paper pasted onto the canvas, bearing a phrase from the Book of Isaiah. A glass brooch adorns the Virgin's throat. Shimmering foil covers the wings of an angel and arms the body of one of the more militant saints. And other small stones and jewels stud the garments of the other spectators, who turn outward to face us as much as they gaze at Mary. Thus does this painting that fills almost the entire east wall—eight by ten meters—seem to move physically toward us as we read the Virgin's answers to our prayers. It is, in short, an imposing physical, three-dimensional presence, deeply rooted in the *terra senese*: glass, foil, armor, paper, gold, rock crystal, and other pieces of earth brought into the Palazzo Pubblico, just as the *terra* gets lugged into the Campo outside to prepare for the Palio. The Virgin's words take on an objective existence too. Her admonition to the proud and her comfort to the weak seem carved rather than painted onto the stairs, assuming just as material and substantive a life form as every-thing else in the painting. So does Simone intermingle not only the sur-face of paint and "things," but sacred and secular, the heavenly patron-ess who is Mary and the civic gathering before her in Siena's public office building. Beneath it all is the seal of the artist himself, painted into the work's frame as though to verify this as an official act of state.

Time has done its damage. While Mary's prayer survives, the words of others have faded—those of the pleading saints with their now empty scrolls unfurled. And in an ironic touch, the salt stored in the basement of the Palazzo Pubblico, so precious that it required a twenty-four-hour guard, sent up vapors that attacked Simone's masterpiece soon after its completion, betraying the modest origins of this civic space central to Si-ena's life as a mere customhouse. Simone was forced to return and redo it, adding six more lines to the Virgin's poetic speech. Traces of the saline damage remain, however, and the colors will never be as vibrant as they once were. Thus, along with the salt, brought in from Siena's territories in Grosseto and the Maremma, the gems and all the very "real things" within its borders have shaped this homage to Mary and her city, invest-ing it with a rare and familiar if translucent beauty. This is what lies be-neath the hills, the mines on which Siena sits, sources of its wealth, but wealth found and fashioned by Sienese hands. Jesus's scroll, which says simply, in Latin, "Love Justice," is glued onto the painting, testament to the papermakers, one of Siena's most prestigious guilds.

The conjoining of *terra* and city generates the creative spark of Simone's painting, here in the basin that defines Siena's civic center, nestled among three hills. And indeed, walking through various points of the city that are likewise in between, or on the ridges of the strange hills—across and behind the perennially closed church of Santo Spirito or in the "Lizza" ("fields to make foreigners delight," according to Faluschi)—you notice this striking intersection of land and the man-made. Particularly noteworthy in Vanni's map are the green spaces. When the penultimate ring of walls was constructed in the first half of the fourteenth century, Siena numbered about fifty thousand citizens. Just as the Sienese made plans for a great new cathedral, so did they build walls to the south and east that would provide ample room for the rapid growth they expected to continue. But the plague took care of that, as of so many things. Vanni's Siena was considerably smaller than its medieval version—perhaps a mere eighteen thousand were left after Florence's siege—and orchards and farms sprang up where homes had been planned. Thus Siena had, and still has, breathing space, green spaces. Color surges from the hills and the valleys closest to the walls, especially in winter when the fields are soaked with the seasonal rains. Even in the most crowded of Siena's streets, Via di Città, you notice the ancient plane tree that straddles the sidewalk outside the Palazzo Chigi where the music academy has its home, and enormous cypresses line San Domenico's eastern side. In a less crowded spot, the park next to Sant'Agostino, children ride tricycles and play on the swings while grandmothers chat on the benches, mildly attentive to their charges. Across the way, close to where Via Duprè sets off to take you down the hill and into the Campo, the stucco is peeling off several of the houses, and one slumps alarmingly out into the street. Here too nature is taking its course, but in the other direction, behind the Fisiocritici's museum, are the expansive fields of the Orto Botanico—the university's garden, which contains a medieval fountain, greenhouses, and an orchard. The gently winding section of the walls suggests just how large the medieval builders intended their city to become.

Here you can linger each afternoon until 3:00 (12:00 on Saturdays, though it used to be 1:00; ignorant of the new schedule, we got locked in and had to call out to parents leaving with their children from the nearby elementary school to see if they could find someone with a key), walking alongside the beautiful rock garden, laced in June with poppies and yellow broom flowers and hovering white butterflies. This is one of the city's quietest places to think, and wander, and write. Beyond the Fonte al Pino is a single basin where washerwomen brought their clothes and where now a few goldfish swim circumspectly around rocks and moss. Beyond that the crumbling fourteenth-century wall sinks almost to the ground at one point, only to angle sharply upward and continue its rise to the edge of Via delle Sperandie, where nuns once did their laundry. The fields are damp; it's been a wet spring, and the grass is green, the flowers grateful. This is Siena at its loveliest and most tranquil, the quiet of high noon, or at least of *pranzo*, lunch, when the Sienese shutter their shops and go into temporary exile in their dark, cool palaces, withdrawing into the vast rooms to eat and sleep and forget for a moment the ravages of the present. (Or not: at the Caffè Diacceto, crowds of locals come for lunch, sitting at the outdoor tables if the sun isn't too bright.) Clouds hover, darkening small patches of the countryside to the south, while other sections remain in the light, exaggerating the checkerboard pattern of the countryside that you find in the paintings of Giovanni di Paolo. Two tourists—I hear some German—eat cherries he plucked from a tree; they're small this year because of the rain.

The Lizza is the other place with wide and open space, although it's flat: just outside and around the hated Medici fort, the Lizza was created as the grounds where the Medici army would train. Now, thankfully, military exercises are no more; there are kiosks where the tourists can buy water and maps, and the area is filled with stalls for clothes and housewares on Wednesdays, the only day when the Sienese themselves are attracted to the place. There are also fairs and concerts here, and in the winter there is a small skating rink. One November evening I go to the "festival of the book" (with the catchy slogan *leggere è volare*: "reading is like flying"), held in a tent set up where in a few weeks the ice rink will be the center of attention. A photography exhibition celebrates a recently published book on Siena's rural territories, called *Visibili tracce*: "visible traces." One photo in particular is compelling: an aging Sienese man with hoe in hand, deeply wrinkled face turned to smile, triumphantly stands over a small patch of cabbages. One would assume he farms his land in the countryside, far from the bustle of the city. But he does not. Behind his right shoulder is the familiar tower of the Palazzo Pubblico, jutting up above olive trees. His farm is just behind the Palazzo, in the gardens of the Pecci, on one of the terraces that step down the gentle hillside, cascading to the plain and the little brook below. I hoped to see the farmer during the evening, when the editors talked about their project, but he wasn't at the front table with the organizers; perhaps he was sitting in a corner, in the back. Below the black-and-white photograph a quotation from the book speaks about the force of "the secret knowledge of the earth" (*la forza del sapere segreto della terra*) that such farmers have been able to unleash so that it springs up in the pavement, through the asphalt and bricks and cement of the city. Seven hundred years ago the project meant to bring new blood into Siena was unveiled, the city's newest *borgo*, hamlet, but within the walls and, like nothing else, planned on a grid; it failed when the plague came in, and the area was quickly reclaimed by vegetation, then bought up by the Pecci family. But now the fields boast a small zoo and a pleasant trattoria with outdoor tables, staffed by former residents of the psychiatric hospital of San Niccolò, which closed in 1983. And its terraces are full of gardens like this one, complete with parsley, lettuce, tomatoes, and even a fan to keep the gardener and his tender plants cool. Such are the results of a life that pulsates upward, from underneath, much as Etruscan and Roman ruins await discovery beneath the Duomo.

So the urban and the natural coexist, cohabit, sometimes uneasily — even in our apartment, where the starlings sleep in the bathroom's air vent. The first few nights we whack the pipe with a broom to scare them away, but by the fourth night we're reconciled to the nocturnal rustlings and the 5:00 a.m whistling, and after a week they've become our unseen companions. They're a reminder that the city is not ours, not even its own, but is surrounded by the constant streams of birds that swoop over our balcony and on occasion alight on the yellow flowers of the tree in the garden below. But mainly they're off to fly around the once imposing tower of San Domenico on the other side of the valley marked by Fontebranda, damaged along with the soft underbelly of the church, which sits on rocks and what seems to be bare sand studded with occasional bushes. To the lower right a gently curved playground now nestles between the quarters of the dyers, Saint Catherine's father among them. Eight-year-olds swing and ride the merry-go-round, dressed in white or red smocks called *grembiuli* (white for the younger ones, red for the older). An elderly, remarkably patient nun ushers them in and out, for lunch, for play, for rest, and only now and then does her voice rise above the sounds of the wheeling birds: "No, qui!" "Basta, Francesco!" "È ora!" Just once did we hear an exasperated "Che cosa hai combinato!" ("What on earth did you do!") Like the starlings, the children flit below, occasionally visible through the leaves of the magnolia tree beneath our window. The years pass, the magnolia grows, and the children are harder and harder to make out through the riot of leaves, especially when we are here in late spring and summer. But their voices persist, and at least for now, the nun is still their guardian.

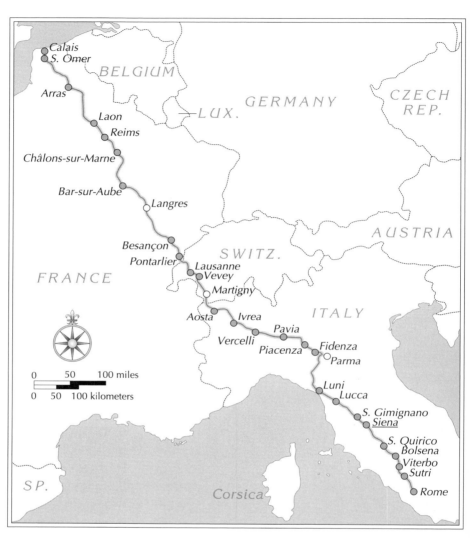

Map 3 ◆ The Via Francigena. Courtesy of Dick Gilbreath, Gyula Pauer
Center for Cartography and GIS, University of Kentucky.

PILGRIMS

2

Pilgrim: strange, wonderful, unusual, rare. A person who comes from a mysterious elsewhere, voyaging through an unfamiliar countryside. *Ager*, from the Latin *peregrinus*, means field, and *per* means through. A star that appears suddenly in the sky, a word that derives from another language and is dropped like a gem into one's own. The pilgrim elicits wonder, amazement, consternation, attention above all—out of the ordinary, not the everyday.

Pilgrims poured into Siena during the Middle Ages, spending a few hours, perhaps a few days, in this town that was famously in between more important sites. Even before pilgrims began to take to the road, Siena had been in between, a nonentity between the Etruscan cities of Chiusi and Volterra, the Roman towns of Florence and Arezzo, the bishoprics of Spoleto and Volterra, while great abbeys—San Salvatore on Mount Amiata, San Galgano in the Valley of the Orcia—dominated the countryside. Yet there was a time when being in between was enough to ensure Siena's growth and prestige, a time when pilgrims walked the earth. Most of them took the Via Francigena, the "French road" that connected the two most prosperous and populous regions in Europe—

Tuscany and Flanders—by way of Champagne, famous for its fairs. The road was thus "the dispenser of wealth," as Italo Moretti has observed— ironically so, given the role that pilgrimage played in medieval spirituality as a state of penitence as well as of suspension: you gave up the comforts of the known world for the unknown in the hope of eventually reaching the divine to ask for pardon, or indulgence, or grace.

For Jews, Christians, and Muslims, Jerusalem was the true destination of pilgrims, and Tobias traveled there when in exile, one of the few to make the trip. But even though Jerusalem was still the privileged center in the Middle Ages—at least when the Crusaders controlled the city or when the Muslims who ran it tolerated visitors—most pilgrimages were more local. Siena became for a time one of the richest cities in Europe by virtue of being en route to holy places. One place was Lucca, the little Tuscan town not far from France that once had over a hundred churches and that still boasts the relic of the Volto Santo, the holy face. This life-size crucifix, it was once believed with more passion than today, was carved while Christ was on the cross by Nicodemus, who supplied his own tomb for the body of God's son. Another place was Rome, with its tomb of Saint Peter and the many sacred sites that a popular medieval treatise called "the marvels of the city." From there pilgrims might go on to San Michele Arcangelo in Puglia, where the angel himself had spent a night, then take a boat to Jerusalem. By the twelfth century, Santiago de Compostela in Spain, not far from the Atlantic and hence on the edge of the medieval earth, loomed as a more westerly destination. This is where Saint James once preached, and where his body was miraculously returned, on a boat from Jerusalem, after he was martyred. Not a drawing card in itself, Siena had no Volto Santo like Lucca, no piece of Saint James's cranium like Pistoia; its own martyr Ansano died outside the city. Only in 1359 did it acquire its first significant relics, such as one of the nails hammered into Christ's foot. It was a way station, a place to spend a night or two off the road. On its strange but manageable hills, Siena's round of walls offered a soothing temporary prospect to pilgrims anxious to escape from the bandits and malarial swamps of the Maremma.

Siena was not born a daughter of the streets, as Ernesto Sestan called her in a memorable essay, but she grew up as one. And as Sestan goes on to say, the hills that Vanni struggled to depict in his maps and paintings hardly seemed destined to become "an urban center. Rather, they're much more predisposed to taking part in the continuity of the rural countryside that surrounds them—among these hills, men built a road."

It's not certain when the road was first fashioned and traversed. No doubt there were many paths that took travelers, farmers, and criminals from and to and around Siena long before pilgrims came; there is a legend that Charlemagne passed through the town. One of the first documented allusions to what would be called the Via Francigena and its passage through Siena is from the late tenth century, notes made by an Anglo-Saxon archbishop's squire as the entourage made its way back to England from Rome. Sigeric, archbishop of Canterbury, had gone to Rome sometime after 989 to accept his pallium, or bishop's cloth, and almost all the places his squire lists are literally way stations. Many of them were abbeys that in the tradition of Benedict were mandated to take in the hungry, the sick, and the *peregrinus*—the Latin word that originally means "stranger" but takes on the spiritual overtones of pilgrim when the Holy Land became a destination for the new religion of Christianity. Three Italian towns are specifically mentioned as part of his itinerary: Rome, "Luca," and an almost unrecognizable "Seocine," the fifteenth spot (out of seventy-eight) where Sigeric sojourned on his sixteen-hundred-kilometer voyage home. The fourteenth spot was the bridge at the river Arbia, some ten kilometers south of modern Siena, where a small park has grown up next to the mill; the sixteenth was the abbey at Abbadia d'Isola. From there, Sigeric hastened north to what are now Poggibonsi and Monteriggioni, the latter built by the Sienese in 1214 as a defense against the ever lurking Florentines.

As the example of Monteriggioni suggests, Siena was more than just a town. As hordes of pilgrims began to travel the road to Saint Peter's, maintenance, security, and assistance were all in demand. "Religious groups were formed in the period with no other purpose than to repair bridges and streets and erect churches and way stations so as to make the holy voyage an easier one for the devout, as laypeople were moved to perform charity by the precepts of Christ and by faith in the forgiveness of sins and the salvation of souls. Such fervent activity took place throughout the contado or territory of Siena." So Giulio Venerosi Pescio-

lini succinctly summarized Siena's importance as more Sigerics went to
Rome. A network of structures—*hospitales*, leprosariums, monasteries,
villages with a house earmarked for sojourners, a room in a mill or in
the bridge keeper's quarters—grew up north and south of Siena. They
were often marked with the cross of the Templars, men who dedicated
themselves to keeping Christ's sepulchre safe for pilgrims in Jerusalem.
Pesciolini rightly notes that the Via Francigena was considered a holy
place: but it took more than God to make it so. It took people who cared
for these strangers in their strange if recognizable garb: a coarse mantle,
a broad-brimmed hat, a pouch, and a walking stick to fend off dogs and
wild boars. In Lorenzetti's fresco of *Buon Governo* you can see a winged
female figure who looks like an angel directly above the gate that leads
to the countryside. Like Tobias's Raphael, she is a guardian for travelers, the figure for "Securitas," holding a sign that reads, "Senza preoc-
cupazione ogni uomo cammina libero / ognuno per la sua strada / finché
questo Comune / conserverà questa Dama [Securitas] in sua signoria."
(Every man will walk freely, each one can make his own way as long as
this City will preserve this woman—Security—as its ruler.) To provide
security means, literally, to take care of someone or something, a job that
extended to humans as well as to angels, and to care not only for those
who found their way within, but for those without.

So in between *hospitales*, there was the road, stretching through Siena and its territory. The city boasts, in fact, the oldest recorded street
regulations in Europe, *Lo statuto dei viari di Siena*—the statutes of Siena's highways, dating back to 1268 and consisting of some four hundred
rules about roads both inside and outside the city. (An instructive comparison: Florence's guide of 1325 had only twenty-four such regulations.)
By 1290 the maintenance of the roads was such that the Sienese created
the *ufficio dello Judex viarum*, the office of the judge of the roads, who
himself had to be a *peregrinus*. In this case it meant a foreigner who came
from outside not only Siena but Tuscany. He was in charge of the path-
ways in city and countryside, punishing those who failed to respect the
streets and policing those who walked them, obliging various communities to carry out work on the roads in their jurisdiction: roads where Madonnas still dot the Via Cassia as one passes wheatfields and sunflower
patches—thousands of yellow petals turned southwest to track the sun.

Over the years Siena's statutes were constantly updated. Their eleven layers make them a maze as well as a gold mine for historians interested in pulling together an image not only of what Siena looked like, but of how and why it worked, another testimony to the Sienese obsession for retaining all traces of their history.

As public assets, the streets had to be protected, both from the citizens themselves (who wanted to build bigger houses, blocking light and access) and from threats on the road. There were plenty of brigands like the terrifying Ghino di Tacco, wanted for murder in the city when he took refuge from the Sienese in the mountaintop dwelling of Radicofani, where he regularly ambushed passing pilgrims from Rome. (Boccaccio turns him into a nice guy on the last day of the *Decameron*, as he cures an abbot he has kidnapped and gives him back his money.) The fortress where Ghino hid, built around the time of Sigeric's journey and long a site of contestation between Siena and the church, is open to visitors. We arrive after hours, but the guard, who lives there and is getting set to watch the semifinals for the European Cup, lets us in anyway. It's much restored but still offers sweeping views of southern Tuscany and the former papal states immediately to its south. Access to the fortress—through a forest of pine where pumice litters the ground, the only trace of this antique volcano—is much as it was when Boccaccio's abbot stumbled up here only to find a terrifying thief.

As it curves toward the top the road is indeed dangerous, safe stops few and far between. A half hour from Radicofani my son and I get out and walk a section of the Via Francigena through a farmer's field, and he calls off his dogs. One recent study suggests, not without justification, that the highwaymen and roving bands of mercenaries were largely responsible for Siena's decline after the tremendous plague of 1348. The petty thieves were one thing, the powerful and unpredictable *condottieri* with their loyal followers were another. These mercenaries were always looking for work, ready to accept bribes in off years not to lay waste a village or lie in wait and kidnap merchants on the road. Saint Catherine of Siena, never known to shy away from dealing with dangerous folk,

Fig. 10 ◆ (*Following*) Ambrogio Lorenzetti, *The Effects of Good Government* (detail of country scene) (1338–39). Palazzo Pubblico, Siena. Photograph: Scala/Art Resource, New York.

NASCE · EL MERITAR COLOR COPERAI BENE · 7 ACLIDIOVI OR DEBITE PEDE

PHILOSOPHIA

wrote a letter to the Englishman Sir John Hawkwood, whose painted image, on horseback, greets visitors to Florence's Duomo. The ruthless Hawkwood was trying to extort ransom money from Siena, a staggering 130,000 gold florins, in exchange for his promise not to attack the city or its territories. Catherine doesn't mince words: "Consider how much pain and anguish you have endured in the devil's service and pay!" Wouldn't it be much better for him to join in a crusade instead? "How cruel it is that we who are Christians, members bound together in the body of the Holy Church, should be persecuting one another."

Catherine's appeal apparently went unanswered. (What would Hawkwood have said anyway?) Pilgrims continued to travel all the same, at least finding refuge within Siena. The road from France brought the Romanesque as well as the Gothic, and French saints came with them along with Spanish: Martin, and Santiago or James. Culinary innovations arrived as well. The French herb *estragon*, tarragon, is a staple in Sienese cuisine (called *dragoncello* and used to flavor fish and eggs). And it's possible—unlikely, but possible—that visitors who came back from Jerusalem brought ideas for Siena's *bottini*, which as Michael Kucher observes are more like the *qtars* or tunnels that conducted water into the high-hilled Jerusalem than the aqueducts of Rome.

The Via Francigena went through Siena on its eastern ridge, and it shaped the city's identity in ways that are still visible. The experience of today's traveler in Siena is not so unlike that of the medieval pilgrim; nine-tenths of them traveled on "Saint Francis's horse": their feet. Vanni's late sixteenth-century map shows the stretch of road a twelfth-century pilgrim would have known, albeit without Pius II's expansive loggia or the current Duomo—then a much smaller church, with the new one under construction. The Campo had not yet come under the new street regulations and was still a muddy basin where men were free to urinate and hogs ran underfoot. But Via Pubblica as it was called included institutions that would be recognizable today: taverns, hospices, tables and kiosks, small churches. And at the center of it all, a building that would become Europe's most famous resting place for pilgrims, the Spedale della Scala, where Vecchietta's traces of Tobias remain.

◆

The entrance into Siena from the north is long and slow, on the flat terrain that the Sienese never could defend. In 1270, after losing at Colle di Val d'Elsa, the Sienese constructed what was called the Antiporta—the gate before the gate—at the city's north end, once enclosed within two circuits of high walls that took the pilgrims to Porta Camollia, the actual gate into the city. Once a densely populated suburb, the area was full of houses, with a *prato* or field that's boasted of in the 1309 constitution as being particularly pleasing to visitors. There were small oratories here too, places for pilgrims to sleep when they arrived when the gates were already closed for the night. Overseen by monks and laypeople, these small shelters were torn down along with the *borghi*, or hamlets, in the wake of the Medici victory of 1555. In his map Vanni portrays the dismal area, by then uninhabited, in ruins alongside the new fort. Now there is a delightful *gelateria* (ice cream shop), a post office, copy shops, and banks: a modern *borgo* that sprang up between the two world wars. The new Porta Camollia—the old one is in ruins on Vanni's map—was built only in 1603, with the Medici seal and its officious greeting put in for a Medici prince. The first thing one sees now on entering the gate itself is the Mercato Rionale, the neighborhood market, which never seems to be open. Here you can find one of the oldest sections of the Sienese walls; the enormous stones bring to mind the Etruscan gate in Perugia.

If they arrived right before the gate swung shut, pilgrims would have gone, perhaps immediately, to the hospice run by the Templars. The church that fronted the hospice was called San Pietro alla Magione, with its twin doors reminiscent of Gothic French cathedrals or the facades of Santo Sepolcro in Jerusalem or the cathedral of Santiago de Compostela, to allow for the orderly entrance and exit of pilgrims, circulating in and out. There were symbolic reasons for the double doors, too. When you left you were not the same person as when you entered, changed fundamentally by the experience of this mini-Jerusalem, this contact with the divine. But this was more than a church: it was a house—*maison* in French (the Templars were founded in Champagne), *magione* in Italian; the place where pilgrims stayed was behind the church, where you can still see the courtyard and a well. Outlawed by a mistrustful French king in 1312, the Templars left this and others of their holdings to the Knights

of Malta, who—a panel tells you—fixed the roof of San Pietro a year after "the war machines" destroyed it in the fateful siege of the Medici,
particularly harsh here in the area of Camollia. Within this dark and silent place in full view of Porta Camollia are faded fourteenth-century
frescoes of women before a tomb, a tree suspended in the background,
colors now subdued to earth tones: the terra of Siena, indented here and
there in soft reds. Faces and hands are uplifted toward a tomb, perhaps
a coffin; angels are hovering, but it is not clear around what or whom.
Lazarus, perhaps, leaving the tomb? If so, this is the theme of resurrection crucial to pilgrimage, the brush with death, the emergence into
the light. The simple pleasures of the new life are memorialized in this
place, with its round apse and unadorned brick arches where the soft
stone crumbled and gave way. Throughout, white crosses remind us of
the *magione*'s original keepers, who tried to make every place they oversaw a Holy Land.

Heading always south, toward Rome, one passes the church of Sant'
Andrea, where the gilded frame of Sano di Pietro's breathtaking altarpiece (a coronation of the Virgin), visible from the street when the doors
were open, supposedly was used to lure pilgrims within. It is one of the
few altarpieces still in its original home. This too once provided a hospice
for pilgrims, complete with a cemetery. Now it's rarely open, at least
during summer. One can catch a glimpse of Sano's gold–suffused colors
only once a week, just before Sunday's 10:30 Mass, over in half an hour.
Afterward a mother and her already elderly daughter walk in compan-
ionable silence. It's the moments of these masses in small churches like
Sant'Andrea that bring the old women out, to then vanish again into
their apartments, a single room or kitchenette on street level. This is
the rhythm of Siena's Sundays, to and from church, to the grocery store,
home to close the blinds against the sun, while the men sit at the bar near
Porta Camollia.

To the right of Via Camollia, almost unnoticeable, is the Renaissance
church of Fontegiusta, home to Vanni's painting of Beato Sansedoni,
begging favor from the divine mother while a Michelangelo-like figure watches nonplussed and the city lies darkening beneath it all. This
stretch of road is rarely traveled by today's tourists. Via Camollia tends
to be quiet, with shops that cater to Siena's residents—hardware stores,

tailors, bread shops. The restaurants cater to the Sienese as well. Il Vinaio (the Wine Seller) has opened recently, with a few tables spilling onto its deck outside. Inside are bookstalls as well as board games for the youths and the elderly men who come in for an afternoon beer; it's open all day rather than just for lunch and dinner. As we dine on *pici*, the broad, flat noodles that are uniquely Sienese, and sample a local white wine, the owner, Davide, explains that he and his brother Bob wanted to capture the aura of taverns of an earlier time. It's no accident that they also reopened the once famous Trombicche, which had been closed for years. It's a tiny eating place in Via delle Terme named for its owner, one-tenth the size of Il Vinaio and recently written up in the *New York Times*. But the *Times* correspondent didn't mention the book of reminiscences about Trombicche by the Sienese writer Euro Gazzei, written after the restaurant closed in the 1960s and before Davide and his brother reopened it in the 1990s. Gazzei reflects on the students, on the peasants who passed through on Wednesday (market day), on strange Sienese "types"—an aristocrat who'd lost his money, a garrulous regular called Nanni—and on his own inability to fit in with the daily crowd, since rather than a noonday glass or two of wine, he preferred coffee. The aging owner (who went by his nickname, Trombicche), "figures out that I don't want any wine, and his expression, at first serious, now hardens. He's never liked people who don't drink wine, and from now on he won't find me very likeable—*simpatico*—just as he didn't find me simpatico when I came here when I was younger." So much for Nanni's claim that Siena "is famous for its hospitality; you'll find yourself treated well here." But Davide and Bob make up for Trombicche's grouchiness, offering us limoncello on the house before we leave Il Vinaio.

Pilgrims with money—and there must have been quite a few—would have stopped at such taverns; Siena was once full of them. At its height there were also some ninety hotels on this road (around the corner from where we live the eighteenth-century sign for the Albergo del Ristoro still survives, if not the hotel itself) and some fifty hospices where you could stay free or for a small offering, with another thirty or forty outside the gates. Via Camollia becomes Banchi di Sopra—literally, "the stalls on the upper road"—where the road arches over a slight hill to swing down toward the Campo. This is where you'll find the highest concentration of stores in Siena, then as now. The Sienese *passeggiata* or evening stroll is the best way to experience the crunch of pilgrims, especially when sales begin in early July and the stores stay open late. (There's also a national *notte bianca*, "white night," in June when everything is open until midnight, and when our favorite bookstore, Libreria Ancilli, where in fact I bought Gazzei's memoir, sells a bag of books for five euros. It's now called Cartazucchero and is on Via Camollia.)

The Croce del Travaglio marks the spot where this road from the north connects to the road that heads south, the Banchi di Sotto that takes you toward Porta Romana. A third road connects here as well, Via di Città, which once led pilgrims around the northern base of the Campo to Via dei Pellegrini and the Duomo. Michael Kucher gives us a nice sense of the more expansive geographical domains of these roads: Banchi di Sopra went north to France, Banchi di Sotto south to Rome, Via di Città to the Tyrrhenian coast. More prosaically, here at the Croce, the three *terzi* or divisions of Siena come together, corresponding roughly to the arc of the streets: City, Camollia, and the southernmost San Martino. More prosaically still, there's a Furla store with its beautiful purses and costume jewelry and, slightly more crowded on a summer's evening, the *gelateria* Grom. (Furla is not an inappropriate choice for this corner. Faluschi's guidebook informs me that one of the side streets was once known as Via dei Borsajoli, named for those who made and sold *borse* or bags. Here brides would buy enormous sacks as part of their dowries, sacks made in the Levant and stored in a warehouse near the Sansedoni palace after merchants purchased them in Talamone.) The crush of people to the right and left suggests how the city now as then would partake in the ebb and flow of major pilgrimages. The jubilee year of 1300 brought thousands to visit Rome's seven churches and receive the promise of a release from purgatory. There was another jubilee in 1350 even though the popes, having become French, were ensconced in the far more civilized town of Avignon. Pilgrims were undeterred. One anonymous chronicler wrote that during that year "everyone became rich in Siena who ran a hotel, or who trafficked in or otherwise used the streets for business." The same wouldn't be true a hundred years later when Pope Nicholas V mandated a midcentury jubilee. It was a flop, and the hopeful hotel and tavern owners suffered.

Where Banchi di Sotto swings to the south, the *terzo* of San Martino begins, territory of the French knight who shared his mantle with a poor man and hence became the symbol of generosity to the needy. Next to his church—closed except for early morning masses and occasional feast days—a crane has been ominously snuggled for as long as I've been coming to Siena. The church sits on an incline to the right of Pius II's *loggiato*, where it oversees, like a knight from his horse, the goings-on of this section of the pilgrims' road as it winds out toward Rome. Here pilgrims would pass stall after stall selling souvenirs as well as cobblers and leatherworkers happy to provide new shoes and rucksacks or repair old ones for these walkers who would sometimes cover twenty-five or thirty miles a day. Via del Porrione—the emporium, and the name tells all—had its origins here, nestled close to the Campo, where you would find additional stalls with food and drink. Via del Porrione runs parallel to Banchi di Sotto, which becomes Via Pantaneto and is now a prime area for college students. The University of Siena maintains several buildings off this road, filling up the vast convents and monasteries that have been largely empty since the nineteenth century. The playwright Vittorio Alfieri lived in Via Pantaneto in the late 1700s ("I have always blessed the day I saw that city," he wrote of Siena, thanks to his meeting "six or seven learned men of sound judgment scarcely credible in such a small community"), and I've met friends at the Caffè Alfieri on the site of his old apartment. Faculty at the university grab a bite to eat here before they head back to their homes in Florence; there is also a lovely garden in the back if you're not in a hurry. The Università per Stranieri, or University for Foreigners, which brings in hundreds of international students to learn Italian and, if they're advanced enough, to read Alfieri, is off this street as well. Dollar stores (or more precisely euro stores) line one side of the street along with a kebab spit, one of the city's few Chinese restaurants, and a new Indian eatery.

Around the corner from the Università per Stranieri's new site—an unkempt courtyard where girls are practicing ballet steps, near the eternally closed church of Santo Spirito—there is the church of San Giorgio, where Francesco Vanni is buried in an imposing but easily missed monument immediately to the right of the entrance. The dedication paid for by his children, set in an otherwise grim-looking assortment of marble skulls and bones, speaks of him, hyperbolically, as the equal of Michelangelo and Raphael. Vanni put himself into a painting halfway up the nave on the left. He appears in the lower left corner, wearing a black cap and black garments, his hands folded in prayer, a somber self-portrait as he gazes sideways away from the Crucifixion and toward, as it were, the monument to his own death. It seems to be this profile that his sons imitated in their sculpture. San Giorgio is a light and lovely church, gray and white, an unusual Renaissance church built not long after Fontegiusta. This is where women come for the Rosary every night about 5:30, one by one. Some of them still wear winter coats even though winter is nearing its end, but the church is cool. This is not strictly a religious assignation; it's social too. One woman leaves early, making plans at the door with a late arrival for dinner at Salvatore's. When they finish intoning the Rosary a stooped priest even more aged than the women shuffles toward the altar and slowly prepares for the Mass.

This is not, however, the route pilgrims would have taken, even if now it is the obvious one, as it leads to the early medieval Porta San Maurizio, and then to Via Roma and out. Via Porrione once fed into a road that has now been blocked off at its northernmost access point, creating a dead end—unusual for Siena. And yet Vicolo degli Orefici, as it is called, virtually invisible (the residents no doubt like it that way) and so narrow that no car could get through, has stones original to the earliest tract of the Via Francigena. Gentle curves take you beneath arches and past dozens of flowerpots in what seems like a secret garden, certainly a secret neighborhood, a *contrada* unto itself. Above me a woman sings as she hangs dishtowels on a line, and an elderly man stumping along with a cane eyes me tentatively. Here the *orefici* or goldsmiths tended to their own secrets, around the corner from Via dell'Oro, where gold was sold, perhaps by pilgrims themselves before they left for the threatening roads. There's the clatter of plates during a family meal; a dog barks as I walk toward the end of the street, and again when I turn back. All around are the smells of winter: cigars, fireplaces burning wood, a pie in the oven.

Pilgrims emerging from Vicolo degli Orefici could have gone one of two ways: to the left meant Porta Romana or, before that was built, Porta di San Maurizio, our landlord's namesake. To the right meant another church, Santa Maria dei Servi, decades in the making.

Fig. 11 ◆ Vicolo degli Orefici, Siena. Author's photograph.

This is my favorite church in Siena, and not only for the simple quiet one finds within this serene Renaissance space or the spectacular view from the gardens of the Società di Castelmontone, the lucky *contrada* that has its headquarters here. It is also perhaps the most representative of Sienese churches, with art extending back to the mid-thirteenth century and into the eighteenth, almost all by Sienese artists: Guido da Siena, Pietro Lorenzetti, Giovanni di Paolo, Francesco Vanni, Rutilio Manetti, the length and breadth of the tradition. Quiet, simple in structure, it projects calm in its architecture and in its solitude. Usually there is no one here save a Servite or, at most, a pair of French tourists. Once an entire troop of Germans filed in to fill the pews, but they left a few minutes later; one woman tripped as she went down the steps.

As usual there is a multitude of Madonnas, but my favorites are in the first two side chapels to the right. In the first, a gigantic smiling Madonna reaches down to help grateful souls out of the fires of purgatory. In a town where Dante had almost instant appeal (Simone Martini adapted Dante's terza rime to his own sacred poem in the Palazzo Pubblico, and one of the earliest illuminated manuscripts of the *Comedy* was made here by Lorenzetti) the image, a rare one for the time, should not surprise. Throughout his poem Dante compares his voyage through purgatory, his second stop in the afterlife, to a pilgrimage, as when he likens his nostalgia for the earth to a pilgrim's longing for his home when he hears the bells at vespers: "It was now the hour that pierces the new pilgrim with love if he hears from afar a bell that seems to mourn the dying day" (*Purgatorio* 8). As Siena's "strangers" made their way through and out of the city, the thought that Mary might raise them from their all too earthly journey was no doubt uplifting. An angel, equally grand, holds her red cape while she benignly reaches out to reformed sinners, their hair garlanded in white flowers. There are an equal number of what look to be girls and boys; one incredulous soul feels the flowers on his head as though he can't quite take in his good fortune. This is only a fragment of what was once a larger work by an "unknown Sienese artist," painted sometime in the late fourteenth century and thus not long after Dante's poem. The tips of Mary's fingers are cut off, and we're also missing the body to the outstretched pair of hands raised toward Mary in what one must presume to be thanks. Two of the figures join hands; another two march forward into heaven, the young girl with arms crossed over her breast like a Mary annunciate. This is happiness, the end of the journey, the end of suffering, even as the six beings dressed in white continue their travel across the bottom of the painting, thrilled to have arrived in this place of grace, the perils of their sojourn in the fiery pit of purga-

Fig. 12 ◆ *Madonna of Purgatory* (detail) (anonymous, fourteenth
century). Fresco. Santa Maria dei Servi, Siena. Author's photograph.

tory at an end. Indeed, farther up in the nave, beneath an altar and easily missed, is a vision of purgatory itself, another fragment of the fresco
that must have covered an entire wall. The bodies of seven sinners are
plunged into fire, while an angel grasps the hand of an eighth, soon to go
on to heaven.

Images of purgatory are rare in Italy. There is an elaborate representation in Todi, another in the Cappella degli Spagnoli in Florence's Santa
Maria Novella. Dante is notable for having turned the undifferentiated
fires of this in-between sphere—the same fires in which the souls are
burning under the altar—into a mountainous landscape with seven ter-

races, in which we confront flame only at the top, where the lustful do penance. This transitory space had been invented a half-century before Dante's birth in 1266 by a church in need of money, though also increasingly interested in condoning middle spaces and ambiguity. Dante gave purgatory a location and turned suffering into a journey, a pilgrimage up a mountain that surged toward heaven with its calm saints and welcoming Madonna. Heaven and hell exist for all eternity, and the notion of change or progress in either place—or even the passing of time—has no significance. Purgatory is a temporary state where souls lucky enough to have escaped hell but not fully equipped for heaven pay their dues in various forms of penance. Dante has his penitents fully experience the rhythms of night and day as they travel toward the top of the mountain where the garden of Eden awaits them, and they sleep in the valley where Dante imagines bells tolling, while angels protect them against a serpent who is still at large.

It was from a kind of purgatory that the painter of the Mary in the second chapel on the right sought to be released: the wide-eyed Virgin of a captive painter, Coppo di Marcovaldo. He was in need of redemption when he was captured by the Sienese during the famous battle of Monteaperti, lost by the Florentine side that Coppo fought for. He was in chains, with some eighteen thousand others being led to various prisons in the city and outside. He apparently bargained with his Sienese captors: If he painted an image of the Madonna to whom they credited their victory, could he go home to Florence? There she sits on a throne, eyes wide, slippered feet on a beautiful exotic rug, a sign, perhaps, of the foreign city Coppo had been led to, one visited frequently by Germans, Frenchmen, Englishmen, and traders from the East. This is his ransom, the Madonna herself, as though she were reaching down to take him in. She is a more serious affair than the Madonna who a century later would welcome penitents to paradise, but Jesus gently touches her collar and she gently touches his right foot. She gazes out at you with a knowing look, one of the first of the multitude of Madonnas who would come to occupy this city and make it their own. It is moving that a Florentine, striving to be released from the Sienese purgatory where he found himself a prisoner, was the one to create her.

Much more awaits in the church: a Vanni annunciation awash in pastels, desperate mothers in a Lorenzetti scene of the massacre of the innocents, a fine Giovanni di Paolo Madonna of Mercy or Misericordia, her face impassive, her arms in richly brocaded silk reaching out like the slanting roof of a church to protect her Sienese people. But like the pilgrim, one must head out of the city and out the gate: Porta Romana, newest and largest of the outside gates, built in the 1320s and once boasting a painting by Simone Martini. The pilgrims returning from Rome might be heartened and certainly impressed by its splendor and stature: here was a city that might vie with the Rome they had just left. For those heading to Rome, the church of Saint Nicholas on the right would have been one of the final stops for prayer (torn down to build the psychiatric hospital protected by the same saint, who became the patron saint for Italy's mad. A friend told me a threatening little rhyme her Umbrian mother once recited to her, about San Niccolò being the last stop for children who didn't behave!) After that there were pauses to be made in Buon Convento, where Emperor Henry VII died; in the Val d'Orcia, where Saint Catherine reluctantly took her baths; and in the little town of San Quirico. Closer at hand are hospices on the river Arbia and at Belem, shorthand for Bethlehem, as though the Holy Land were just around the corner. Farther ahead pilgrims encountered Mount Amiata just before arriving in the territory of the papal states with the abbey of San Salvadore and the fortress at Radicofani, then the road down the other side that heads to Rome.

◆

Born as a city meant to provide hospitality, Siena is full of lore about good and bad forms of the hospitable. Its saints start out doing small works of kindness and charity, giving clothes to the homeless, food to the poor, lodging to pilgrims. One of the most frequently illustrated events from the life of Catherine of Siena is when she gives her father's best cloak to a beggar who turns out to be Christ. In one of the earliest works of art in the Pinacoteca, Andrea Gallerani, a murderer banished from Siena who vowed to make good is seen welcoming Jesus at a gate of the city, possibly Porta di San Maurizio. One of four fellow travelers, Jesus seems indistinguishable from his shivering and impoverished companions. Gallerani's legend—he eventually was beatified—has him offering lodging to a poor pilgrim who, like Catherine's beggar, turns out to be Christ. He founded

the Casa della Misericordia, now in Via Porrione but originally near the
towering church of San Domenico where the town's communal library
sits. Misericordia means mercy, and a list of the seven acts of corporeal
mercy in which Jesus instructs his disciples is affixed to a column at the
threshold of the Misericordia's little chapel.

Tobias had these rules down first, and he put them into action burying the dead, feeding the hungry, and giving alms. When Jesus tells his
disciples that every time they feed the hungry and clothe the naked they
are in fact feeding and clothing him, he is counseling them to follow in
Tobias's path. They act astonished: "How could it be, master, that we're
really helping you?" But two of his disciples have the chance to do just
that in the days immediately after Christ's Resurrection. Duccio di Buoninsegna depicts it in one of the more stirring of his scenes from his own
spectacular *Maestà*, completed a decade or so before Simone's. It is now
in the Museo dell'Opera del Duomo, in a room almost all to itself where
the lights are low and voices are hushed. It's as though we were still in a
church—the Duomo, to be precise, where the *Maestà* occupied the space
above the altar until 1505, when Pandolfo Petrucci, temporarily Siena's
dictator, thought it too medieval and had it taken out.

In one of the twenty-six panels depicting the life of Christ that
would have covered the back of the large single painting of Mary on
her throne—thus visible only to the cathedral's canons, not to the hoi
polloi—three men stand in profile outside a city gate, the stone path sloping up and into what seems a dark tunnel; behind it at a right angle are
two green towers with pink roofs and a third one all in yellow. The first
two men wear the simple robes typical of the disciples, while the third
wears a coarse woolen overgarment. He is a pilgrim, a man on a journey, and given that it is Duccio's *Maestà*, he is Christ on the day after the
Resurrection, having just come upon two of his disciples on the road to
Emmaus.

In all other scenes from Christ's life after the Crucifixion—his descent
to limbo, his appearance to Mary Magdalene—Jesus is dressed in a shimmering red robe with a blue mantle, both garments embroidered with
gold thread as though to suggest a divine light playing on the creases and
folds of his clothes. The only time he was dressed so resplendently in
life was at the Transfiguration on Mount Sinai, to which James and Peter

Fig. 13 ◆ Duccio di Buoninsegna, *Christ and Pilgrims on the Road to Emmaus* (1305). Panel from the back of the *Maestà* altarpiece. Museo dell'Opera Metropolitana, Siena. Photograph: Scala/Art Resource, New York.

were witnesses along with Moses and the prophet Elijah. In the scene on the Emmaus road, however, Jesus is dressed in simple pilgrim's garb: coarse brown mantle, hat resting on his back, pilgrim's stick in hand. Tokens of his visits to holy sites are pinned to his hat like souvenirs: the Volto Santo from Lucca, the palm from Jerusalem, the scallop shell from Santiago de Compostela. The most telling detail in the entire panel is the welcoming hand of the disciple as he turns to the gate: Would you like to join us? Would you like to come inside these walls to eat and stay the night?

The story is from Luke's gospel; he dwells on it in some detail in the final chapter. The disciples who stand just outside the city, ready to go in, can't believe how clueless this stranger is: he hasn't heard the big news sweeping Jerusalem, the death of Jesus. But once updated, he launches into a lecture on scripture that persuades the disciples he has something to say to them and their friends, and they want to learn more. One might ask, why does Duccio clothe Jesus in pilgrim's garb, anachronistically arriving from the Holy Land and hence from a visit to his own tomb? In the Latin Vulgate, one of the disciples, Cleophus, addresses this unknown man as *peregrinus*, which in the days of the Roman Empire simply meant stranger: you must be a *peregrinus* in these parts, since you don't seem to have heard of Jesus's death. Yet all pilgrims are strangers, and welcoming pilgrims is always a gesture of unknowability as well as a test: Who really knew the stranger being invited in? As in the *Odyssey* or in Ovid's *Metamorphoses*, it could be a god; as in the gospels, it could be Christ. The disciples don't seem to suspect this, even as they linger with Jesus before the city gate. Night is coming on; the faint golden light in the background that cleverly intersects with Jesus's halo and renders it virtually unseen suggests a sunset. They stand on flat gray stones, but bricks line the street within the gate. In the late 1200s there were new regulations that all Siena's streets must be paved with bricks as soon as possible; Duccio himself sat on one of the city's commissions that passed such rules. The warm red tones define the urban landscape as it had so recently defined itself, and soon Jesus will disappear within, as so many pilgrims disappeared within Siena.

Jesus is, in a sense, the first pilgrim: the first to travel to his tomb, the first to leave it, the first to tell about his journey. But in the interim, before he reveals who he is, he needs a place to stay. On the other side of Duccio's great painting Mary welcomes saints to paradise as she sits on her glorious throne, and in Santa Maria dei Servi she welcomes penitent sinners newly arrived from purgatory. Here the disciples offer a terrestrial foretaste of that eternal resting place, the hospitable space within a city's safe walls. Old Tobias welcomed strangers to his home in such a way, and so was the younger Tobias welcomed on the road.

A number of Duccio's panels for the *Maestà* focus on the travels of Christ and Mary alike: the flight into Egypt, with accompanying angels; the procession to Calvary; the especially large panel of the entrance into Jerusalem for what would become Palm Sunday, commemorated in Siena by large processions through the city. The *Maestà* itself was part of such a procession when it was completed, carried first around the Campo and then into the Duomo from Duccio's shop just outside the gate of Stalloreggi. Feet are prominent throughout the painting. The sandals the disciples remove on Holy Thursday abut the frame of the panel like large ants, their straps at angles that look like arms and legs. In the scene where he denies he knows Christ, Saint Peter tries nonchalantly to pretend that he just wants to warm his feet in front of the fire and that the question about Christ is an annoyance. Upstairs in the same panel—to convey contemporaneity Duccio connects two scenes by a stairway— Christ is questioned for the first time, having passed through the very courtyard where Peter now sits in comfort. Jesus's feet are always bare, and not only after he becomes a pilgrim.

But most pilgrims wore shoes. Hence the legend that grew up in the late Middle Ages: the Spedale della Scala was founded by a poor cobbler named Sorore, whose mother dreamed he would build a place to welcome not only pilgrims but abandoned children. Vecchietta depicted the dream and Sorore's telling of it in the most fanciful painting in the Spedale's Pellegrinaio—and the only one for which Vecchietta was responsible in the new cycle. Three muscular babies (they could be cherubs save for the absence of wings) climb a ladder to a Mary as welcoming as Duccio's, or that of the anonymous artist in Santa Maria dei Servi. She reaches out from her heavenly domain to pull the first baby in, while below the humble cobbler in black frock and little white cap kneels before a kindly man seated on a chair to whisper the dream in his ear. The elegant loggia teems with straining listeners, from an old man who looks like Moses to two well-dressed young courtiers who frame Sorore, contrasting with his humility.

Along with the Duomo, the Spedale occupies the same piazza as the Museo dell'Opera del Duomo where Duccio's *Maestà* now sits, on a slice of land that once was a hill, flattened out to create Siena's sacred center. Splendid Duomo and (now) plain Spedale coexist comfortably in the same space, it seems, though it has not always been so. A thin white line, still visible, crosses the piazza to delineate where the Duomo's land ends and the Spedale's begins. This is the result of a long-standing feud between the cathedral's canons who founded the Spedale and the laypeople who ended up running it. Even today the archbishop is not willing to include the Spedale in the list of "diocesan" stops in Siena and thus help boost its numbers of tourists (47,000 visitors came to the Spedale in 2012, a million to the Duomo). But for those of us who sit in this fabulous space, where the setting sun lights up the cathedral's facade, such squabbles are of no account. In the late afternoon light the Duomo glows, reassuring us that in centuries to come, or at least the next time we visit, it will still be here: there is so much that anchors it to the ground. The church is dedicated to the Virgin on the feast of her assumption—her magical ascent into heaven—but the sculptor Giovanni Pisano carved scenes of Mary's childhood in the lintel above the main door. These are tales of birth and youth, with no sign that she will be marvelously lifted into the sky. The gothic arches may point upward, but the three arched curves below each ascending point deliver your eyes back to capitals and columns and to the steps, the *scala* for which the hospital is named: the Hospital of Santa Maria della Scala, Saint Mary of the stairs (although some suggest it's named for the *scala* the children climbed to Mary in Sorore's mother's dream). Muted colors, Siena's white and black, *bianco e nero*, stripe the campanile, the body of the church, and the adjoining bishop's palace. Pink tones lighten the facade, making one think of Assisi's soft colors. Yet this is Sienese soil, *la terra*, used sparingly as background, to fill the spaces between.

The best place to view the cathedral's facade is the stone benches in front of the hospital. It's not only the facade that you see. A bare wall juts out at a right angle from the right transept: two arches meant to be inside the church exposed to the elements, like the children once left at the Spedale. Had things gone better during the plague years of 1348–49, had the architects had a better grasp of the land's terrain, Siena's ambitious extension to the Duomo—optimistically called even today the Duomo Nuovo, the new cathedral—might not have been pronounced unworkable by a Florentine in 1355 and left to the elements. Duccio's *Maestà* is now in the area that would have been part of the new Duomo's nave. Instead it became the place for generations of marble workers and sculptors to carve their stone. This is where Jacopo della Quercia made his Adam and Eve for the Fonte Gaia, where Michelangelo carved his statues for Pius II's tomb. When you come up the precipitous steps from the baptistery below and, panting for breath, walk under an arch, you are going through the spectacular side door of the nave that, in the words of Zbigniew Herbert, has the sky for its roof.

Flautists and accordion players serenade us from under the arches, and the sound echoes, amplified in this naturally resonant space. We can hear it on the benches outside the Spedale where tourists exhausted from their day make phone calls, drink water, read a paragraph or two from a guidebook. You must turn around, though, to see the stark walls of the building that houses Vecchietta's paintings of Tobias and Sorore, walls that betray little sign of what they harbored in the past; Lorenzetti's frescoes of the life of the Madonna, still visible in Vanni's Fontegiusta painting, are long gone. These benches were built so the city's magistrates could have a privileged view of the relics shown outside the chapel of the Spedale each twenty-fifth of March—a nail from the cross, milk from Mary's breast. This was the day Mary had promised an angel that she would do what God commanded; nine months later she gave birth to Jesus. Thus, in this space that the eyes easily traverse, we move from a girl's promise to save the world to her reward in heaven as celebrated by the Duomo dedicated to her assumption.

The story about Sorore is a fifteenth-century fabrication. But the tale quickly took hold, and today scholars are still uncertain about the hospital's precise foundation. It may date back to the late ninth century. By 1090, when a pious couple donated some of their lands to the "Xenodochio et hospitale de Canonica Sancte Marie domui episcopio senese," the institution was already established. Of all the monumental buildings in

Fig. 14 ◆ Spedale di Santa Maria della Scala, Siena, northern wall.
Author's photograph.

Siena, this one has seen the most change since its creation a thousand
years ago, and long before it existed it was the site of Siena's most ancient
civilization, as archaeologists are discovering. Gabriella Piccinni and Giuliano Catoni suggest that with respect to the excavations, "they were
looking for the history of the hospital and they found the history of the
city": not only its Etruscan and Roman roots—signs of a thermal bath,
the construction of artificial terraces—but also its Lombard and early
medieval legacy. It is here, behind the walls Vanni made so luminous in
his painting, that one comes to see a Siena in miniature. A city within a
city, over the centuries the Spedale absorbed into itself streets, orchards,
warehouses, and even sections of the city wall: all for the purpose of *ac-
coglienza*, or hospitality. By a strange act of cannibalism, the hospital

engulfed the city to make the city open itself to others; and yet the hospital too learned to make its services a source of wealth. It made enough money on the plague to buy the relics the magistrates could glimpse once a year, preserving the goods and money of pilgrims who died on the road as well as collecting the pledges that Sienese recorded, in the presence of two witnesses, in hopes of a shorter stay in purgatory.

If the Spedale started as a place for pilgrims to spend the night, it wasn't one for long. The Pellegrinaio, once the large entrance hall for male pilgrims (the women were taken elsewhere; one of the first instances in medieval Europe of a separation of the sexes in the vast network of hospices), represents the Spedale's imaging of itself to itself and to its guests and patients. In this secular pictorial cycle, virtually unique in Italian Renaissance art, the protagonist is the institution itself, painted by Vecchietta and two other Sienese painters, Domenico di Bartolo and Jacopo della Quercia's brother Priamo (no match for the sculptor). From the mass of humanity that covers the walls only two identifiable pilgrims emerge, both waiting in a breadline and marked by the familiar signs of sacred journeys: a floppy hat and a scallop shell that, like that of Duccio's Jesus, attests to the distant cathedral of Saint James. Now they're standing patiently in line with others. The poor, single mothers, the homeless, all wait for the bread that would have been stamped with the Spedale's characteristic seal: the ladder with three rungs, topped by a Latin cross. Another painting shows care being given to children left in the middle of the night on the *pila* or basin outside the Spedale's main door; after ringing the bell, the mother—or father, or some other relative—would disappear into the darkness. Children of the Spedale were tattooed on their feet with the official logo, like the bread. The crowded painting takes us from their entrance into the world of this strange, sprawling institution to their education—girls learning to read, boys to write—and eventual marriages: a coy young woman marries a man who has asked for her hand, the successful transition into society of an orphan entrusted to the mercy of the Spedale. Fulfilling the dream of Sorore's mother, the children arrive and grow up, their entire life span encompassed by the building's welcoming gates. Brought in as abandoned infants, they are ushered out lovingly as spouses after the hospital has found them husbands, or as workers when the hospital has found them jobs. In between they are breast-fed by the *balie* or wet nurses who lived in a communal home connected to the Spedale by a covered alleyway; bells rang when a new baby arrived, and a nurse would run up the stairs. In Bartolo's painting a nursemaid of ample and exposed bosom holds an infant to her breast while a grinning toddler reaches around from behind to squeeze her other nipple; she gives him a look of fatigue and exasperation. Once weaned, babies were fed on the produce grown in the orchard outside the Spedale, perhaps prompting the name of the *contrada* whose territory surrounds the hospital's bulk, the *selva*, or forest, and a servant at the top of the painting plucks grapes from a vine just outside.

A third painting, ruined by a window carved into its midst, features a weekly meal for the poor; a fourth shows us the workings of what today we would consider a "real" hospital: an almost nude man is tended to as blood seeps from an open wound on his thigh, and a hospital worker kneels before him to wash his feet, evoking Holy Thursday's ceremony with the disciples. To his left, a physician shakes a tube of urine to see if it is cloudy or clear, and to his right a man is brought in on a stretcher while a priest hears a deathbed confession. The painting doesn't show the new cemetery that was just being built behind the Spedale in the direction of the Fosso di Sant'Ansano; it would be in use until the middle of the eighteenth century. As Beatrice Sordini comments, the hospital should focus on healing—not death.

Nonetheless, this was a whole system of misericordia, from birth to death. Even in the wake of plagues and fiscal crises, even with Siena's fall to the Medici, funding for acts of mercy was never cut back. The setting for these humble acts is elegant and ornate. The paintings are brightly colored, occasionally awkward as they wrestle with how to portray all that went on here, from birth to death, to make the place seem less an *asilo di tristezza e di dolore*—a nursery of sadness and pain—as described in a plaque outside the pilgrims' quarters, and more a vibrant community, a city within a city. Once it served only pilgrims, but eventually the hospital came to welcome all who were wounded in life, *by* life: men, women, and children scarred by natural and human disaster, from earthquakes to plagues and political crises.

The paintings' vibrancy conceals a reality darker than they suggest. Indeed, the Spedale becomes more somber as you descend into its depths,

Fig. 15 ◆ Domenico di Bartolo, *Preparations for Adoption of Children*
(detail) (1443). Fresco. Pellegrinaio, Spedale di Santa Maria della Scala,
Siena. Photograph: Alfredo dagli Orti/Art Archive at Art Resource,
New York.

now being readied for exhibits. When we take a tour to learn about the
building's underground quarters—Saturday mornings at 10:30—we see
the traces of a modern heating system and an enormous well that contained water for the pilgrims and the sick, dug thirty-five meters into the
earth; the land here was too elevated for *bottini* to reach it, so the wells
had to go deep. Our talkative guide, Giulia, tells us that the sturdy beds
were made of iron, not of wood, and food was carried on trays to the

pilgrims and the sick, ushering in the furnishings and practices of modern hospitals. As one walks through this mostly empty structure, the space seems huge, but there were times when it wasn't big enough. During waves of pilgrimages to Rome—the jubilee years of 1450 and 1475, or the pestilence that struck in 1463, right between the two jubilees— many could not find room, and indeed, the paintings in the Pellegrinaio give a sense of enormous crowds jostling for space. In other years when leprosy broke out the Spedale paid for a small *lazaretto* in Vallepiatta, a kind of waiting room for triage. You can see in the lowest levels the warehouses and the granary where provisions were stored, the areas where dirty laundry was delivered, and the most somber setting of all, the *ossarium* or *carnaio*—the charnel house, a term that brings to mind grim Dickensian images. During plague years bodies were unceremoniously dumped into pits. Giulia shines her flashlight into the corner to show us bits of clothing and jewelry in the jumble of bones and dust, all that is left of Sienese and their visitors from the fourteenth century. In those years what was once an extensive herb garden for the pharmacist, destroyed in 1730 for a new infirmary, wouldn't have provided enough medicine for the many who sought shelter. Nor would the neighborhood normally teeming with butchers (hence the nearby Via Galluzza, after the chickens raised there). In good times the diet of the sick was surprisingly sumptuous: lots of meat—those Via Galluzza chickens—as well as eggs, bread, and wine. Domenico di Bartolo's painting shows two bottles at the head of the sick man's bed, probably one for wine and the other for water. You can still see niches in the walls for these bottles and colorful painted headboards in a room adjacent to the Pellegrinaio.

How can we imagine the shadowy community that embraced life in such a place, where poor health or death was often the payment for charity? In a hospital in San Gimignano, another pilgrim town, a marker from the early thirteenth century refers to one Santo Bartolo, who had leprosy but continued to work in "lo spedale di Cellole." One could pledge a lifetime commitment to the Spedale and so dwell for the rest of one's days with the sick and needy within the walls of this enormous place, donning the black cape and cap to become an oblate—literally an oblation, turning one's life into an offering to God. Or one could take a lesser vow and live at home, devoting a generous amount of time to the Spedale and willing one's goods to the Spedale after death. These were acts of mercy, lived out daily: welcoming pilgrims, tending to the sick, taking in and raising orphans, lodging the city's poor as well as nobility who fell on hard times, giving alms to families in need and to the poor every Sunday and on feast days, and feeding the entire citizenry of Siena in times of famine. There are accounts of miracles and sudden healings, such as Catherine of Siena's saving a woman by sucking pus from her tumor. There were tensions not only with the church—hence the white masonry line that separates the Spedale from the Duomo—but with the state. The rector Giovanni Battista Tondi resigned in 1505 rather than submit himself to what he considered the tyranny of Siena's leader, Pandolfo Petrucci. For his bravery he is buried in the wall of the Pellegrinaio, where a marble sculpture shows him lying comfortably on a pillow, smiling in death. There were young men and women—*figli dello Spedale*, or children of the hospital—who, grateful for the care and education they received, devoted their lives to the place. The orphan Giovanni Macchi was in charge of the Spedale's records for over thirty years and left a detailed design of its facade, noting the doors for the horses' stalls and the granary, where one would leave alms so the hospital could buy grain, the basin where newborns could be left in the dead of night, the principal entrance into the Spedale, the house of the rector, the carpenter's shop. But by the late eighteenth century reforms forced the Spedale to concentrate more on the work we identify with modern institutions and less on the sprawling system of medieval charity that began its life. A *policlinico* opened here in 1880, one of the first teaching hospitals in the new nation of Italy. As its mission became almost exclusively "health care" rather than life care, specialized fields of medicine moved to a new hospital outside the walls. After 1975 babies were no longer born in these cavernous halls, although there was an emergency room and patients were seen at an eye clinic through 1996, when it closed.

Vecchietta, painter of the shy Tobias and of Sorore's dream in the Pellegrinaio, was called the painter of the Spedale for all the work he did here over three decades. He covered the sacristy with his frescoes of the Apostles' Creed and painted a wooden cabinet, now in the Pinacoteca, that held the precious relics acquired in 1359 from Byzantium and taken out once a year for display. He left a modest self-portrait, almost

completely faded, on the lower part of the sacristy's north wall. Just below, one can make out the faded ghosts of hospital officials at prayer.
Vecchietta donated his few goods to the hospital, signing his will with a
simple cross. He asked to be buried in the Spedale, and though his final
resting place is unknown, the bronze statue of the risen Christ that he
may have designed for his own tomb is in the Spedale's church of the Annunciation, where Mass is said daily.

This stunning piece, possibly his last work, looks black against the
light blue background of the church's tribunal, and rays of light pass
from the painting in the apse behind to Christ's head in a wonderful
juxtaposition of baroque and Sienese Renaissance. The painting itself,
by the eighteenth-century Neopolitan painter Sebastiano Conca, depicts
the pool of healing waters mentioned in the Gospel according to John: the
infirm gather by the dozens near a pool, and more are coming in from
the countryside, where there is an ancient temple. A young man carries
an old man on his back, a visual reference to the Stanza of Raphael in
the Vatican, where Aeneas carries his father from the burning city of
Troy; another young man guides a blind woman. But the real powers
of healing belong to Jesus. He has just cured an emaciated cripple, who
waves his crutches above his head in triumph. This is a place of healing, consolation, even magic, like the Madonna's plucking a soul from
purgatory or young Tobias's restoring his father's sight with the gall and
liver of a fish.

Vecchietta lived and died for the Spedale, and even as he took on other
occasional projects, for decades this was his center. His staying attests to
a certain humility, shared by all those who chose to serve the sick. Unlike the pilgrims who came and left, yet no less modest than they, they
lived perpetually suspended in between, waiting to greet whoever came.

◆

Cathedrals were once temporary Jerusalems for pilgrims, the places
where they were closest to the experience of the resurrected Christ they
hoped to partake in more fully on arriving in the Holy Land itself. Even if
the Spedale put them in direct contact with those who emulated Christ's
life on earth, the Duomo offered a place where things of this life should be
cast aside. Yet there is something distinctively earthly about the Duomo,

Fig. 16 ◆ Vecchietta (Lorenzo di Pietro), *Risen Christ* (1470s). Bronze. Ospedale di Santa Maria della Scala, Siena. Photograph: Scala/Art Resource, New York.

even as it aspires to replicate Jerusalem's temple with its marbled floor and walls and the Pantheon with its weightless cupola rimmed by stars: it is anchored to the *terra*, a church that is a place not so much of intense piety as of self-conscious historicizing. This is a space not of overwrought mystical fantasies but rather of calm acceptance of its place on earth, where the busts of 172 popes look down quizzically but kindly from the nave. Far from imperious, the coronas gracing each small head convey the serenity of continuity, as does the rest of the church, especially the figures on its spectacular mosaic pavement, which the Florentine Giorgio Vasari pronounced "the largest, most beautiful and most magnificent floor ever made."

The German historian Friedrich Ohly offers a more poetic image as he rhapsodizes on this "mighty expanse of parti-colored marble pavement [that] stretches out before us like a brilliant sea flowing into the great space." Unable to paint on the austere marble walls and columns—there are no frescoes in this nave, as in so many Gothic and Renaissance churches—the Sienese undertook a singular project that lasted for centuries, overseen by various *capomaestri* of the Opera del Duomo. The inlaid pavement has now in certain places been utterly consumed, as under the chair of the canons behind the altar, where an emblem of Misericordia has almost entirely disappeared beneath the scrapings of chair legs and shoes, along with an image of "the old Tobias," according to Faluschi's guidebook—perhaps the most visible link to the Spedale across the way. To protect from further damage, much of the marble is regularly covered with inelegant cardboard mats, removed only for the Palios of August 16 and several weeks following. (I finally got to Siena in mid-September and saw the astonishing vision of the marble pavement as it was meant to be seen, its inviting colors of yellows and pale rose softening the harsh monochromes of the pillars and walls and letting the eye reassuringly linger not above, but below, at ground level.)

But even with the mats in place, the pavement that *is* exposed still has something for everyone. A Persian sibyl in sandals nonchalantly waves her hand before a prophecy about Christ's birth, now virtually illegible, the letters faded to a series of pointillist dots. At the foot of the altar is the Hebrew king David, seated on his throne among musicians and singers who are performing his psalms, while roundels depict on one side the

Fig. 17 ◆ Duomo, Siena (interior, facing west). Author's photograph.

young boy with his slingshot, and on the other a towering but vulnerable Goliath. There is the Egyptian Hermes Trismegistus, an allegory of Fortune featuring Roman and Greek philosophers, and a wealth of stories from the Old Testament, including the siege of Bethulia and Judith returning triumphant with Holofernes's head. There is only one scene from the New Testament, the killing of the innocents, the massacre of male infants by a jealous Herod in the months after Christ's birth. Matteo di Giovanni's soldiers are positively gleeful as they plunge swords into babies' necks and chests; at the center a startled child watches the tip enter his cheek and seems to twist his head around to see where it emerges, behind his left ear. More horrifying than the pile of bodies littering the floor is the spectators' reaction: not only is a turbaned Herod glorying in this gory ritual, but from small windows that give them privileged access to the scene, little boys—perhaps just a few years older than the ones visited by death—watch in fascination, even delight. Is this a well-produced play? Are they future minions of Herod, or of Roman emperors like Nero? When we look at Matteo's painting of the same subject in the Spedale, this return to Herod's pernicious deed makes sense: the Spedale, like the church, protects the innocent, welcomes in the babies who without its guiding hand would be subject to exposure and death from the Herods of an unkind universe.

All are here—Jews, pagans like Aristotle, ten enigmatic Sibyls whose ancient words supposedly predicted Christ's birth. Next to the Hellespont Sibyl, a lion and a wolf tentatively touch paws. Even Florence is welcomed: some art historians contend that the lion here stands in for Florence, but even if not, there is a clear reference to the Florentines in the wonderful wheel that places Siena's nursing wolf at its center, the founding twins tugging at her teats—two *gittatelli*, castaways, rescued by a merciful animal—and "Florentia" with its lion as one of its spokes, joined by a unicorn (Viterbo), an elephant (Rome), and a stern leopard for Lucca. This is the Duomo's own *Mappamondo*, perhaps not unlike Lorenzetti's tattered rotating disk, with Siena as its center. The church too is about the here and now, the horizontal light and dark lines of the columns, white and black to match the colors—or noncolors—of the city's seal. The monochrome is deceptive, however. For over six centuries Duccio's great rose window reflected light through six scenes of the

Madonna's life. Worried about American bombs in the dying days of World War II, the Sienese moved the window to safety, and it's now on the ground floor of the Museo dell'Opera, where upstairs you can see the equally colorful scenes from Duccio's *Maestà*. But both *Maestà* and window were once on—and above—the main altar. All could see Duccio's glass, while the Mary he painted on her throne solemnly faced the worshippers, and the panels of Jesus's life with the pilgrimage to Emmaus were turned to the priest and his canons and the choristers.

Now there is no separation between the sacred space of the priest and the hoi polloi, at least when Mass is over. One Sunday afternoon I witnessed a typical scene: two little sisters, no more than six, carefully lighting candles for the Madonna del Voto, who has guarded Siena since the victory at Monteaperti in 1260 (although guidebooks will tell you the real Madonna is the "wide-eyed" and, one must say, wild-eyed Madonna in the Museo dell'Opera del Duomo). A kind female custodian helps the girls, temporarily distracted from scraping the dried wax from the basin before replacing old candles with tall new ones. She is gentle, patient, anxious lest they burn their fingers. They are quiet and subdued. When they finish they run off, their sandals slapping the marble loudly as they run to tell their mother in excited Spanish that the job is done.

Along with the Campo, this is where the lives of tourists converge most serenely with that of the city. We hear hushed voices, the occasional clink of coins, and subdued exchanges like this. Figures lean out from the walls to engage us, not in excitement or animation but gently, the way the woman cleaning the candles treated the children. Here we are, and you are here too, part of this grand sweeping space with its calm assertion that human activity and achievement do matter. The heavy green travertine keeps us rooted in the earth, the *terra* of Siena. There isn't much light, making the space inviting in the heat of summer, so the tourists come to spend minutes or hours in its welcoming embrace. There are chairs, lots of them. It's cool. There are fiercely detailed battle scenes on the pavement for children to study, and you can marvel at the immense wooden poles that used to prop the doors closing off the altar from the populace. You can step into the side chapel with the Madonna del Voto and Gian Lorenzo Bernini's statues, or into the marvelous Libreria Piccolomini, or into the bookshop or the toilets.

And there is always room for discovery, searching for something overlooked no matter how often you return—coming to one or more of the many Sunday masses is the easiest (and cheapest) way. A ciborium by Vecchietta is here, a heavy bronze canopy above the altar, stolen from the Spedale to replace Duccio's *Maestà*. A small side chapel dedicated to John the Baptist—the baptismal font is in its midst—has an extraordinary portrait of a knight praying in a forest, and to his left is the image of a man who was *operaio* or superintendent of the artists who worked in the Duomo, as well as one Alberto Aringhieri, commander of the church of San Pietro alla Magione, that hospice for pilgrims, with a view of Rhodes behind him. Like all men who took vows to be Rhodian knights, defenders of pilgrims and fighters of Turks, he must have spent several years on the island, where he would also have taken a vow of chastity (not kept; he had at least one illegitimate son). The task of painting him fell to Bernardino di Betto, called Pintoricchio, who depicts him in the Knights of Malta's characteristic black robe and Latin cross, the port to his left and boats with billowing sails to his right. Across the nave, just above the eternally closed stairway into the campanile, lies the supine figure of a Piccolomini bishop, Tommaso, who died in 1483. Some of my favorite sculptures are here, almost always ignored by the visitors who, as in Eliot's "Prufrock," flock to see the Michelangelo across the nave. But here there is a modest series of marble plaques on the life of Mary and her parents, and just to the right of the tomb is one of the earliest representations in stone of a bucolic scene: a peasant kneels to hold the rear legs of a sheep while, contentedly perched on a rock above him, a shepherd plays his pipe and his dog watches the exchange. The hills take a gentle dip behind them, and in the valley's curve you can faintly glimpse a tower, a sign of the civilization that is never far from Sienese scenes of the countryside. Next to this scene an angel converses with the shepherd, who then embraces a woman while a cluster of men whisper among themselves: This must be the life of Mary's father, told by an angel to meet his wife at the Golden Gate after the two had lived celibate lives for so many years. She would go on to conceive late in life, as in so many Old Testament narratives, and so open the way for a new testament.

Tourists now gather in this vast, echoing space as they wait for the next bus back to Florence, or for shade to cover the bars on the Campo.

Pilgrims would have lingered here too. But before pilgrims entered the Duomo—before the Duomo as we know it now was finished—they would have come into what is erroneously called the crypt. Rediscovered only in 1999 after centuries of neglect, this sacred space probably served as an anteroom for pilgrims who had just arrived on Via dei Pellegrini, becoming a storage area when the baptistery was enlarged in the late fourteenth century. The *orefici* or goldsmiths from the neighborhood then claimed its westernmost area as a workshop. By the 1500s it was entirely sealed up, and its frescoes, probably by Guido da Siena, teacher of Duccio, were sequestered from offending light, dust, and oxygen. When you enter now, through a side door halfway up the steep stairway that leads to the unfinished nave, the hues of the Duecento, the thirteenth century, come alive. Holy figures in marvelous blues, reds, yellows, and greens burst across and through columns in a medieval hodgepodge of biblical stories, the top row bisected by the walls of the baptistery just below. They prefigure the harmonious intersection of biblical testaments in the church directly above. (A glass panel in the ceiling lets you see the visitors walking just outside the chapel that honors the local knight of Malta.)

In this dimly lit room covered by some 180 square meters of painting, with awkwardly placed pilasters and a fifteenth-century kiln erupting through the floor, the stories of the Old and New Testaments converge in the vibrant colors Duccio, Giotto, and Cimabue would have used. The upper register, in various stages of disrepair, belongs largely to Genesis: a remarkably intact ark, animals peering serenely from the windows; a hungry Esau robbed of his birthright; hints of an Edenic garden in which we see only the feet of Adam and Eve. And beneath, there unfolds the life of Christ: an ethereal Mary greeting a pregnant Elizabeth, a nativity scene in which mother and baby are sealed in a bright blue bubble, and across the room the stark, byzantine movements of Christ being taken down from the cross like a stack of wood as soldiers strain and women weep.

These works are all about touch, hands extended toward others: a weightless, bounding Gabriel reaching out toward Mary; blind Isaac grasping for his deceptive son; Jesus—in a moment of touch fulfilled—holding out his hands to pluck a grateful Adam from the depths of hell and bring him to heaven. Even in death Jesus is compassionate toward others: his arm is bent at an unnatural angle toward Mary Magdalene's face as she bathes his hand in tears. There is also Jesus learning to write, extending a hand toward a woman, possibly his mother, while another youth, possibly John, calmly inscribes letters in a little book like any thirteenth-century boy learning to be a merchant. This scene, like others, comes from popular materials such as the apocryphal Gospel of James, in circulation while Guido and maybe a very young Duccio painted these images, and they focus lovingly on scenes omitted from the canonical gospels. Thus in chapter 31 of the apocryphal Gospel of James, one finds the story of Jesus at school, where he was supposed to learn his letters from the elder Levi. The fresco depicting this writing lesson is on an octagonal pillar and shows old Levi seated on an imposing chair while he turns to Jesus, intent on writing along with the other boys. Michele Bacci notes that they've found some musical notations on a wall near this column, suggesting that for a time this underground space with no windows might have served not only pilgrims but those eager for musical as well as theological instruction, suggesting that "they may also have prayed before these very images, from time to time lighting candles, as is seen from the burning left by the wax on some sections of the frescoes."

But surely the most remarkable work dealing with hands and touch is one of Mary, Joseph, and Jesus escaping Herod's wrath during the flight to Egypt (exhibited elsewhere in the crypt as terrified children stare at swords plunging into their throats just as they do in Matteo's scene in the Duomo above). Mary, Joseph, and Jesus are safe but hungry, huddling beneath a date tree on the crypt's southern side; the tree miraculously bends toward the solicitous mother, whose name is painted in Greek letters above her head as "Mary the Goddess" (*theon*). This story too is found in the apocryphal gospel: tired from the long journey, Mary rested under a date tree and, being hungry, tried unsuccessfully to reach the dates. She asked Joseph to reach them for her, but he couldn't do it either, so they left things to Jesus, who climbed down from Mary's lap and ordered the tree to bend its branches down to the Virgin's feet. Immediately the tree lowered itself, and they ate the fruit. Thus we see Mary gathering the date palm's fruits as it bows down before her, while Joseph points to the miracle, his finger crossing the bright orange-and-red border on

Fig. 18 ◆ *Miracle of the Dates* (anonymous, thirteenth century). Fresco. Cripta, Duomo of Siena. Photograph: Giulo Andreini/AGE Fotostock America.

the octagonal column that separates him from his spouse, so mirroring the tree's gesture. This is life in the desert, responding to a miracle. Suddenly fertile branches break through the artificial divisions of a painting's border, moving around the pillar that pilgrims would have leaned on and may have slept by, in this twilight world that prepared them to enter the fully lighted space of the cathedral above. When I escorted a group of teenagers from Abu Dhabi into this place several years ago, they got excited as I told the tale, and finally one interrupted: they already knew the story, not from an apocryphal Gospel, but from a sura in the Qur'an.

Atop another pillar across from this one, an angel in white opens his hands to Mary and Jesus, offering protection while they are still in flight. Or perhaps it is an act of gift giving: the promise of more dates, of respite in this now dark and once purgatorial place where pilgrims gathered en route to the place of penitence. As Dante and the Sienese painters affirmed, the journey itself was eminently penitential, as old selves were thrashed out and new ones emerged.

MONEY

3

Although his feet are pointed forward, Vecchietta's Tobias looks back, a sign of his reluctance to leave home and of his concerns about the journey ahead. Yet for others, Tobias's hesitation might have meant something different. Consider Agostino Chigi, son of a wealthy Sienese merchant, who himself made a considerable fortune as a banker and businessman in the early sixteenth century. Chigi chose for his personal medallion the figure of Prudence, who looks both backward and forward and, like Janus, was often depicted with two heads. Aristotle in his *Ethics* suggests that "Prudence is the measure of all virtues because she is the correct reckoning of what is possible." This idea of "reckoning the possible" was crucial for a man like Chigi as he slowly and determinedly gained a monopoly on alum in Italy (and almost in all of Europe) and became one of Italy's most powerful men.

Chigi succeeded for many reasons, not least because he was good at twisting popes around his finger. The fierce Julius II and the culture-loving Medici pope Leo X excommunicated Chigi's enemies and debtors and elevated his nephews and friends to positions within the church. Such prudence thus was not without ruthlessness. The Spannocchi, whose delightful Renaissance palace is immediately to the right of the Monte dei Paschi's headquarters in Piazza Salimbeni, had been the chief bankers to the Sienese Pope Pius II and his nephew Pius III. But when the latter died after only thirty days in office (like William Henry Harrison, who survived only a month as United States president, Pius gave too long an acceptance speech and caught a cold that he never recovered from) the Spannocchi were displaced by the aggressive Chigi, who had earlier lobbied for Giulio della Rovere to become pope. After Pius's death, Giulio did indeed become Pope Julius II, and in gratitude he made Chigi his privileged banker. Chigi's wealth and connections in Rome enabled him to commission chapels in Roman churches and build the Villa Farnesina, and he was patron to some of the sixteenth century's greatest artists, Raphael among them.

Chigi seems a far cry from the Tobias story—perhaps the archetypal Old Testament story about the golden rule, doing for others what you would like done for yourself. As the angel's presence attests, these works are graced by God, who at the end rewards those who have loved their neighbors. Still, there is an interesting tension in the story between those who go out and those who remain. Old Tobias can receive his reward only if his son ventures outside the city of Nineveh to reclaim what is rightfully his. And what is rightfully Tobias's is money: apparently a great deal. Part of this reward involves seeking to get back only exactly what was lent, a sum he writes on a slip of paper and gives to the angel. Tobias, that is, asks for no interest. Church fathers such as Ambrose would contrast this worthy Jew with the contemporary Jews of fourth-century Rome, who charged usurious rates. But Ambrose omits an important point: Tobias was lending to other Jews, members of his tribe. The Jews of Ambrose's day charged interest only to Christians, since they were strangers. And over the next thousand years, Christians themselves would become moneylenders, the Spannocchi and Chigi among them. They racked up fearful rates to borrowers, despite the church's sanctions against usury. Thus in 1525 a down-and-out Sienese captain of the guard with the unfortunate name Pochointesta Petrucci (Dimwitted Petrucci) would protest during his trial for outstanding debts that the fellow Sienese to whom he owed money should learn from a local Jewish moneylender, who "spesso me ne presta con bono pegno" (often lends me money at a good rate).

In point of fact usury—the unnatural begetting of money, exploiting the vulnerable to make a gain for oneself—defined much of Sienese business practice. It might help to explain why the energetic new director of the Spedale della Scala ultimately chose to depict in his grand hall, the Pellegrinaio, not the story of Tobias but that of his own institution, focusing on the charitable works laymen and laywomen were doing in the hospital in the mid-fifteenth century. On the one hand, the charitable acts of Tobias père—burying the dead, giving food to the hungry— were hardly at odds with the deeds promoted by the men and women who worked within the hospital's walls. On the other hand, the simple, difficult life the elder Tobias led may have been seen as a reproach to the rich men who helped build the Spedale and made it what it became, not only in the city of Siena but in its territories: a vast network of farms and castles that funneled the products of the countryside into the city to provide for the urban needy. The boy Tobias nonetheless remains on the Pellegrinaio's southern wall, smartly dressed in boots and tunic, hesitating before he goes out on his great adventure, prudently looking back. In the meantime Vecchietta, the artist who painted him, left all that he earned to the Spedale. In contrast to this artist who gave his modest life savings to the institution where he spent most of his working life, other beneficiaries who made much more may not have wanted to be reminded of the honest Jewish elder who refrained from asking his relative Gabael for interest. They were the ones who, like the young Tobias, took to the road.

◆

The portrait of the enterprising banker who brought Siena into contact with the rest of Europe to establish its own centrality emerged with a legal scholar from Prague, Ludovico Zdekauer. In the early twentieth century, he wrote about this adventurous soul in his *Mercante senese del Dugento* (The Sienese merchant of the thirteenth century). With the zeal of the convert—he made Siena his home for over forty years—Zdekauer depicted the quintessential Sienese banker as a secular pilgrim and low-ranking knight, often a young man willing to take risks that his elders would not. In short, he was a worldly Tobias. Equally important for Zdekauer was that this young man would eventually return to pour his wealth into the city, a wealth derived from the only thing the Sienese had to hand: money. Stranded on hills without ready access to water, deprived of the resources that by the late thirteenth century had made Florence a center for wool production, the Sienese realized they had to use their in-betweenness strategically. Unable to manufacture cloth—one of Tuscany's most valued resources—Siena became good at buying it, dyeing it, then selling it for high prices, with its merchants heading west to the fairs in southern France and Flanders and traveling east as far as the Levant. The oldest surviving document of such a transaction goes back to 1193. One Piccolomini, ancestor of Pius II and Pius III, is said to have sold cloth in Rome to the abbot of Passignano, a town on Lake Trasimeno in nearby Umbria. But at some point these itinerant merchants turned themselves into bankers, in Zdekauer's terms, "endowed with an exquisite artistic sense and furnished with an excellent means of exchange, the Sienese coin. In the absence of a flowering industry, money became the principal merchandise in which the Sienese trafficked."

This merchandise owed its very existence to Siena's hills, or at least the hills at the southern reaches of its territory. Metal for coins was mined from extinct volcanoes like Mount Amiata to Siena's south. By 1226 Siena was delving into the silver mines sold to the city when the monks in the abbey of San Salvatore, having barely survived an earthquake, had to unload their properties. Thus German deutschmarks were exchanged for silver florins at staggering rates. But it was a cost others were apparently willing to pay. Less than a decade later, the Sienese Angelieri Solafico was listed as exclusive *campsor domini papae*, money changer for the pope. The Sienese brothers Orlando and Bonifazio Bonsignori would soon take over, building the most powerful banking organization in Europe. In an epoch marked by what Edward English has called a "commercial revolution," dependent on the availability of credit and easy money for entrepreneurial types, Siena was the Wall Street of Europe. Its seventy towers formed a skyline not unlike that of lower Manhattan, while its families were for generations the preferred bankers of popes and princes—such as Edward I after he expelled the Jews from England in 1272.

Much of Siena's predisposition to changing and lending money came from the presence of its pilgrims—not only the ones who came to be housed in the Spedale, but those with money to spend at the taverns that sprang up in the center of town. Sitting in the Campo one June evening, Gabriella Piccinni tells me that the best lens through which to examine Siena is not pilgrimage per se, but voyage and travel more generally. Siena's sudden extraordinary growth in the thirteenth century was hardly due just to the throngs of pilgrims crowding the streets. The city was an obligatory stopping place for anyone going to Rome: archbishops, kings, diplomats, caravans of merchants, adventurers. And to be sure, when considering Ambrogio Lorenzetti's *Buon Governo*, in the next room over from Simone Martini's *Maestà*, one notices that there is not a pilgrim in it.

Lorenzetti's fresco principally documents travel in and out and through the city, and its main protagonist is a road. In the precise middle of this work that spans an entire wall is a gate that separates well-governed city from well-governed countryside: Porta Romana, the formidable gateway leading to Rome, barely completed when Lorenzetti started his painting. A bourgeois couple is entering the city astride their horses. A shepherd driving his goats is on his way out to pasture. The only stationary figure is a beggar squatting outside the gate, while above him Securitas spreads her wings to utter her lines about protecting those who travel in her domain. As her prominence suggests, despite the scenes of movement taking place in both country and city—harvesting, planting, and falconry on the one hand, teaching, building, and dancing on the other—the fresco is really about movement *between* worlds. This is a painting about entrances and exits, the necessary order that the city brings to the country, the necessary goods that the country brings to the city. It's also arguably about the way those worlds mirror one another. The energy and productivity found in the countryside parallel what occurs in the city: the work zones of Lorenzetti's fresco show us business as usual on the ground and construction in the skies. Three men work on top of a bright pink building, while two others bring them bricks and slate on trays and in baskets balanced precariously on their heads. All is activity, including the nine figures who dance in a circle while a tenth taps on a tambourine, precursor to the music that will fill the city streets before, during, and after Palio season.

Fig. 19 ◆ Ambrogio Lorenzetti, *The Effects of Good Government* (detail of trade in the city scene) (1338–39). Palazzo Pubblico, Siena. Photograph: Erich Lessing/Art Resource, New York.

Entrate e uscite. Entrances and exits: these are accounting terms, used by bookkeepers today as well as eight hundred years ago, tracking the flow of money and the bodies who brought it, made it, paid it, carried it out. Everything that came in or went out had to be *gabellato*: filed and taxed. From hogs to wine, stored in large jars and sold in places where women and children under fifteen weren't allowed to go. This was how the city procured and preserved its identity, guarding intake and outtake, closing the big gates by night so that nothing should enter or go out under cover of darkness and thus be unseen, unaccounted for, unrecorded.

To understand money and its uses is to grasp a great deal, in medieval and modern worlds alike. For a time this monetary expertise distinguished Siena, and the value of the silver coins that circulated throughout the city was understood and used to advantage better here than anywhere else. Lorenzetti's city is a place where money changed hands. There is only one vague sign of its religious dimension: the cathedral's striped campanile, which flashes in the upper left corner, and in any case more than likely is a belated addition to a supremely secular scene. Highlighted instead is the city's third pivotal space after the Campo and the Piazza del Duomo: its undisputed commercial center, represented by the Loggia della Mercanzia and located at the meeting of the city's three major roads, the Croce del Travaglio. The latter word is perhaps a mangled version of "three roads," but it also suggests the French and Spanish words for work. Here, a stone's throw from the Campo, the elected members of the Arte della Mercanzia and the Arte della Banca had their official home.

The Loggia itself is an elegant fifteenth-century structure, built a century after Lorenzetti painted his *Buon Governo*. But it marks the place where commerce and banking overlapped and nurtured each other long before the 1400s, and they had their official recognition here, in one of the most prominent places of Siena. It sits behind the palazzo dedicated to commerce, which faces onto the Campo and which, until shoddy eighteenth-century restorations destroyed it, was the most beautiful gothic palace in Siena.

The side street where the Loggia sits, thankfully unchanged, thus links itself directly with the city's crowded arteries where they met and became—and remain—most crowded. This space was designed to bring together "merchants and other honorable citizens" to engage in "discussions on commerce and other related affairs," as the city mandated in 1417 when it enhanced the open loggia on this site. But much more than discussion took place here in the years when the loggia was being constructed. The Mercanzia had what now may seem (or, perhaps, depressingly not) an extraordinary degree of autonomy in its own affairs: its own police force, its own tribunal, its own prison for those who could not pay their debts. Vecchietta worked on the new loggia, and it is curious to think that here too he created a work of art that alludes to something torn down to make way for something new: in this case, his statue of an emaciated Saint Paul, a reminder of the church destroyed so the Loggia and the fine palace behind it could be constructed. Paul nonetheless protects the Loggia with his sword, angled out into the passageway that takes you down into the Campo.

Yet the Loggia would be nowhere near as elegant, the Palazzo nowhere near as grand, were Siena's wealth and *banche* to depend solely on local traffic. The modest origins of the word *banco* are telling. It comes from the bench or table where money was counted and exchanged. The earliest "banks" were little more than roadside stands where money changers awaited the arrival of pilgrims; our English "bankrupt," as Penny Marcus once reminded me over lunch, comes from *bancarotta*, or broken bench, meaning that the bankers' money had run out. If pilgrims and others were coming in, the Sienese—not just the falconers and priests portrayed by Lorenzetti—were going out, and had been doing so for several centuries before Lorenzetti's fresco. And as Zdekauer elegiacally maintained, and like the young Tobias leaving to recoup his father's losses, they also came back.

Thus one might return to the Via Francigena and see it with eyes different from those of a pilgrim intent on religious transformation. The road still preserves the homes of two families who in turn were, for a time, phenomenally successful at harnessing the one commodity Siena had to offer. On Banchi di Sopra, and hence on the old Via Francigena, these two palaces dominate the road, each framed by piazzas that were cleared only several centuries after the families made their fortunes. The first is the seat of the Monte dei Paschi, originally the home of the

Fig. 20 ◆ Looking north to Banchi di Sopra. View from the Museo
dell'Opera del Duomo. Photograph: Alex Klein.

Salimbeni, who boasted Germanic roots and claimed they participated
in the First Crusade and played a key role in taking Antioch. The trip
to the Holy Land whetted an appetite for travel and for spices, and the
knight came back a merchant. The second palace, farther down the hill,
where the Banca Firenze now has its Sienese headquarters, is the home
of the Tolomei, who in a claim even more grandiose than the Salimbeni's,
linked their family to the Ptolemies of Egypt and Greece, and hence to
kings and an ancient Hellenic civilization. They competed to be the central bankers of kings and popes as well as abbots and aristocrats, and the
street was usually not big enough for both.

A history of Salimbeni-Tolomei relations throughout the Middle Ages
reads like a Tom and Jerry cartoon. One day the Salimbeni are burning

down the Tolomei's palazzo; the next day the Tolomei are inviting the Salimbeni to a feast and poisoning them (at the villa of Malamarenda just south of the city—literally, "wicked snack"). One day the Salimbeni are being chased out of town by their enemies, retreating to vast and ever-increasing holdings in the Val d'Orcia; the next day the Tolomei are fleeing to the Maremma to wait out the hostilities. And on one rare occasion, as told in the *Fioretti di San Francesco*, a collection of popular legends about Saint Francis, the gentle Umbrian himself brought about a temporary truce when he visited Siena in 1212. Now we just have the usual enmity between Siena and Florence represented by these two imposing buildings: the one sits behind a statue of Sallustio Bandini, an enlightened eighteenth-century economist, that in December is set off by an enormous Christmas tree with lights wishing the world *buon natale*. The other, made of a darker, heavier stone, is flanked by a somber plaque recalling one tragic member of the family, Pia Tolomei, whom Dante memorialized in *Purgatorio*. The line, "Siena made me, the Maremma undid me" alludes to her death at the hands of a jealous husband who threw her from the window of their country home. Siena's banks are in crisis, but you wouldn't guess it from seeing the bankers in immaculate white suits who ignore the flow of tourists on all sides while leisurely smoking cigarettes under the gaze of Bandini or beneath the statue of the wolf and the fatherless twins, symbols of Siena.

At the same time, these imposing *palazzi* represent only a fraction of the land that was held by these powerful tribes. And tribes they were. Over a hundred Salimbeni relatives once lived in the family's fortress. Coming west from the church of San Francesco toward Banchi di Sopra, you notice the disquieting hulk behind the Monte dei Paschi's Renaissance facade, a surging polyhedron that seems out of place with the rest of the neighborhood. The *castellare*—literally "castle"—consisted of an enormous collection of buildings that included palaces, towers, a warehouse (known as the *fondaco*, an Arabic word), factories, an abbey, and a church. The Salimbeni's fort—for so it was—was the biggest in Siena, its towers the highest of the city's seventy in the mid-thirteenth century when the family was at its financial height. It also owned land around Porta Camollia and the church and hospital of Sant'Andrea. The enormous mass that served for several centuries as the customhouse and that now holds the Monte dei Paschi's meeting rooms and art treasures was the Salimbeni's warehouse. Behind it is the church of San Donato, where the family members would presumably come to confess their hatred of their deep-pocketed neighbors as well as any sins committed in the course of making "good money from bad money": not counterfeiting, exactly, but exchanging Sienese coins for Turkish or Turinese currency or for English sterling for a high fee. (Here too they confessed illicit liaisons. The small Oratorio di Sant'Onofrio now sits on a site where there once was an orphanage devoted exclusively to raising the illegitimate children of the Salimbeni men.) During the fifty years from 1230 to 1280, they had a contract to collect the taxes for the Holy Roman Empire itself; Charles of Anjou, the pope, and finally the city of Siena asked them to be their primary lenders. Another branch of the family oversaw mining of precious metals as well as imports of precious goods such as spices and silk from the Orient and cloth from Flanders. Their land in the countryside came in handy for storing wheat and other cereal grains, and they exacted tolls from pilgrims and other travelers crossing the bridges they controlled.

It is no small irony that when the Monte dei Paschi—or as it was originally called, the Monte di Pietà—was established in 1472, it was set up to relieve the dependence of the Sienese both on the Jews, traditional lenders to individuals of modest standing, and on families like the Salimbeni, whose usurious practices were decried by popes as soon as the politics of their city conflicted with papal ambitions. By then the international banking family had been reduced to "regional merchants," their palace long rented out to shopkeepers and family members. The Monte di Pietà was short-lived, but when it was revived under Cosimo de' Medici a century later, it took up holdings in the Salimbeni palazzo (where the widow of one Salimbeni descendant was allowed to stay on in a basement apartment until her death). Appropriately, to celebrate the bank's new life, a *Cristo risorto*, or a Jesus leaving the tomb, was commissioned. But this Christ, designed by Lorenzo Rustici, emerges from a tomb that resembles a safe, while two serene angels watch. As our guide puts it, we thus witness the resurrection not so much of the son of God, but of a bank: of money itself, which the Medici hoped would wind up in their grandducal coffers. (Much of it no doubt did.)

You can see Rustici's painting on one of the few days a year when the Monte dei Paschi opens its doors to the public: the days of the Palio, when tours are arranged for those who want to visit the bank's opulent vaults, renovated in the 1960s, its archive made to look like a ship sailing through calm waters—or, as the guide explains, a ship in which we have placed our trust. Of the seventeen thousand artworks the Monte owns, some two hundred are on exhibit, in the archive itself and in the bank's boardroom. Among other imposing pieces is a large-scale painting by Francesco Vanni, asked by bank administrators to paint a subject in which "Joseph repaired the sterility of Egypt." It has darkened over the past four hundred years, but Vanni also intended to give his work a twilight ambience, with buildings reminiscent of Siena—or Rome— glimmering in the background. Indeed, in this scene based on the story in Genesis, Joseph, still in disguise, greets the strangers who are really his brothers, who had tried to kill him first by throwing him into a pit and then by selling him into slavery. As if by magic, this man has come back from the dead to save the world from famine and rule Egypt as Pharaoh's right-hand man. Thanks to dreams from God he has had Pharaoh store surplus grain for seven years so that something will be left for the coming seven years of hardship. Vanni paints Joseph reaching out to the men before him, whom he has recognized as his family though he does not yet reveal himself. Tests are still to come for these brothers, desperate to feed both themselves and their father back in Canaan.

Key to Vanni's painting are two surviving designs in pencil. One is of the brother who throws up his hands in supplication, kneeling before the man he does not know as Joseph. The drawing shows him holding a staff, suggesting that he is a pilgrim seeking charity in a foreign land. The other drawing has largely been preserved in its details in the final painting. It shows two figures to Joseph's right, who seem to have little to do with the family interaction but a great deal to do with the Monte dei Paschi. A man calculates a sum and extends money to the figure before him, who wears a pilgrim's hat with tokens from all the usual places: Lucca, Santiago de Compostela, Rome.

Vanni's painting presents the ideal that the Monte at least used to aspire to: charitable work. But its charity is not unlimited or excessive or without measure, as the presence of the accountant suggests. Arguably, the Spedale extended the same kind of measured charity, and Vanni's work returns to the concerns of the Tobias story. Like Tobias, Joseph is also a young boy who has left his homeland, though under duress—sold by his brothers—and without the guidance of an angel. This boy endures the perils of a foreign place, far stranger than those Tobias sees, where he is always greeted by friendly fellow Jews. Arriving in this new world of Egypt, Joseph even spends two years in prison. When he emerges, he has mastered the language of Egypt as well as the language of dreams. Attaining a stature he'd surely never have imagined possible—as Pharaoh's governor—he saves himself and his family from famine, from poverty, from death. Joseph's journey is a reverse pilgrimage, as Israel comes to Egypt to find salvation and new life. The forgiving brother, like Christ, offers charity to his brethren, but only after putting them through some terrifying moments, as when he accuses the beloved Benjamin of stealing his silver cup.

Or perhaps it is Siena that offers new life, dispensing with Jerusalem as a secondary place. Surely this is what Vanni, or his administrator-commissioners, must have intended. Perhaps surprisingly, this is also the gist of a conversation recorded in a letter earlier in the sixteenth century. It concerns another Sienese banker, the Jewish Laudadio Ismael da Rieti and was written by the false messiah and adventurer David Reubeni in 1524. Reubeni was from Jerusalem, and while paying a visit to Rieti's splendid palazzo in the heart of Siena, he was troubled by his fellow Jew's comfortable life and his evident attachment to his place of birth. As he describes his sojourn in a letter now in an archive in New York, he asked Rieti, "Toward which city do your affections most turn, to Jerusalem, or to the city where you live now?" And, he continues, "I was shocked by Laudadio's answer: 'I don't want to go to Jerusalem, I love only Siena.'" While Laudadio da Rieti was better off than many other Sienese, his response nonetheless suggests that Siena had been a relatively good place to live for Jewish families—at least until the Florentines defeated the Republic. By 1573 Cosimo de' Medici had ordered the creation of a ghetto—a small area behind the Campo, the gatekeeper to be paid for by the Jews themselves—confining some 130 families that had formerly been dispersed throughout the city and prompting a chastened Rieti to say, "I see no hope, I see no future." Long before that, however,

an edict had gone out following a plague that many Christians blamed on
Jews, banning Jews from the Via Francigena as well as the road that went
from the Croce del Travaglio to the westernmost gate—and hence from
the commercial heart of the city.

One morning we go the synagogue, newly renovated and reopened
as a museum, with hours from 10:30 to 3:00 except on Saturdays. It is
between two large parallel streets: Via del Porrione and Via di Salicotto,
a name once thought to originate from the Hebrew *selihot*, or prayer, but
more likely to come from a German word for poor or muddy land (*scholle
kot*). Only the Vicolo della Manna seems to allude to the several centuries of Jewish life in this quarter before the 1930s brought in a period
of "cleansing" that tore out the older buildings and widened the narrow streets. (Until the mid-nineteenth century there was a bakery on
the little street that made unleavened bread—the "manna" God sent to
his people in the desert.) Still, a tailor shop and a small antiques shop
squeezed to the right of the ramp leading from Via del Porrione down
to the synagogue bear traces of this thirteenth-century community. Our
entertaining and energetic guide, Anna di Castro, shows us the bright
and spacious large room upstairs where services have been held since
the mid-1700s; the columns that flank the ark of the covenant have inlaid
marble that came, she tells us, from Jerusalem. Unlike Florence's more
imposing structure with its gold dome that competes with the Duomo's
when seen from the Piazzale Michelangelo or the church of San Miniato,
Siena's synagogue is slight and unpretentious, but it is significantly older
and its neoclassical style is unforced. There is nothing on Vanni's map
to indicate its existence—or even that of Cosimo's ghetto; the houses
in what would have been the densely populated areas between Via del
Porrione and Via Salicotto look like the houses everywhere else in the
city. (Current maps of the city inexplicably follow Vanni's footsteps and
largely fail to mention the synagogue, although in his 1784 guidebook
Giovacchino Faluschi makes special mention of the ghetto on page 123.)
There is still much work to be done before the synagogue will be a prime
exhibition space, but Anna and her colleagues are trying. In an upstairs
storage area with grates looking down into the sanctuary from the wom-
en's gallery, we see posters in both English and Italian that describe the

Jewish community's roots in Siena and Italy and explain Judaism more generally to what one suspects is a largely gentile audience.

Anna herself is full of fascinating facts. Once the community was so large that it needed a second synagogue, but that is long gone. Siena's university, the Studio Senese, had Jewish students and at least one Jewish professor; Jewish doctors were allowed to practice even after the ghetto was forcibly established. The city's relationship with the Jews who were the traditional bankers is thus contradictory, not always straightforward or positive. San Bernardino, the fifteenth-century preacher whose image is ubiquitous throughout Siena, was vicious in his sermons against moneylending Jews, and the Monte dei Paschi of 1472 may partly have been inspired by his anti-usury rants. A riot in the late eighteenth century, in the wake of both the earthquake and revolutionary activities in Paris, led to the lynching of nineteen Jews, to which the small synagogue off of Via Salicotto bears somber witness with a plaque outside its door. During World War II Siena's Jews hid in the *bottini* beneath the city, using the abandoned system as a refuge. This later tolerance seems more characteristic of Christian Sienese attitudes toward the Jewish population, which at its height ranged around two thousand.

But where did this community go? Across from the escalator that takes you up to San Francesco (its walls covered with colorful tiles made by local high school students), there is a lovely ridge with modern apartment buildings—which is to say, late nineteenth-century—in Ravacciano, where much of the Jewish community moved after the destruction of the ghetto in the 1930s. The buildings on Salicotto were torn down and reconstructed in what has been called, justifiably, a bizarre medieval style, with the exception of the synagogue and, from the looks of it, the tailor shop. Anna herself lives on an extraordinary rural property seven kilometers from Siena's walls, built just after Italian unification, in the days when Florence was capital of all Italy. She tells me her husband's family left Rome in 1942 right before the city's Jews were rounded up, arriving in Siena before their names were placed on official lists of "undesirable citizens," and so escaping detection. Even so, the monks of nearby Passignano hid them for six months. Now Siena's Jewish population is quite small, although the synagogue attracts Jews from around the world—you can buy a general ticket to the three synagogues in Venice, Florence, and Siena—and a week of films held for the Giorno della Memoria, Day of Memory, has brought attention to this tiny community and its history,

Aemuli Iudeorum, emulators of the Jews, was the attack thrown at the Salimbeni and other families who were accused of usury—of making money from money. It has an ironic ring, and not only because of Petrucci's claim that the Jewish lender charged him much less than the Christian one who had Petrucci locked up. The floor of the Duomo, much of it carved in the years when Laudadio da Rieti was singing Siena's praises, is full of stories from the Hebrew Bible: Judith and her maid carrying Holofernes's head; Elijah waits for the Lord on a mountaintop; Moses comes down from the mountain with his tablets, railing at the people who have fallen away. And in front of the altar itself King David presides over a choir of angels as he sits majestically on his throne: "Rex" is the simple word beneath him. To be sure, the Old Testament stories had their allegorical twins, their Christian doubles, in the gospels: Judith was Mary, the savior of her people; David—in any case Mary's ancestor—was Christ, slayer of giants. And yet the old Hebrew tales one ponders most in Siena are precisely those that inspired emulation among Christians and their institutions, Joseph and—uncanonical though he may be—Tobias among them.

◆

The scribe in Vanni's painting of Joseph—the man writing things down, lending money to a pilgrim in need—takes stock of entrances and exits, applicable to people and things passing through cities, transformed into data faithfully recorded in the books of the Monte dei Paschi or the Spedale. These ledgers attest to a long history of Sienese preoccupation with recording *entrate e uscite*, "comings and goings," especially of money. And while no one other than Securitas is at the gate taking stock of these ins and outs, one of Lorenzetti's buildings opens onto a schoolroom where a professor lectures to a captive audience. Could this be a teacher from the Studio Senese training future notaries, pressed into service by a city that has one of the earliest surviving documents of any European financial transaction, from a ninth-century fair? That the document survives is thanks to Siena's great archival impulse, and the Archivio di

Stato itself is now in the Piccolomini palace that angles into the Campo on its southwestern side, its terrace a perfect place from which to watch the Palio. But there are other reasons to go there.

In the mid-1100s, possibly earlier, the Sienese began maintaining ledgers recording "entries and exits" produced by the office of the Biccherna. That term is thought to go back to the name of the palace in Constantinople, center of the great Byzantine Empire, that regulated the domain's finances. The Biccherna was the agency that saw to the city's "well-being," as a constitutional clause puts it in the fourteenth century, in charge of the ins and outs of money, what was taken in and how much was spent. Every city had such offices, of course, and still does. But what makes Siena unique is the attention given to the books themselves that contained the documentation, and in particular to their covers, which beginning in 1257 were illustrated with images of the man who attended to such serious affairs. This was the *camerlingo*, another strange word, from the Frankish tongue: someone authorized to enter the *camera*, or room, of a sovereign or bishop, and hence someone who knows secrets.

The earliest covers depict these knowers of secrets in their little rooms, seated at tables with stacks of coins, the Sienese coin that was silver to Florence's gold florin. The *camerlingo* was typically a monk from the nearby abbey of San Galgano, respected perhaps for his moral austerity, his ability to keep a secret, his allegiance to a higher order than the town itself. (Although the abbey's founder, Galgano Guidotti, had an interesting purgatorial past. A spendthrift knight, he was en route to Jerusalem to kill Muslims and make money when an angelic voice drew him to a hillside in Montesiepi, not far from Siena, and told him to dedicate his life to solitude and penance. To symbolize his change of heart, he thrust his sword into a stone—possibly a source of the King Arthur legend. San Galgano is now a towering, roofless shell of a church in a place that once throbbed with hundreds, possibly thousands, of monks and peasants and their families. Now the sunflowers wave in the light evening winds that keep you company as you drink a glass of wine in the dying sunlight while gazing at the ruins on one side and the looming Mount Amiata on the other.)

But back to the covers of Siena's account books: often seated alongside the monk is a secular figure—a notary—taking down the sums and the

Fig. 21 ◆ Mount Amiata, seen from San Galgano. Author's photograph.

subtractions patiently counted out by his monastic partner. The *tavo-lette* or covers of the *Biccherna* (now simply referred to as "*biccherne*") depict a steady history of the town's preoccupation with memorializing the acts responsible for creating and maintaining a city's well-being and identity. Michele Pellegrini takes me and a few students through the collection in the Archivio di Stato, open every morning save Sunday. He suggests that little by little the portraits of the monkish distributors of money gave way not so much to the recording of sacred events deemed timeless by the Sienese and by all medieval Christians—Jesus's birth, Jesus's death—as to their direct bearing on Siena. In one fifteenth-century cover, the Virgin steadies the city from above as though it were a boat on a tempestuous sea; in another, from 1480, she supports it from below as though it were—and in the image, it indeed seems to be—a miniature town that is sitting neatly inside a feeding trough or a grand piano. *Hec Est Civitas Mea*: "This is my town," she says to Jesus as she gestures toward the unpleasant-looking swamplands from whose grip she has preserved it, high and dry. By the mid-fifteenth century the covers were reflecting current events. Perhaps the most curious is Vecchietta's painting of the coronation of Aeneas Silvius Piccolomini as Pius II, in whose family palace we are standing. This is not the actual coronation that occurred in Rome in 1458, but the version that happened simultaneously in Siena's Campo, long before television made it possible to see the real thing. Someone dressed as Mary placed the papal crown on someone else dressed as Pius II, and there was "great feasting and celebration in the streets." A cover from about ten years later shows Siena terrorized by threats of the *terremoto* or earthquake that sent Sienese into tents around the city. This scene was depicted by the young Francesco di Giorgio Martini, already fascinated by Siena's unpredictable geology. The earthquake of 1467 never happened, possibly because the Virgin invoked in the upper reaches of the painting—holding a little flag of Siena's white-and-black colors, like a cheerleader—did her work, and the city, vacated by its citizens, was unharmed.

These wooden covers transform financial transactions into art. This is the alchemy that the *biccherne* enact, as though Ludovico Zdekauer is proved right. Far from being simple examples of a way of painting surfaces to give them color, they produce the ultimate "return" of money flowing through the city: beauty. Even the paper the accounts were written on was produced by the artisanal company Arte del Libro, which made a prized paper called *bambagina* used by the Biccherna from 1229 on. Meanwhile the writing school run by the notaries produced masterpieces as well: the beautiful ligatures or buckles used to fasten the books. Perhaps boys were apprentices in such a craft in one of the artisans' shops that Lorenzetti depicts near his classroom in *Buon Governo*.

The Sienese painted their covers for the *Biccherna* throughout the seventeenth century. Ultimately they became large panels independent of the account books themselves, and hence works of art freed from their more prosaic ministrations. From the genre's humble beginnings emerge elaborate pictures of processions through the Campo and a grand celebratory image of the destruction of the Spanish Fortezza in

Fig. 22 ◆ Francesco di Giorgio Martini, *The Virgin Protecting Siena from an Earthquake* (1467). *Biccherna* cover, oil on wood. Archivio di Stato, Siena. Photograph: Universal Images Group/Art Resource, New York.

1552, followed by a dark, bleak image of the siege three years later. One fascinating painting shows the arguments in 1582 Rome about the new Gregorian calendar. A gesticulating scientist waves a banner with two symbols of the zodiac—Cancer and Libra—while monks, laymen, and cardinals engage in animated debate and a bored pope sits on a dais away from the action. The 1571 battle of Lepanto against the Turks; a naval battle in the Peloponnese; the treaty signed at Cateau-Cambrésis—these are world events, and their images take us far from Siena, as though their detachment from the registers themselves loosens the city's hold on what its artists can produce. Indeed, the fundamental relationship to the *entrate e uscite* that determined Siena's wealth and hence, according to Zdekauer, its beauty, is gone. And yet so much of this beauty was bought with the same thing that more recently brought down the Monte dei Paschi: fiscal speculation, often in foreign lands and foreign banks, the lands to which the Salimbeni and the Tolomei traveled, indulged in by families who were forced out of their glamorous roles as entrepreneurs just about half a century before Lorenzetti painted his *Buon Governo*. Perhaps Agostino Chigi, "richest man in Rome" in the early 1500s, was more successful because he was more prudent, placing his faith largely in concrete things such as alum, with which Monte Amiata was flush.

◆

More than just a city, Siena was—and is—a territory, with the shape of what the eighteenth-century scholar Giovanni Antonio Pecci called in his history of his native land "an imperfect oval." His great work lists rivers, bridges, hospitals, lakes, baths, bishoprics, and every town in Siena's domain, even if that domain was overseen by the grand duchy of Florence—which in 1737 had just come to its end. Pecci complains in his preface about the indolence and inefficiency of the Medici governors. He plans to be far more efficient and thorough, if only in the realm of scholarship, and he has sent out a questionnaire to the communities that were once Siena's, asking the respondents to touch on all areas—political, cultural, geological—so that he might write a history "from the periphery": the small towns and villages and hostels that make up the rural lands running all the way to Mount Amiata and that Siena, despite its ferocious attachment to self-sufficiency, depends on so intensely.

It is a largely glowing view of city and country relations that Lorenzetti paints in his great fresco in the Palazzo Pubblico. His country is
marked by fertility and by the very rivers and streams that eluded Siena
itself. The Arbia is probably one of the several rivers that Lorenzetti depicts, the word itself from *ara*, "fertile." Lands to Siena's south and east
bear the river's name today, as they did in Lorenzetti's time (Taverne
d'Arbia, Monteroni d'Arbia, Lucignano d'Arbia). In the foreground men
and women work in the fields gathering olives and wresting the tender
grapes from their vines, while farther in the background they're harvesting the wheat: an improbable conflation of several seasons in a single
stretch of fresco just like the ghostly wedding masque in Shakespeare's
Tempest: "Spring come to you at the farthest / In the very end of harvest!" (4.1.112). Two peasants bring a mule and a pig—the famous "Cinta
senese," black with a white stripe around its middle—uphill toward
town, as two noblemen with their falcon and dogs amble down the hill.
Yet despite all the activity, there's a perfunctory feel to the countryside,
as though the farther Lorenzetti got from the city the more he lost interest in his subject. The figures at the extreme right of the fresco seem
mere sketches in pencil, flat cartoons: a pair of peasants guiding a horse
over a bridge and two people chasing a dog are merely stick figures. They
have none of the life or presence of the five workers atop the roof who
will shortly be breaking for lunch. Large swaths of the fresco are empty
except for vast fields with sheaves of grain, as though Lorenzetti realized
he'd devoted too much space to *la campagna*—fully half of the wall—but
it was too late to change. (See figure 10.)

   At the same time, Lorenzetti's peaceful if occasionally vacant fresco
belies the uneasy relationship that the city had with the inhabitants of
the countryside: not so much the peasants seen laboring in the fields—
they would revolt only in the early twentieth century—but principally
the nobles and their families who lived in hill-town castles. To choose
just a single decade shortly before Lorenzetti began his fresco, in 1331 the
Aldobrandeschi counts of Santa Fiora had a "disastrous war with Siena,"
forcing them to sell two of their holdings for eight thousand gold florins,
a tremendous sum; Grosseto repeatedly resisted Siena's efforts to encompass her within its borders and submitted only in 1334, after numerous skirmishes; Montieri, a prosperous mining community whose roads

and hills are now being torn up because of the new industry of frack-
ing, fell to an invading Siena in 1341. Frequent raids by the Sienese on
aristocratic towers caused unending stress for the countrymen caught in
the middle. And once a town or a castle was conquered, it was subjected
to harsh taxes and regulations. Possibly the oldest fresco in the Sala del
Mappamondo, directly behind Lorenzetti's circular map, depicts hand-
ing over a castle. It looks like a perfectly civilized exchange, but this is
no doubt after the threats, the bloodshed, the coercion exacted by the
hired mercenaries who traveled up and down Italy looking for work.
The defeated lord, one hand in the air—in protest?—and the other on
his sword, stands before the member of the Sienese republic who has
presumably come to seize his lands. (See figure 1 in the introduction.)

Yet these tensions that resulted partly from the magnates' wealth
expressed themselves in another way: a surprising way. If Lorenzetti's
countryside looks orderly, it is not just through sleight-of-hand, a con-
venient forgetting of the violence that marked its hills. (Shown on the
other side of the room is Lorenzetti's opposing fresco of *Mal Governo*—
bad government. Despite the damage wrought by time, we can still make
out the devastation of the fields by mercenaries.) Part of Siena's mark
on the countryside, and by no means a minor one, was its network of institutions and farms associated with the Spedale. Its presence extended
for miles to Siena's south and east, rendering the country more secure,
more productive, less strange—and Siena, certainly, closer. The Spedale had local sources for food—its extensive orchard, its stockyard and
butchers—but it was hardly large enough to accommodate all the hospital's pilgrims, orphans, and needy: in 1555 alone, the year of the siege,
some 138 *figli dell'ospedale* or orphans were taken in. Thus outside Siena's walls there arose an extensive system of granaries—called *grance*,
from the French *granche*, or depository for grain—a network of farms
that fed the needs of the growing Spedale and of Siena at large. The *grancia* was in many ways a secular monastery as well as a castle and small
village, a hub for hundreds of people. By the fourteenth century there
were more than a dozen directly associated with the Spedale. Such was
the level of organization that one is not blamed for (erroneously) translating the Italian word for farm, *fattoria*, as "factory." These farms that
covered Siena's southern territories *were* factories, where the peasants

gave half the fruits of their labors to the city and the notaries trained to record *entrate e uscite* had full-time work.

The Spedale had its own account books, their covers painted like those of the Biccherna. One fifteenth-century cover by Sano di Pietro depicts a *casa rurale*, a modest pink house and a wall, the ladder and cross sign of the Scala beneath it. Sano painted only one side of the house. The roof extends to the left and disappears under the book's metal hinge, while the wall goes off to the right and past its wooden border. He thus leaves open the possibility of something large-scale, far beyond the book's cover; and indeed the *grance* were enormous.

One of the largest fortifications was at Cuna, only a few miles south of Siena. You can distinguish the shimmering buildings of the city from the fields surrounding this now almost deserted spot. Immense walls encircle a number of smaller structures including barns and office space, with signs warning passersby about the fragility of the entire compound. Even so, five families still occupy apartments in the *grancia*, and as recently as 2010 outdoor films were shown here; there are still chairs stacked against the walls. One of the earliest and best organized of the many *grance* that dotted the Sienese countryside to the city's east and south, Cuna once had three floors—the first two for pilgrims, the third for artisanal work in silk and wool, and since it was Siena, offices for the makers and keepers of registers and documents, the accountants, and the officials who visited twice a year from the Spedale to check the books. And in the world immediately beyond it, the farmers who had to give not only half their harvest to the *grancia* but the best of what they had to the *grancia*'s overseer: chickens, eggs, peaches, wax. A smiling townswoman (not one who lives inside the castle; it's too dangerous, she says) unlocks the door to the tiny church, just beyond the *grancia*'s walls, dedicated to Saint Christopher and Saint James, two consummate travelers: the giant Christopher who bore Christ across the river on his massive back and Saint James the Greater, whose body awaits pilgrims in Santiago de Compostela in Spain, not far from the sea. A badly restored fresco in the church shows James saving a pilgrim who was on his way to his cathedral when he was falsely accused of theft and hanged. The saint rescued him just before he breathed his last.

Already in existence in 1152, Cuna's *grancia* originally contained

Fig. 23 ◆ The Grancia of Cuna. Author's photograph.

a hospital for pilgrims who needed a place to stay near the Arbia, a river in Lorenzetti's fresco. But its independent life would not continue for long. Within forty years the *rettore*, or director, of the Spedale was giving lands he owned near the Arbia to the Spedale, and by 1295 another *rettore*, Ristoro Menghi di Giunta, paid cash to buy Cuna and Castelluccio—the little castle—so as to donate them in turn to the hospital. In an interesting phrase, he claims he does so for the "salvation of souls": not those of the pilgrims or the needy, but his own soul and his brother's. What's more, the wording of his testament suggests he is giving to the Spedale "every earthly good that he and his brother had acquired in illegal fashion." What this illicit gain may have been is not specified. But contemporary documents by equally wealthy figures suggest that the language of "ill-gotten gain" and the desire to save one's own

soul and those of one's loved ones is not unique to this Sienese. Buying
up the countryside, then giving it over to the Spedale upon one's death
to feed the orphans, the hungry, and the pilgrims who crammed its halls
enabled many men like Ristoro Menghi di Giunta to have their cake and
eat it too: to enjoy their ill-gotten gains in life, then to proceed to the
afterlife knowing those gains would be handed down not to their own
families but to the needy.

Thus the charitable works undertaken by the Spedale and the *grance*
were supported, even rendered possible, by uncharitable behaviors. The
bribing or usury of Ristoro Menghi di Giunta allowed for the construction of the vast factory, which expanded to include three mills, and like
its mother city, a series of walls to protect it from the surrounding turmoil: mercenaries throughout the fourteenth century, the Spanish riding
north after the sack of Rome. The Scrovegni chapel in Padua is the most
blatant expression of a merchant's anguish at a life wasted in accounts.
Through Giotto's magnificent brush he procured for himself an entire
chapel, a place of beauty full of spiritual lessons for those who would
come after him. Many have heard of Enrico Scrovegni, so his gesture
bought him a certain fame. The lands around Cuna go largely unmarked
by the family names of those who pledged to give away acres of rolling
fields near the Arbia. Only those who labor in the archives, like our guide
Michele, patiently unraveling the handwriting of notaries who scrawled
their figures in the *biccherne* or the registries of the Spedale, know the
stories of these unquiet souls. The *stilema* or emblem of the Spedale—
the ladder with a Latin cross—marks the property consigned to its new
owner, reminding the peasants as well as travelers of the constant presence of the city to their north, the institution within which the gains of
its donors, illicit or not, were transformed.

Today the *stilemi* remain, along with more recent signs leading to
the Via Francigena, which runs along the fields behind the *grancia*, and
then down the street in front of the church. Possibly because it's the
lunch hour, a vast silence hovers within this magnificent structure that
looms up from the fields like a cathedral. In this desertlike space, however, no crowds cluster anymore. Pigeons roost in an old shed, a garter
snake slithers out from behind a rusted motorcycle, and a watchful cat
stirs restlessly on a hay bale. There is no human activity save ours; two

years after our first visit, there is no one here to open the church, and
an aging farmer in his truck suspiciously circles the parking lot where
we've left our car, then returns to whatever fields he's come from. Farther out, little towns jump at you from just off the road. The entry to an
eleventh-century church or a bar is less than a meter from your car door;
if you swing it open you'll hit someone on the sidewalk. In these towns
clustered around old bridges on the Arbia, recent immigrants from Ni-
geria and Morocco tend to congregate. Farther away, on a farm near Asciano, one feels the utter isolation of the true countryside, farmhouses
topping hills encircled by cypress tress that provide shade from the late
afternoon sun and protection against the winds that whistle menacingly
from November through March. Huddled within this natural fortress,
a forty-five-year-old bachelor named Lorenzo, friend of a friend, oversees the terrain that became his grandfather's after World War II, when
the centuries-old system of sharecropping or *mezzadria* finally came to
an end.

Bored as he may have been by the more rustic spaces of his fresco,
Lorenzetti nonetheless acted on his hunch that the Sienese countryside is the product of the same extensive social organization one finds
in the city—or found in the late Middle Ages. In another image from a
century later, a panel by Giovanni di Paolo now in the Pinacoteca depicts the passage of the Holy Family into Egypt. These were the original
pilgrims, fleeing Herod to find peace, a subject already encountered in
the crypt of the Duomo, where a thirteenth-century octagonal column
bears witness to the story of the date tree that miraculously bends down
in the desert. Here, though, no magical date trees are needed. Rather, as
Mary and Jesus sit astride the donkey and Joseph follows, his staff over
his shoulder, they find themselves in the midst of a genuine harvest: two
peasants plow, a third wields a hoe, and a fourth threshes wheat. On the
other side of a river is an odd machine that scholars have recently identi-
fied as the newfangled mill described by the Sienese professor Mariano
Taccola, possibly a teacher of Francesco di Giorgio, in his *De ingeneis* of
1433. Two cities dot the landscape as well as a mountain that might be
Mount Amiata. Studding the terrain are strange-shaped gray hills that
for Giovanni di Paolo are a veritable fixture: the misshapen lunar sur-
face that calls to mind the area to the city's southeast called the Crete

Senesi (nothing to do with the island). In this Tuscan setting, Mary and Joseph haven't yet made it to Egypt; they've been sidetracked, taken on a detour through central Italy. There is no need for miracles in this landscape less real than metaphorical: this is the landscape of human effort, of the *grance*, of the network of labors that maintained the just society that was Siena's. Mary and Jesus will be more quickly supported by their fellow beings than by an act of God, and even the two maidens who follow them, dressed in delicate colors and holding sheaves of grain that match the color and texture of their hair, embody this notion of plenty, of wealth, even of ease. They could be out for a country stroll.

Making cities appear out of the countryside, sometimes in distinctly unpromising sites: this was the dream of Pius II, the pope financed by the unlucky Spannocchi family. He wanted to transform his lowly hill town of Corsignano into an ideal city to be named Pienza after himself, and he hired the great architects and artists of his day to do so. The town that emerged, however, was a far cry from the pale walled medieval towns of Giovanni di Paolo's paintings. Instead, it was the Renaissance city that Leon Battista Alberti was the first to envision. The bastard son of an exiled Florentine, Alberti grew up in Venice. His first trip to his family's native town in 1432, where he marveled at Brunelleschi's dome, still brand-new, filled him with gratitude for having escaped Venice's backward Byzantine art. Engaged in the plans of Pope Nicholas V, two popes before Pius II, to restore Rome to its status as a glorious ancient capital, Alberti had little stomach for the excessively wrought artistic works of late medieval piety. The merchant-patriarch of his dialogue *On the Family* discourages his naive young wife from going on pilgrimages, preferring that she stay at home. Much of Alberti's architectural work was inspired by classical norms, such as the Malatesta Temple in Rimini or his tribunal for Santissima Annunziata in Florence. He was the first since Vitruvius to write a treatise on the art of building (Francesco di Giorgio would be the next), and the first ever to write one on painting.

The little square of Pienza was built by men influenced by Alberti rather than by Alberti himself. It was not quite constructed ex nihilo; dozens of homes were torn down to achieve the humanist's aspirations—and Pius's. The long, well-lit nave of Pienza's cathedral that slopes toward the valley, the low walls behind and alongside it, the comfortable palace to its right—no signs here of the militant fortifications of the Salimbeni's *castellare*. Looking down into the countryside below, toward Monticchiello, one can almost imagine Mary and Joseph crossing the field.

Not a merchant himself, Pius II—in secular life Aeneas Silvio Piccolomini—came from a family of merchants, and he owed his own way of life to their successes: traveling to Germany as a fun-loving courtier and diplomat, writing a racy novel in Latin, fathering a pair of illegitimate children, then becoming Siena's bishop and finally Christendom's pope. More than anyone, he strove to make Siena a Roman city. In the mid-fifteenth century that meant a Renaissance city, and Pius sought to make the area his family occupied, to the southeast of the Campo, sufficiently "modern." The great palace with the museum of the *biccherne* (and a balcony that gives you one of the best views of the Palio) was expanded during his reign as pope, and dozens of family members lived there before it became a school. The Palazzo delle Papesse in a prominent spot in Via di Città was commissioned by the pope's sister and built by the same architect who designed Pienza; the Loggiato that he dedicated to his descendants is an imposing structure that housed a printer's shop and is now an outdoor restaurant in the summer. This was Pius's attempt to replace the anonymity of Siena's medieval buildings with edifices that would be suitably impressive, his latter-day version of the Salimbeni's *castellare*. Pius was a forceful and imposing man, but after a while the Sienese stopped taking orders and he had to take his architectural obsessions elsewhere—to Pienza. (Even so, at least early in his papacy the Sienese were happy enough with having a Sienese pope to inscribe on the interior of the Duomo Nuovo—a century after giving up all hope of matching Florence's duomo—"MCCCCLVIIII a di V di Ferriaio PPA.P.II. VENE. I[N]QUESTA. BUTIGA": On the fifth day of February, 1459, Pope Pius II entered this workshop. You can still read the sign, behind the ticket office for the Duomo and near the accordion players who occasionally play in the unfinished nave.)

The best place to seek out Pius in Siena, though, is not the buildings that bear his stamp but the Libreria, the ample side room in the Duomo. Ten paintings ring the room testifying to Pius's life as well as to Agostino Chigi's influence. Chigi was the one to suggest that a painter he'd met in Rome, Pintoricchio, might be best suited to depict the life of Siena's fa-

mous son. In the first scene from Pius's life, a tempest tosses the ship that
the young Aeneas Piccolomini boarded for the north. But like the Roman
Aeneas he will be saved—though temporarily stranded on the coast of
Libya where Queen Dido once ruled Carthage. As in Simone's *Maestà* in
the Palazzo Pubblico, the scene gleams with real things: stirrups, bits,
belts, and knives, the scabbards of swords glued into the painting so that
it brims with tangibility and light. In the back an improbable rainbow
leaps from the cloud, promise of things to come. In another scene we see
the marriage of Eleanor of Portugal and an emperor, Frederick III, outside the gate of Camollia at the Antiporta, where a tall monument marks
the site both today and in Pintoricchio's painting; in another Pius is ar-
guing as an orator before Pope Callixtus III, whom he would succeed, as
to the necessity of fighting *ad bellum asiaticum*—in the Asian wars. And
finally we see the setting for Pius's death. His papacy had been defined by
the fall of Constantinople to the Ottoman Turks in 1453, and he managed
to persuade a warring Europe that the threat was imminent, as educated
Greeks and Byzantine priests streamed into Italy to attest to the death of
the eastern empire of Rome. Aging, racked with gout, he accompanied
the crusaders as far as Ancona, where he died after catching pneumo-
nia. Without his extraordinary personal powers the crusade quickly fell
apart. The Latin inscription under this last painting (you see it as you
round the corner in this small and almost always crowded room, which
is oddly secular in a cathedral, thanks not only to Pius II's own secular
ways but to the lovely classical statue of the nude Three Graces in its
center) is almost a boast: "His body was carried back to his country and
buried within the city," *inurbem*. And so it was, at least for a time, on the
other side of these walls, in the monument for which a young Michelangelo helped to carve one if not two statues. (Pius is now buried at San
Andrea della Valle, in Rome.)

Was Pius II haunted by the sins of his dissolute youth? Is the great cathedral in Pienza, or his rush to call for a new crusade, a way of atoning
for the "illegal" gains of his own life? Would they be blotted out by zeal,
by art, by building a beautiful city to honor God? Would these places—
the "Libreria Piccolomini," Cuna's *grancia* rising high above the road as
though it were a cathedral, the abandoned, roofless San Galgano—exist
at all without sin, failure, and remorse, sheer terror before the inevitable

that is death? Others would choose more radical alternatives. Pius, after all, continued to live in splendor in the papal palaces that had recently been constructed by his predecessor Nicholas V, and his children would eventually live in his palace in Pienza. (The "last Piccolomini," Count Silvio, died there in 1959, stained by accusations of complicity with the Fascists, grieving over the death of his only son, a pilot in World War II, and embittered by the peasants' successful efforts to end the centuries-old system of sharecropping. One of his final acts was to preside over the enforced dismantling of his massive holdings, once the property of a pope.) The Sienese Giovanni Colombini was a wealthy and, sources said, unscrupulous merchant who gave up everything in 1355 despite his wife's protests. He begged in the Campo for months as a way of doing penance for his sins and was directed by God to found the Gesuati, a mendicant order. (His business sense was not put to waste, however; the Spedale asked him to become rector, and he helped to negotiate the purchase of the Byzantine relics.) Colombini recognized that the games the merchants played were finally too unsettling and hypocritical; you could not reap spiritual gain by giving up your financial gains only in death. One had to be jettisoned for the other, so Colombini abandoned his wealth, his home, his family. A member of the wealthy Tolomei family, Bernardo, abandoned the city itself earlier in the century, founding the abbey of Mount Oliveto above Buonconvento, in the Crete. He would be joined by at least one member of the Salimbeni clan, the Tolomei's mortal enemies. Their collaboration in forging this lonely but lovely and admittedly comfortable home in the hills represents the renunciation not so much of earthly goods, although it was also that, as of long-standing hostilities based on property, commerce, and money: an unlikely instance of enemies' coming together just a few decades after the events at Radicofani.

And so this steady back-and-forth between lives of rejection and those of immersion in money and what it could buy. Saint Catherine was preoccupied with the "fruits" of one's labors, and she tells a story about a monk whose superior asked him to plant a dry, dead stick in the ground and water it. When it brings forth leaves and fruit, it is said to be a symbol of the fruitfulness of obedience. How, though, to explain the miracle of leaves and fruit coming from the dry stick that was money? How might one really know the outcomes, or even the origins, of one's

efforts? Money grows in unnatural ways. All the "economic machinations" of Agostino Chigi, as Ingrid Rowland suggests, "all his grand ex-
penditures, had at their root a vehement faith in the essential piety of
his actions"; he built a chapel to the "wandering Madonna" at one of his
alum sites, in Tolfo, and had masses said there in his name. His wealth
and that of other family members enabled the last Chigi—Guido Chigi-
Saracini—to dedicate the fine palazzo in Via di Città to music making;
it houses the Accademia Chigiana as well as the artworks that Agostino
commissioned. Others could not sustain the two kinds of life and gave
themselves up completely to only one of them after knowing the other
intimately: Colombini, who begged in the Campo; the Tolomei and Salimbeni youths who went into the Crete for a life of abjection.

◆

And so the Crete. Wild, exhausting, earth baked for millennia, the heat
reflecting off this savage-looking land draining your body so that you
repair to Asciano, to the shade of a welcoming bar serving salumi and
pecorino only mildly seasoned. We had looked from afar before, posing
at the roadside in front of these untamable hills that from far off seem the
color and consistency of an elephant's hide. This time we went to them
directly, leaving the car at the *castello* of Leonina d'Asso with its four-star
Relais hotel and walking down the dusty hill back to highway 448; we
turned onto a farm road where the path was supposed to be, according to
a guidebook written in French, then we headed toward the hills, the gray
protuberances that line the landscape in Giovanni di Paolo's painting,
rising above the fields where farmers reap and strange new machines
harness waterpower while Mary ambles toward Egypt on her mule.

Only they're not, in fact, so grim as they'd have you believe: Charles
Dickens for one, who said in 1846 that they were "as bare and desolate
as any Scottish moor." The eighteenth-century Sienese linguist and editor Girolamo Gigli comments on the three products the Crete is good for:
truffles, wine, and grain. There are no signs of grapes until we return by
the back road to Leonina, three hours later, but in the dried mud near
a water hole where a lone tree stands vigil we debate over hoofprints—
deer or cattle? The pigs we spy in a farmer's barn on the slopes of Mon-
testigliano, the highest point around, are boars, and most likely they
search for the prized truffles. But it's the grain that catches your eye,

Fig. 24 ◆ Scene from the Crete; abandoned table possibly used for winnowing wheat. Author's photograph.

golden in the late spring/early summer of June, dancing in the wind to unwritable rhythms, making sounds that can only be called music. In Roman literature one encounters constant personifications of grain, in Virgil, Catullus, Horace, and the Italian *bruscelli*, rustic songs from the Renaissance, are about bringing in the grain. But when standing in the midst of it like this, the literary efforts seem forced.

All this is to say that the countryside is not barren. The gray hills are hillocks, really, some of them only clumps of mud, springing up out of green, gold, and an occasional blue, spotted with tufts of vegetation. Man-made lakes shimmer below us as we steadily ascend and then level out on a ridge that takes us to the eerie bronze sculptures called *Site Transitoire*. In 1993 the French artist Jean-Paul Philippe made molten projections that frame this variable landscape, providing a bench to view it from, imitating a tire half-rotted into the ground, a pillar that pretends, cheekily, to be more than it is. Concerts are performed here on occasion in the summer, and the name brings to mind the transitory state of humanity itself against this backdrop of ancient, aging volcanoes. To the south is Mount Amiata, ever present, ever looming, bluish gray against the clouds. But one might also consider the transitory site of the purgatory Dante created as a realization of pilgrimage, and the pilgrims would have passed through here too as they gazed on the mountain that marks the southern border of Siena's province. The city itself is to our northwest, the tower of the Palazzo Pubblico unmistakable in its longing for everlasting status. The Duomo is fainter and less precise, but all the city is like a wall, comforting, not soliciting our gaze or once upon a time the pilgrims', but simply there.

The lake below, water that returns me to the Lorenzetti fresco, is too recent to have been a part of his work. But there is blue in his fresco, buried deep in one of the valleys of *Buon Governo*, and it is marked by the only word in the painting other than those spoken by Securitas: TALAMON. These shimmering waters seem, nonsensically, to be the destination of the road that is the Via Francigena, yet that's impossible: this is Talamone, not a lake but the sea, on the edge of the Maremma. Siena's interests in building a port there go back to the thirteenth century, and Dante makes fun of the city's maritime ambitions just as he laughs at its attempts to find a river beneath the streets of Castelvecchio. A thriving port would certainly have transformed Siena, and for at least several decades, starting in 1303 when Dante was just beginning to think about his *Divine Comedy*, the Comune put considerable money aside to create what amounted to a colony—but one that didn't survive the plague. So one expects to find a ruined coastal town at this southernmost tip of the Maremma rather than the vibrant place that gave Garibaldi his first entree into Tuscany. Today it offers wonderful alternatives to the Sienese diet heavy in meat and serves as a gateway to the island of Orbetello. I wonder if this too was just another concerted effort by rich and possibly ruthless Sienese to speculate while attempting to surpass the Pisans in shipping. In fact, though, the Comune's real goal was simpler, and perhaps more venial. They needed salt, a commodity so precious that when it was brought back, heavily taxed, from the Papal States or from Pisa it was stored in today's Palazzo Pubblico, guarded twenty-four hours a day in the cellars, from which it managed to eat away at the paint of Simone Martini's *Maestà* directly above. The first recorded commercial society was formed when eight merchants brokered an agreement with the city of Siena and the powerful Aldobrandeschi, counts of Grosseto (not far from Talamone and the site of some fine beaches where Romans go for the weekend) to supply salt to Sienese citizens.

En route to the Palazzo Pubblico, salt is likely to have entered the city even in Roman times through what Fabio Bargagli Petrucci called the "Arco of Porta Salaria": roughly where you find the bridge that is Via Diacceto, around the corner from our apartment. But despite his immense knowledge of the city's history—Bargagli Petrucci wrote a magisterial account of Siena's fountains in 1906—he was wrong. The bridge was late medieval, and there are records for its construction, in part to accommodate the ice stored there, packed in sea salt. As to exactly where the Roman gate into the city—hence the way out to the sea and its salt—was located there is still disagreement. But it seems there was a double arch at the top of Via Fontebranda, similar to the double doors into the pilgrims' churches. One had the choice of going either right toward Castelvecchio and the hills or left toward what would eventually become the Duomo, and hence on the route to be called Via dei Pellegrini.

Here on Palm Sunday processions would pass out, and then back in. Thus one left the city—the neighborhood tucked on top of a hill, secure and untouched by the Via Francigena, and hence by pilgrims and strangers—then returned to go on to the Duomo. This symbolic exiting and entering fulfilled the need to go outside, to be touched by the lifeblood of the sea, before reentering the city walls. But the point of Palm Sunday, too, was that the people bowed and sang hosannas to a Jesus who had rejected the title of an earthly king, remaining untouched by the glory and wealth that would characterize such a monarch. A Jesus, that is, as simple and as valuable as salt.

Contrada: a street with habitations: *"Strada di luogo abitato, caseggiato"* NICCOLÒ TOMMASEO

Who has no house has no *contrada*. PROVERB

NEIGHBORHOODS

4

In the beginning was the road: *la strada*, as in the title of Fellini's film. And from the road came the *con-strada*, which eventually contracted to *contrada*: a road with (houses). Not just a means for going from point A to point B, the road became a place where you live, and where others live too. It becomes, in short, a neighborhood.

"Neighborhood" translates variously in Italian. *Quartiere* is the generic term and certainly the more modern, meaning "quarters," assuming that cities are squares and can be divided evenly into four equal parts; Venice has *sestieri*, a city divided into six. Not infrequently, borders are natural and hence inflexible. The serpentine Grand Canal determines the Venetian *sestieri*. Trastevere is literally the area on the "other side" of the Tiber in Rome, just as in Florence the Oltrarno is the other side of the Arno. In Siena, however, the *contrade* are man-made kingdoms, fixed forever at seventeen (down from an all-time high of over fifty), their borders precisely delineated in 1730 with a stroke of Princess Violante Beatrice of Bavaria's pen. Kingdoms that, as a Dominican nun once said to her flock of tourists as they stood outside the Casa di

Santa Caterina, you need a passport to enter—an exaggeration, but not wholly untrue.

For those who are not Sienese, these neighborhoods are perhaps the most inscrutable and hence most fascinating aspect of the city. Most notably today, these neighborhoods are the forces behind the famous Palio, itself a two-minute horse race. But while the race might seem straightforward, the bewildering rituals that surround it are not, at least not to a stranger. They include the *sorteggio* or lottery to choose which *contrade* will compete and another lottery to choose which *contrade* will get which horses; pre-Palio dinners; the *prove*, or dry heats; the processions, parties, and banquets feting the victorious *contrada* in the wake of the event—all of which serve the paradoxical function of enabling a city to publicly display itself to itself in the midst of thousands of uncomprehending others. For forty-eight weeks a year, tourists travel the city as though it were their own, especially in the winter months when the few who are lucky enough to be there can experience without lines or fuss the fog that is still settling over the Campo well into the late November morning, or the colorful Christmas stalls lit up by night. For the one week before and after each of the two Palios, however, the Sienese take back their city from the prying eyes of modern pilgrims. They occupy its streets and piazzas with tables and processions, making them sometimes impossible to pass through (although, it's being Siena, there's always another way to go). And at night, the packs of drummers roam the streets, often ending in the Campo, *facendo bando, battendo cassa*, "claiming space by making noise." This too was legislated by the princess in 1730, even while she limited the official *feste* of a neighborhood to "those roads and piazzas within a *contrada*'s boundaries" (although the waves of sound from *facendo bando* cannot be stopped by the princess's edict, and they keep awake even the heaviest sleeper in an adjoining *contrada*). At its most outward moment, at its most crowded—fifty thousand people packed into the Campo, although this past year authorities lamented that from a helicopter you could make out some empty space—Siena turns inward: a breach, it seems, of more than a millennium of hospitality, at least ever since the bishop Sigeric eased his caravan up into Siena's strange hills from the borderlands of the Maremma.

If the *contrade* are all about secrecy and self-sufficiency, the Palio

Fig. 25 ◆ Selvaioli at a pre-Palio lunch. Author's photograph.

offers the occasion to make this especially clear. The original reasons for forming the *contrade* may have been defensive. Their common link was that they were inside Siena's ever-shifting walls, and they began as administrative units organized around the need for military recruitment with an eye to maintaining peace both inside and outside the city. Roberto Barzanti calls them an urban police force, responsible for executing orders from the authority of the Comune—making sure that citizens within a given district paid their taxes and that services were carried out. When the "enlightened" Hapsburg prince Leopold II banned the city's zealous lay confraternities along with all other pious organizations, the *contrade* began absorbing religious practices as well. And when half a century later Napoleon closed most of the churches and monasteries, the suddenly empty chapels and convents became places for rituals both secular and sacred, housing the cloth or *palio* that gives the Palio its name and serving as the *contrade*'s headquarters or *società*. But long before the eighteenth century, the *contrade* boasted distinctive emblems that continue to define them today, drawn from animals and nature: dragon, giraffe, wave, among others. (Many of them appear, emblazoned on banners for a procession for the Madonna, in a little book printed by the first Sienese publisher, one Simone di Niccolò di Nardo: *The Magnificent and Triumphant Celebration and Hunt That Happened in the Renowned City of Siena on August 15, 1506.*) After the Medici victory of 1555, the neighborhoods quickly took on what Piccinni and Catoni call "the jealous custodianship of the spirit of Siena." Or as Barzanti says, "When the unwieldy military companies were dissolved, the Contrada assumed into itself the mission of remembering the history of a great city and took on the job of organizing the Palio, which began in the mid-16th century to be what it is today: a celebration about survival, the celebration of an illusion."

What is this illusion, you might ask, while passing from one *contrada* to another (effortlessly, it seems, and without a passport)? Borderlines invisible to the casual tourist are sharply drawn during Palio season, when all the flags come out at a prescribed moment, making clear the passage from one territory to another. The illusion persists in the negotiation of these at times blatant, at times subtle boundaries: the *contradaioli* all know, if the tourists don't, where the borders begin and end. "Every land and every *contrada* has words all its own, different from those of other lands and *contrade*": this a quotation from a Sienese phrasebook. For years—for centuries—a member of Tartuca, Tortoise, didn't marry a member of Onda, Wave, even though the two *contrade* abut each other on Siena's southern side. Istrice, Porcupine, which extends from Porta Camollia, stops short at what was once the enormous castle of the powerful Malavolti family, now the post office, where Drago, Dragon, takes over, and the Porcupine people cannot climb the stairs into the only part of the convent of the Sisters of Paradise that remains habitable, the oratory of Paradise. This is Drago's religious center, dedicated to Saint Catherine. Meanwhile the church of San Domenico in Dragon's territory, which houses Catherine's head, hovers over Catherine's home, found in the enemy territory of Oca, Goose.

Yet just as Siena has never really been self-sufficient, neither are the individual *contrade* really isolated. Residents travel to each other's homes not only when they've won a Palio but on the feast days of their patron saints. So on July 8 the Bruco, Caterpillar, dutifully visit Selva's oratory of San Sebastiano, in their shiny green-and-gold costumes, where the drums cease and they sing a hymn; then they're out again to toss a few flags to admiring cheers and head up Vicolo delle Balie, pressed between the Spedale and the adjoining building to the next *contrada*. Two hours later they are sweating and less adroit as they leave the oratory of the Dragon for Porcupine. Later that day the Onda, having just won the July 2 Palio, take yet another victory march through the city, displaying the *palio* with its soft earth colors and Franciscan theme in this year of austerity and the eight hundredth anniversary of Saint Francis's visit to the city to make peace between opposing families. This time their procession brings up the rear of a parade of homemade floats on which members of the other *contrade* ride and make fun of Onda. "Let this be the last time Siena will be washed out by a wave," say the signs on the Tartuca's float, which is piled high with washing machines, comparing the victorious *contrada* to a cheesy laundromat. Another *contrada* sings about how easy it was to win a Palio when only seven horses were running (at the last minute three of the ten were declared unfit to race): "Who can't win with only six competitors?" (The Onda will defy probability and win again in August 2013, this time against the usual nine.) The solemnity, even the dignity, of the Onda's members contrasts with the raucous music and banter edged with jealousy (Nicchia, Seashell, was supposed to have won, having been granted the favorite through the lottery), as well as the knowledge that no one *contrada* will, or should, always win. That all seventeen *contrade* never race at the same time is sufficient insurance against this, as are the notorious bribes to the jockeys to lose a race on purpose, or to trip up someone else's horse—deals negotiated in backrooms or over cell phones while sitting in Bar Palio in the Campo.

These ongoing demonstrations assert the obvious: Palio is not a race but a season, a way of life. Or as the T-shirts from the Contrada della Selva say, "Il Palio è vita": Palio is life itself. These green-and-orange shirts are sold to us foreigners for ten euros during a pause in the lunch where six Selvaioli officials are watching a pre-Palio interview; a little disgruntled at the disturbance—we shouldn't be in their headquarters at all—the only woman in the group makes her way to the cash register to take our money. We're something between guests and intruders in this scene, much as we will feel several nights later at the big dinner or *cenetta* before the Palio—temporary points of interest for a community brought together so often that they are intrigued by the novelty we represent. We're not real Selvaioli; pleasantries are exchanged and quickly worn out. But my husband is invited by the man sitting next to him, a wine seller, for a late-night espresso at the Selva's headquarters where we'd bought our T-shirts, and he's ushered off into the separate, privileged world of men. And, in fact, thanks to a friend from the Selva and our local newspaperman Andrea, who is also a photographer, we procured the tickets to this special festive meal. (The meal will take place at the exact moment that Italy is playing in the finals for the European Cup. The Sienese are forbidden to watch the finals during the pre-Palio dinner, by order of the mayor, the former prefect from Perugia, but they will glance surreptitiously at their phones for text messages throughout the evening.) When three tickets suddenly become available, they go to us after a series of frantic phone calls and texts, and I have to run to find a different Andrea in the crowd of Selvaioli as they are setting up for the dinner outside San Giovanni Battista, the baptistery at the foot of the Duomo, where the steep stairway begins that will take you first to the crypt and then to the church itself, high on the hill.

Here below, where an orchard once supplied the Spedale's residents with food, outside the baptistery where Florentine and Sienese sculptors vied to cast the best panels for the baptismal font itself (Donatello handily winning with his dramatic scene of Salome's dance before Herod, whom she will soon ask for John the Baptist's head), the narrow tables are laid out, the silverware and tablecloths made ready, the gates eventually closed, just as they will be in the Campo tomorrow, when the horses are finally allowed to parade in. This time, this once, we are within those gates, to hear the excited speech by the Selva's captain, who enjoins us to "transmit our love for each other to the horse"—a love that is exemplified in the *contrada: La cosa più bella, più unità:* "There is nothing more beautiful, nothing more unified." Women wipe away tears after his speech. Then a few terse words from the jockey, followed by the prefect's restrained speech. He remarks on the Franciscan theme of the Palio and suggests that the Selva—the smallest *contrada* in terms of people if not territory—is the most "Franciscan" of Siena's neighborhoods and so deserves to win: "We are small, but strong!" But Selva won, after all, just two years ago, and Franciscan humility demands that they think about things other than winning a horse race, even as they all stand at the end of the evening to sing rousing choruses of their song, with a lilting melody that sounds southern—Neapolitan, or perhaps Spanish:

> O Selva, Selvina va!
> il Palio si vincerà
> e quando in cielo saliranno le bandiere
> la Selva prima giungerà nelle carriere.
> O Selva, Selvina va!
> il Palio si vincerà!
>
> [O, Selva, little Selva, go!
> You'll win the Palio
> and when the flags sail up to the sky
> the Selva will come in first at full cry.
> O Selva, little Selva, go!
> You'll win the Palio!]

◆

The earliest known neighborhoods in Siena were secluded from what would eventually become the pilgrims' path, the ridge to the city's eastern side, so leaving the western hill protected. Strangers to Siena, as welcome as they may have felt, saw only part of the town. What pilgrims didn't see was where many—in fact, most—Sienese actually lived: the old Castelvecchio or the original city within the earliest set of walls. It seems that what many people feel as the city's inaccessibility is most pronounced here, in areas off-limits or at least inhospitable to pilgrims, where the roads take on a very different pattern. No longer are they the straight, flat embankment leading to Rome. The winding streets constitute a symbol central to medieval pilgrimage: the labyrinth, found on the pavements of cathedrals like Chartres and on the facade of Lucca's

Duomo. One might venture that the rigid neighborhood structure that defines Siena today and provides the basis for its most enduring traditions is in part a defense against the constant presence of strangers in the town, even as the neighborhoods embrace everything within the eighth circuit of walls, including the stretch of the Via Francigena well known to pilgrims.

A twisting little road off Via di San Pietro, just past the Pinacoteca with its collection of art dedicated almost entirely to Sienese painting and its inviting marble benches out front, takes you to the heights of Castelvecchio, the old castle, with a few surviving signs of its medieval structure. Castles along or just off the pilgrims' route belonged to wealthy families—the Tolomei, the Salimbeni, the Ugurgeri, their spacious quarters now serving as the home of the Civetta, Owl, in what is the city's best preserved *castellare*, on Via San Virgilio. But Castelvecchio constituted the original settlement, where ordinary Sienese from the eighth and ninth centuries gathered in the years before Sigeric made his journey from England. The sixteenth-century historian Bartolomeo Benvoglienti would define the original castle area as neither *molto grande, nè molto piccolo*, not very big or very small—not a helpful gauge in determining its extent. How much Benvoglienti can be trusted is in doubt, but what is known for a fact is that much of the topography of the zone was altered first by Franciscan nuns who built a convent in honor of Santa Margherita and persuaded the Comune to lower the original walls of the castle. They were lowered again for the once famous institution for deaf-mutes founded by the Genovese priest Tommaso Pendola, for whom one of the main streets in Castelvecchio is now named. *Siena e il suo territorio*, the book in which Professor C. Toscani wrote about the city's geological formations, was published there in 1862. The thriving school was designed to educate deaf children for work in the outside world, and typesetting became one of the occupations in which hundreds of youths were trained.

But the Vicolo di Castelvecchio—*vicolo* because it's little and narrow—is the most representative street of the ancient high nucleus of Siena, from which one could once view all the surrounding territory, snug within the once high walls. But that was before there were Franciscan convents and schools for the deaf. The area is circumscribed now by Via

Pendola, Via San Pietro, the flat and broad Piano dei Mantellini, and the steep Via di San Quirico. As Roberto Cresti maintains, you only need glance at a map of Siena to realize that "the castle is still there, notwithstanding the changes that took place over the centuries, with its inner streets, its elevated courtyard still perfectly conserved, and the towers, such as the one cut off behind the Piazza del Conte, called the Tower of Voltaia."

One document from 1010 that Cresti cites places a Count Bernardo as a renter in a house owned by the Viscount Guido *ad locus ad castello vetero*, or on the site of the old castle. Even a thousand years ago, the castle was already considered old. But just how old is still to be determined. Similarly, "Via delle Murella" as it was once called—now Via Tommaso Pendola—is said in thirteenth-century records to show traces of ancient walls, or *murellos*. The imagination instead can run wild on this hill, where at least from the north side the view onto the Duomo is yet unimpeded, or when coming down onto the Piano dei Mantellini where the bright yellow and blue flags of the Tartuca wave lazily in a breeze during Palio season. To the left of where the road emerges onto the flatter, broader Piano, on Via di San Quirico, one sees the oratory called the church of Sant'Ansano, where Ansano, the youth who brought Christianity to Siena, is said to have been imprisoned. The supposedly Roman tower called the Rochetta is testament to the ancient origins of the building—even though the tower was clearly built in the fourteenth century. Now the oratory for the *contrada* of the Pantera, Panther, the church served as Siena's first baptistery before the great structure at the bottom of the hill from the Duomo was built.

Going the other way on the Piano dei Mantellini, you pass San Niccolò del Carmine, once a great center for the Carmelite monks, whose white stoles (*mantelli*) over brown garments gave the road its name. Nurtured by their geographical link to an Old Testament prophet who was taken up into the heavens, the Carmelites were forced to leave the Holy Land when the crusaders failed to keep it and subsequently fanned out through the Middle East and southern Europe. Their solemn, plain, enormous church in Siena was built in 1262, in the glorious decade when Sienese were basking in their victory over the Florentines at Monteaperti and the Tolomei and Salimbeni flourished as papal bankers. Once in the city, they renounced their desertlike isolation to run a scriptorium and a school—though smaller than the one in Florence, Santa Maria del Carmine, where Masaccio's frescoes have made the chapel famous. Now it's locked up to all but university students; a peek into the library lets you see sixteenth-century paintings of Salimbeni and Beccafumi. Meanwhile the cloister has been turned into a lovely hotel, and the courtyard offers a spacious garden that conveys instant calm. To the left of the Palazzo Pollini, an imposing Renaissance structure by Baldassarre Peruzzi just to the cloister's left, you can see a stretch of the oldest layer of the walls.

Continuing on Piano dei Mantellini, you come to one of the most distinctive inner gates of the city, the Archway of the so-called Due Porte, or Double Doors, the westernmost entrance into Castelvecchio. Those who want to see the signs of a Roman encampment in the area maintain that the arch is made of a stone typical of an era earlier than medieval. One gate is now blocked, marked only by a small wooden door with a No Parking sign and a single cyclopian window. The other door opens to Via Stalloreggi; a sign indicates that Duccio's studio was here, although the workshop where he painted his dreamy *Maestà* before taking her in procession to the Duomo was another one, right outside the Due Porte. Artisans' shops still line this section of the road. SATOR, a shop dedicated to the craft of book and manuscript production, has a view out the back window onto the Spedale's hindquarters, and Piergiorgio Caredio Bartolozzi, the shop owner, offers college students internships to learn the dying arts of illumination and bookbinding. He sells homemade cards featuring Siena's art—panels from the *Maestà*, *tavolette* from the *biccherne*. They brighten the room, along with books that he publishes in limited editions and bookmarks and posters in Hebrew; I bought a card for a friend, inscribed with the traditional blessing for a Jewish house, to be placed over the door.

Farther up Via Stalloreggi, where you turn off to take the road to the top of the old castle, you can see the painting commonly called the Madonna of the Crow, by the sixteenth-century painter Giovanni Antonio Bazzi, called Il Sodoma. It shows a dead Christ in Mary's arms—an unusual outdoor image in a city where mother and newborn are much more common. No crow is to be found, but it was here, some say, that lightning struck the bird, infected with plague, that flew into the city. Or, others say, it was here where the bird struck its first victim, bringing the Black Death to half of Siena. If you continue straight on Stalloreggi, you arrive at the crossroads of the Quattro Cantoni—a flat, open piazza where, sure enough, four roads come together and where some have divined the existence of an original Roman forum. From here you can go left to the Duomo, but if you turn to go back out through the Due Porte, you'll descend the hill that goes behind the Spedale and so gain a spectacular view of this once densely populated town within a town, not bound by the rules of any *contrada*.

Here you are behind the city: south of the Duomo, west of the Spedale, without even a glimpse of the ubiquitous tower of the Palazzo Pubblico, unless you find yourself coming down the hill from Castelvecchio on its southern side to arrive at the Church of Sant'Agostino. There, suddenly, through the gate of San Giuseppe on the far reaches of the Tartuca's *contrada*, the tower briefly, miraculously, juts forth. Sant'Agostino stretches out across a long plateau between San Giuseppi's gate and another one just to its west, Porta all'Arco. Just below Sant'Agostino is the university *mensa*, or cafeteria, in the old and now deconsecrated church of Sant'Agata, patron saint of metalworkers. On its other side are Siena's elite high school, named for Pius II, and a police station. Sant'Agostino is open on a limited basis to the public, and now and then it opens for cultural events, such as a summer performance, sponsored by the Accademia Chigiana, of Mendelssohn's *Elijah*, about the Old Testament prophet who ascends to heaven in a fiery chariot at the end of the oratorio.

Inside the dark, humid church we strain to make out the works of art still decorating its walls. Pietro Perugino's *Crucifixion* is to our right as we listen, so we have ample time to study it, but the Il Sodoma *Epiphany* over the main altar is too dim to make out, and the famous Lorenzetti Madonna is inaccessible. As we leave, a boisterous, noisy crowd has gathered in the field directly in front of the church, where there are children's swings, a little carousel, and a view out to Santa Maria dei Servi. Hundreds of members of the *contrada* of the Tartuca, who won the Palio a

Fig. 26 ◆ San Giuseppe or Sant'Agata Arch, Siena (ca. 1920). Torre del Mangia can be seen in the background. Courtesy of Touring Club Italiano/Alinari Archives Management. Photograph: Ermanno Biagini.

year earlier, are packed onto benches before a gigantic television screen, set up at the edge of the road that leads down to the botanical gardens so that the two-minute race can be shown repeatedly during the evening.

There are many more of them than us, and the worlds are not mutually exclusive. But for this one night, at least, as the huge, windowless basilica marks the boundary of the Tartuca's feasting, the two groups of concertgoers and Palio fans do not seem to coincide in any way. The evening provides a far less dramatic version, to be sure, of the image of civil war in Lorenzetti's *Mal Governo*: a figure sawing herself in half as she holds a shield of Sienese white-and-black. Bad government is civil war, self-hatred, the self against the self, a form of suicide. Thus in Giovanni di Paolo's *Martyrdom of Saint Ansano* from a century later, the Roman soldiers hold a tattered flag and shields painted with Siena's crest, rising up before a ditch in front of which Ansano is kneeling, ready for decapitation. Perhaps Giovanni is conflating two scenes here: the scene of Ansano's actual martyrdom, outside Siena—the knobby little hills of the Crete punctuate the desertlike landscape of Giovanni's panel—and the scene of his torture, a ditch in Siena behind what is now the Spedale. (We now have a road called La fossa di Sant'Ansano, with a little cross marking the spot.) But Giovanni's point is this: that the Romans are torturing one of their own, an idealistic youth who had also made his way north, and that in the same way the Sienese too often turn against themselves.

One of the things we wouldn't have seen in Sant'Agostino even had the lights been brighter was an altarpiece about the life of a man said to have inspired Saint Augustine more than any other: Saint Anthony the Abbot. Once a multitude of churches and small hospices were dedicated to him, including a church in Fontebranda, and the Spedale spent a large sum in 1359 for a piece of his cranium. Now the church is gone and his cranium is virtually invisible within a large reliquary in the Spedale's depths. But the altarpiece was temporarily reconstructed almost in its entirety for an exhibition we went to see in the Spedale one summer. Its panels, dispersed by Napoleon, now are housed far afield in London, Washington, DC, and New York. Painted in the mid-fifteenth century by the mysterious artist called the "Maestro dell'Osservanza," possibly a young Sano di Pietro, the panels were (almost) all brought together in the Spedale to tell the story of this inspiring hermit's life.

Anthony, a wealthy Egyptian who lived in the third century, gave all he had to the poor so he could live a life of perfect contemplation. The earliest panel shows him distributing clothes to the blind and the poor, then going to a monastery that looks like the hermitage in Lecceto, not far from Siena. He is then shown living alone in the desert, where he was visited by the usual congeries of demons, in the form of beautiful women as well as beasts. My favorite panel shows him taking a little trip, presumably to break up his lonely desert sojourn. We follow a twisting dirt path in and out of woods as Anthony progresses on his journey. In the upper left corner he sets out with his belongings flung over a shoulder, like a boy running away from home. Midway along his path he encounters a centaur, who seems to be giving him directions as he stands on the edge of a dark forest. Then in the bottom right corner we have the point of the panel: his delightful meeting with another hermit, Saint Paul of Thebes, sealed by an embrace. In Saint Jerome's telling of this story, bread is delivered by a solicitous angel, and the two stay up all night, each pleading courteously for the other to take the first bite after these many months of fasting. (The angel reappears to end the discussion, deciding they should break and eat the loaf at exactly the same time. In other accounts a raven delivers them food.)

These hermits may have set out to lead solitary lives, but they are not in essence solitary men. The serendipity of community emerges in that neither really expected the other, yet both are delighted to find the other there, beyond forests and centaurs, in a place where no human habitations are supposed to exist. Paul graciously shares his local space, carved out of the elements, with the man who has come so far to find him. Yet it is Anthony who will become a patron saint for hospitality and emerge, especially in Siena, as associated with the acts of mercy or *misericordia*. Like Tobias, he gave freely to the poor and cared for the dead, providing the cloak to wrap Saint Paul's body when he died; one of the panels from the Sant'Agostino altarpiece shows him in the company of lions, burying his companion. And he is in fact the patron saint not only for the Augustinian order, but for the Misericordia, the "other" hospital in Siena, founded about 1250, a century or so after the Spedale, by the former criminal Andrea Gallerani, seen in a painting in the Pinacoteca welcoming Jesus and other pilgrims to Siena.

Fig. 27 ◆ Maestro dell'Osservanza, *The Meeting of Saint Anthony and Saint Paul the Hermit* (mid-fifteenth century). Courtesy of the National Gallery of Art, Washington, DC.

Unlike the Spedale, the Misericordia—which has chapters throughout Italy and southern Europe—is still in operation. And so on January 17, Anthony's feast day, new members of Siena's Misericordia are invested into this fraternity; now women are welcomed too. The Mass in the usually closed church of San Martino, just off Via del Porrione and behind the loggia dedicated to Pius II, is a spectacle of brightness, much of it borrowed from the baroque—angels zooming out from angles uncharacteristic of most Sienese sculpture—as well as darkness: the confraternity's members are all in black, with only their faces showing. The archbishop speaks of Anthony's compassion and of the need to see the hard times Sienese face as occasions for learning, not for lamenting. In the next-to-last row of the church the four-year-old son of a new initiate—she is proudly dressed in her black robe and hood—is wearing a child's version of the bright orange vests donned by the men and women who run the ambulance service in Siena. The Misericordia's emblem—a cross inscribed into what looks like an omega—is sewn onto the shoulder. The little boy nibbles on a "Saint Anthony's roll," for sale at the back of the church. The new initiates are presented to the community to applause and song, and everyone spills out into the courtyard in front of the Loggia of Pius II to bless two new ambulances. Earlier in the day the Misericordia members' pets were blessed, since Anthony is also the patron saint of domesticated animals. Some of my favorite devotional images show him with a crook and an impressively long beard, standing next to a contented pig. You can still find images of Anthony in country homes and barns and on the facades of the low buildings in Fontebranda, where the butchers used to have their shops. And in fact later in the evening each *contrada* will have its currently empty stalls blessed by the bishop so that when the horses come for the first Palio in July, Saint Anthony will have already graced their dwelling. We had seen a raucous group of Selvaioli preparing earlier in Vicolo delle Carrozze, cleaning out the stable before heading to the Società for dinner.

Three nuns break away from the crowd outside San Martino, and I follow them into the Misericordia's little museum in Via del Porrione, though I've been there before. One day the previous summer I stumbled into the hospital, not far from the synagogue and what was once the Jewish ghetto. Orange-vested men and women were waiting for emergency

calls in a room just beyond a lobby where a nineteenth-century ambulance is on permanent view, though minus the horses that would have
pulled it. But there was clearly a more extensive museum next to this
hospital that didn't seem at all like a hospital. (I learn that it's simply
where the paramedics congregate, their modern ambulances waiting in
the alleyway outside, ready to transport victims of motorcycle accidents
on the ring road outside the city or heart attack patients within to the new
modern hospital near the train station.) But the museum wasn't open;
and after several cordial exchanges with the receptionist I'm introduced
to a man with the key, who will turn out to be my guide to the institution,
which fills vast spaces on the eastern side of Via del Porrione, as well
as to the objects filling the darkened lobby: paintings of the members of
the Misericordia in procession, hooded like the Ku Klux Klan to ensure
anonymity lest they be tempted to boast about their charitable works;
child-sized coffins from the eighteenth century; medals and plaques;
the axes used when they served as Siena's firemen (through the early
1900s); the black armbands worn for funerals; statutes contained in
sixteenth-century manuscripts with miniatures of Saint Anthony himself, staff in hand.

The organization, now numbering some twelve thousand members
in its Siena branch, has its roots in the golden rule practiced by Tobias
and Saint Anthony alike, and in the chapel that dates back to the eighteenth century their duties are affixed to two columns. In a basement
room next to the ambulances that serves as a sculptor's studio sit registers of the Misericordia that go back at least to the eighteenth century: I
can make out the dates on the binders, "1758 no. 1; 1758 no. 2." And in the
newly renovated room on the second or third floor of the Misericordia's
modern wing, in a climate-controlled space that contrasts both with the
archive and with the Pinacoteca's open windows and sweating paintings, there is a Francesco Vanni canvas of Anthony on his deathbed. He's
not in the desert where his predecessor Paul passed away, but on a sun-
swept hill, flanked by Saint Catherine of Alexandria and others, his arms
open to greet angels who swoop down to take him to the heavens where
Mary awaits: a much more triumphant version than the muted funeral
cortege painted by the Maestro dell'Osservanza almost two centuries
earlier for the now dismantled altarpiece.

In short, the Misericordia is not the Spedale, whose oblates disappeared within its walls and, in a certain sense, never returned to the world outside. But there is a sharper difference when thinking of the city's neighborhoods. The Misericordia functions in many ways like a *contradaless contrada*. It offers its services to everyone, those within the city as well as those outside, and Misericordia members attend the Palio not to cheer on a favorite horse but to stand, arms crossed over their bright orange vests, declaring their allegiance not to a particular neighborhood but to a different conception of neighborhood. They are watching for victims of heat, of dehydration, or—though it's unlikely—of a stampeding crowd. They provide a number of services to the city, such as taking meals to the homebound, coordinating blood and food drives, running an antiusury group and drug treatment center, and—one of their more solemn tasks—burying the dead. Federigo Tozzi writes in his *Bestie* that as a young boy the sound of the accordion would alert him to a funeral procession, and he remembers the pallbearers' eyes peering out from their white hoods, the medals on their belts jingling as they walk.

While the Misericordia ministers to the stranger, like the Spedale of old, the *contrade* minister to their own, offering the hospitality for which Siena is best known, but a hospitality turned inward, to nurture the city itself, even as the city's numbers are in decline. They are a buffer for generations above and below, the frail eighty-year-old widow protected by her young neighbors, who walk her home through the dark and mostly silent streets after a dinner at the *società*; the six-year-old boys throwing a basketball into the makeshift hoop on the wall next to our nearby restaurant, Il Divo, supervised by a doting but critical grandfather: *Più in alto*, throw it higher! he calls until well after midnight. In the same way, the *contrade* ensure that the horses are taken care of when they no longer run in the Palio. There's a farm outside Poggibonsi, unique in Italy, where they're sent when they are ill or old, to be tended well into their dotage. These are miniature communities in action, and clearly something more positive is at work than resentment over Florence's domination. They are communities based on both pride and *misericordia*: mercy, also translatable as sympathy or, more strongly, compassion—what you feel when you enter, as the columnist Maureen Dowd once put it, "into the chaos of another."

But there is something else at work in Anthony's life. In his biography of the saint, Saint Jerome claims that Anthony, already 90 years old, was motivated by vainglory and presumption, supposing that *he* was the first hermit. Discovering the existence of Paul of Thebes, at the time even older, at 113, put such pride to rest. Anthony's life militated, that is, against exceptionalism. And in fact the angel's intervention (or the raven's) ensures that Anthony and Paul are equals, after each politely refuses to eat first. Thus the Misericordia members' hoods ensured that they were not outwardly recognized for performing charitable works. The *contrade* too seek to minimize individual achievement. To be sure, a *capitano* oversees the *contrada*'s involvement in the Palio, while the happenings of everyday life fall to the generally more senior, certainly more somber, prefect. Yet the *contrade*'s very organization undoes once fiercely maintained distinctions of class: the captain may be the butcher, the secretary a lawyer. Like Paul and a subdued Anthony, *contrada* members learn to put others of their tribe before themselves, and the Palio ensures that they share Anthony's devotion to animals, especially horses.

◆

Siena's "collective genius," in Gabriella Piccinni's phrase, is not limited to the *contrade*. Siena was the first town to have a cultural academy, the Academy of the Intronati, a group of well-off, educated men who decided in the 1520s to make themselves deaf to the world around them—*intronato* means thunderstruck—and write plays and treatises as a group. Its first play, *The Deceived*, one of the most influential comedies of the Renaissance, inspired Shakespeare's *Twelfth Night*, and it has no author other than the Accademia degli Intronati. A corresponding organization, the Congrega dei Rozzi, "the association of the uncouth," consisted of artisans who, bound together in their common ignorance of Latin, "use their leisure time productively" to write plays and poems, many of them about peasants, whom they saw both as figures of satire and as worthy of compassion. The Rozzi took an oath that no one would ever perform without the consent and participation of his fellows. One Salvatore, a tailor, was penalized and temporarily expelled in 1542 when he performed one of the Rozzi's plays in Rome without express permission. The Accademia dei Fisiocritici, first housed in the Spedale and then in its comfortable home near the Orto Botanico, is another example of purposeful community, priests working side by side with deists to achieve a common, scientific good: "the distinguishing of the true from the false."

The origins of this collective ingenuity may lie in the rugged commune that rose up in the twelfth century to throw off its bishop, then crystallized in the popular government of the Nove—the Nine—which commissioned Lorenzetti's *Mappamondo*. They refused to allow aristocrats or rich magnates a voice in their government, which endured from 1287 until 1355, fostering a rule of the *meça gente*, or "faceless middle class," instead. Sumptuary laws were more stringent in Siena than in many other towns, and the towers that were the mainstay of Siena's important families when they were free to live in the city (not often) are still unlabeled; one can only guess at who lived where, and only the occasional quotation from Dante gives a vague clue as to provenance. And the great home on Via dei Pellegrini of the *magnifico* Petrucci, who tried to model himself on his contemporary, the more successful Lorenzo de' Medici, is now remembered primarily by the bakery called Il Magnifico, which makes the best and freshest *ricciarelli* in all of Siena—soft cookies made with almond paste, better than macaroons. There's nothing left to see of his palace, and even the *braccialetti di bronzo*, bronze hitching rings, once used to tie up horses outside have been moved to the atrium of the Palazzo Pubblico. (Petrucci himself was memorialized by Machiavelli, who in his usual wry fashion commended him for having good advisers—possibly a backhanded compliment to a man who had his father-in-law murdered and who attempted to deceive Machiavelli by suggesting they meet so he could impart secret information about an upcoming French attack on the Florentine republic. There was no such attack; he was simply trying to learn about Florence's military plans, and Machiavelli smoked him out.)

This resistance to commemorating Petrucci or to letting a Sienese take over the town (better to invite in the Milanese Visconti, as they did in 1398, or the Spanish in the 1520s when the Intronati withdrew from the world to form their group) is an at times twisted expression of what Mario Ascheri has recognized as Siena's long-standing commitment to full political participation by the *meça gente*. The Sienese republic existed as a dream of the Sienese, even if it could not always be a reality, with laws in place that allowed each propertied male citizen to have his say: unless you were a Salimbeni or Tolomei, or a member of one of the other eighty families on the list of those excluded from public affairs for fear they would turn the republic into a tyranny. Eventually this dream would become what Ascheri defines as an "anachronistic luxury of full political participation" during a certain period—the sixteenth century. This was the century of Siena's final defeat, marked elsewhere in Europe by principalities and oligarchies, such as Petrucci's brief and anomalous reign. This "Sienese syndrome," as Piccinni and Catoni have called it, caused continual tensions and in-fighting. Yet it was deeply embedded in a Sienese insistence that no single member of their city should be authorized to make a decision alone. All requests had to go before one of the ruling bodies of the republic: by way of the committee, the guild, the Nine, the Twenty-four, the One Hundred. In Lorenzetti's fresco of the allegory of the *Buon Governo*, twenty-four men hold the "cord" of *accordanza* or agreement in their hands to symbolize a perfect number for a ruling body that would, in fact, rule for only two months, then be replaced by twenty-four other men. When I applied for permission to tour Siena's underground *bottini* in the heat of July, it took weeks to get approval. This was not because my request was ignored, as I'd feared, but because it had to circulate among the members of the mayor's office, finally coming to a vote of the Comune, who decided—grudgingly (by a single vote?) that these Americans who had to go home soon after the Palio should be allowed to prowl the tunnels beneath Via Camollia, in the hope that only minimal damage would be done by opening the doors to the ninety-degree heat outside.

But as idealistically democratic as the Sienese may be, their attitude is also deeply rooted in suspicion of the individual: not simply the loner taking the government into his own hands, but anyone who is different, who tries to rise above the norm. Saint Catherine was worried that her greatest "sin," or so says her hagiographer, was *superbia*, or pride: and indeed she was attacked by her fellow Sienese for trying to get attention by her mystical spells, or for drinking the pus from a woman's tumor in the Spedale. Dante may have gotten it right in his *Purgatory*. Of the seven sins punished there, two are illustrated with examples of Sienese citizens: pride and envy. The two mirror one another: the envious, who rejoice when a neighbor falls on hard times and plummet into despair

when he's visited by good fortune, would like to be exceptional themselves. So Sapia dei Salvani, her eyes stitched shut in punishment so that
she can no longer gaze on others and thereby envy them, remembers
how happy she was when her fellow-citizens were routed by the Florentines at Colle di Val d'Elsa, not long after the victory at Monteaperti.

One of those routed was her own nephew, Provenzano Salvani, who
helped lead the Sienese to victory at Monteaperti in 1260 and who, after
the defeat at Colle ten years later, was taken prisoner and beheaded by a
Tolomei. Provenzano is in purgatory too, on the terrace of the proud; and
Dante expresses surprise that he is there at all—Dante's contemporary,
the Florentine historiographer Francesco Villani, called him "a man who
presumptuously sought to get all Siena into his hands," and one suspects
that Dante thinks he should be in hell, or at least still languishing on the
shores of ante-purgatory. But there he is, already on Mount Purgatory,
albeit suffering silently beneath the stone he is forced to carry around
the mountain. According to a fellow penitent, he has been saved because
Provenzano once humbled himself in the Campo. Dressed in sackcloth,
he begged for alms to raise money and release a friend from the clutches
of King Charles IV. He "affixed himself to the Campo," in Dante's words,
the phrase that adorns a wall in the Campo itself. As another historian
recounts, "when the Sienese saw this man, whom they thought of as
their lord, usually so proud [superbo] begging so pitifully, they were
moved to pity. Everyone helped, according to his means. So that, before
the time had expired, he was able to buy his friend's release." By debas-
ing himself before all eyes in Siena's most public space, dressed in rags,
head lowered, hands upturned, he became the beggar Lorenzetti would
paint half a century later in the Buon Governo, sightless gaze raised to the
knight who leaves the city—proudly—on horseback.

But even as he rejects self-esteem and pride, Provenzano exhibits the
Sienese characteristic of tenacity, affixed as he is to the Campo. And
Sapia's closing lines suggest that she too views her fellow Sienese as a
vana gente, a vain people, who persist in impossible pursuits. It is in
fact through Sapia's voice that Dante makes fun of Siena's quests for a
thriving port at Talamone and a river beneath the city. The coupling
of such behaviors with resistance to the individual means that these
organizations—comune or contrada—can be suspicious of change. And

while change will eventually come, it comes slowly. Hence, for example, the long and painful process by which the Contrada dell'Oca admitted women as voting members. Some women—as well as some men of the *contrada*—lobbied for women's right to vote (ironically, in the neighborhood of the outspoken, fearless Saint Catherine of Siena). Fellow *contradaioli*'s resistance to what they saw as selfishly motivated designs to secure the vote for women revealed itself particularly in the numbers who attended the two court cases held in the city's tribunal. The second time, the court voted in favor of the women's proposition, one that came from decades, even centuries, of the Oca women's recognition of their status. Some of the women have been embittered by the drawn-out battle and the way they were attacked. But as of May 2012 all of them have been allowed to vote: mothers, daughters, grandmothers. Somewhere Saint Catherine approves.

One night after the Palio victory, women of the Selva take to the streets, bells ringing in the *contrada*'s oratory, lights flooding the tiny piazza that once belonged to the secluded nuns of the Gesuate and is now their own. The girls practice the drumbeats they've heard incessantly since they were born, brandishing and tossing the colorful flags—hitting stray passersby who try to dodge—and a little before midnight they charge into the city on Via di Città, and across the Campo. The men follow, laughing, feeling superior. The coveted *palio* is in their hands. Behind them straggles a crowd of neighbors, with worn green-and-orange bandannas around their necks. This is a double claiming: the city as the Selva's, and the Selva's—almost—as the women's, all except the Palio itself. And yet the jockey who won the Palio for the Selva is from Sardinia, like most of Siena's jockeys, and their horse, Fedora, assigned to the Selva through the lottery, was borrowed for the occasion. What, that is, belongs to the *contrada* itself except its buildings, mostly dark and austere except for colorful laundry hung out a window that overlooks San Domenico and the wide stretch of road that winds around behind the Spedale to the place where Sant'Ansano was tortured?

◆

Once Anthony finds Paul in the desert, he doesn't leave him. Similarly, the *contrade* protect against not simply solitude, but isolation, in the same way that one can't go to the Palio alone. Solitude has little chance of withstanding the onslaught of community. In the face of the *contrade* banding together in the Campo, that you might be alone, unable to lay claim to a neighborhood, or in possession of the camouflage that lets you pretend—a hastily bought scarf with the colors of the Porcupine or Tortoise—is only amplified. This is the city of guilds, gatherings, associations, academies, neighborhoods grown into the soil that is carefully scattered over the bricks a week before the Palio so that the horses can run the *prove* or trials without losing traction or damaging their hooves. Bringing the soil in is a collective labor too: one night teams of workers arrive to unload caravans of dump trucks full of earth. Steamrollers do the rest, along with an army of men with shovels and spades, packing down the soft dirt of the Sienese countryside. Thus does the race course magically come into being one morning. Several days after the Palio, it will just as mysteriously vanish, allowing the red bricks to reappear. (This is almost impossible to envision outside Palio season. A group of retired Australians seated next to us at a table in the Campo one May morning spent some time discussing how the horses could run on these uneven bricks without stumbling or getting hurt, finally coming up with the solution: "They must wear booties!" "A great town this is, eh?" closed the conversation.) And if you are in Siena for Palio season but have nowhere to go—not to one of the dinners for which they are still assembling the massive tables, fathers and their young sons trying to be helpful—you can only go home to regret that you are not a part of this great production. You are limited to watching the grown children long gone who return to Siena the night before the Palio, dragging suitcases as they come off the escalator from Fontebranda to fall asleep in their parents' homes.

Yet when the starting gun finally goes off, the horses sprint around the Campo and the cheers rise up, it may no longer be just about Siena, but may encompass something else. Eternal *giovenezza*, eternal youth, Pope John XXII said, or the beauty of speed, of color, of a throbbing crowd, eyes and necks strained for two minutes to watch a sight that is both joyful and potentially violent, merciless in its speed and ruthlessness. Hence a poem on the Palio by Corrado Forlin, whose explosive, futurist painting of the Palio I mention in the introduction (fig. 2). The offensive beginning of his poem, which appeared in the Sienese newspaper the day after the August Palio in 1937—"Vita imbecile / Vita odierna inacidita" (feeble-minded life / sour modern life)—and its comparison of the town's urinals to cathedrals for pederasts caused an outcry led by former mayor Fabio Bargagli Petrucci. (Partly as a result, Forlin's fabulous painting was not exhibited publicly in Siena until 2009, part of an exhibition at the Pinacoteca devoted to *macchine*, or machines: I still recall my surprise at seeing motorcycles from the thirties sharing space with Vecchietta's reliquary cabinet and Simone Martini's Madonnas.) But it was another futurist poet, Farfa, present at the same Palio, who conveyed perhaps the more authentic sentiment of a first-time Palio attendee rather than a young man's posturing: "Ora potrei morire io t'ho detto / ma salvami, concedimi un'altro anno / per vederlo una sol volta ancora!" (Now I've told you that I could die / but save me, give me another year / so that I can see it again, just one more time!)

And that first Palio may be the most memorable, especially if the *contrada* where you happen to be living wins. We got to the Campo early—roughly 3:00 in the afternoon—to find some choice standing space (in the shade, to the west of the Campo). Most of the *contradaioli*, however, couldn't have cared less about where they would stand but were off at their oratories, where the priest said the Our Father and blessed the horse, asking God to protect it in an unexpected act of tenderness. But we were there, beneath the stands, across from the Palazzo Pubblico decked out in the flags of the ten *contrade* in the race, below the tower completed moments before the plague struck the city in 1348. You can imagine the shiny new bells in the brand-new tower tolling for the dead. Not unlike these few hours before the Palio begins: the bells are solemn, almost funereal from the beginning. Earlier in the day, about noon, I had been surprised by an equally funereal procession as I walked on Banchi di Sotto from Banchi di Sopra to the university. The tower on top of the rector's building, usually reserved for meteorological experiments, was open to the public for a rare visit, so I was off to take in the aerial view. A mournful drumbeat accompanied eight Sienese in armor, complete with helmets, holding swords and flanking a page who bore the Madonna on her silk standard, shimmering in the light breeze. No one was at the corner of Banchi di Sotto and the Campo, as they crossed the street to head toward the Palazzo Pubblico, where the banner would await the procession later that day. Perhaps twenty tourists who had been listening to the drums now watched, amazed that the *palio* was within their grasp, all of us stunned by the unexpected appearance of this prize.

But now in the Campo the *palio* is nowhere in sight, and we wait, the space filled to bursting, with people hanging out of the windows and balconies above us. And waiting, it turns out, will define the afternoon as much as anything. Trumpets will finally disrupt the bells' hypnotic beats after a gun goes off at 5:15, startling the starlings and the elderly, announcing the entrance of officials, followed by noble families on horseback and then representatives of the city's guilds as they once were, symbolized by shields and flags: the guilds or *arti* of masonry, of wool, of architects or engineers or whatever is meant by a geometer's compass. Minor dignitaries, secular and ecclesiastical, follow suit as the campanile of Siena's cathedral winks above the Campo's western side in the approaching sunset. Only when this slow procession makes its way almost all around the Campo do selected men, women, and children from the *contrade* enter to bring in more energy, fiery drum cadences and flags tossed to the third floors of the palaces, magically caught to impressed applause. The six "ghost *contrade*" are here too, neighborhoods incorporated into other ones after violence broke out in the Campo one night in 1675, and the wise princess of Bavaria banished them forever with her *bando* of 1730. Still, their bestiaries survive them, and their representatives—a knight with a helmet that completely conceals his face, a looming bear, a cock—must slowly circle the Campo to the monotonous beating of drums. Last of all, just before the horses arrive, comes the large painted carriage drawn by impassive oxen with the *palio* hoisted on it. The prize for this year was designed by a Lebanese artist who studied in Siena and now lives in Milan. His olive-skinned Madonna—the image all *palios* must bear in honor of Siena's patron and protectress—is a portrait of his wife, while the turbaned warrior standing before her is the artist himself, submissively planting his scimitar in the ground. A verse from the Qur'an, in Arabic, attests to Mary's presence in Islam's holy text, and over the past month has occasioned criticism from some of Siena's less open-minded citizens, including the archbishop. As they, too, solemnly round the Campo, always, throughout, the bells toll, D, C, D, C, an in-

Fig. 28 ◆ Campo, procession of the *palio*. Photograph: Nathan Klein.

sistent, somber background, reminding us of the divinity that underlies these colorful gestures: the reason for their existence.

From then until the horses erupt from the Palazzo Pubblico to ready themselves at the starting line there is mounting excitement, if not irritation. They are wild, beautiful mixed-breeds. Thoroughbreds, with their easily broken legs, are no longer allowed to run this narrow course with its abrupt curves. By now the Sienese themselves have arrived, including those who have spent 290 euros for a seat without a cushion (it's slightly more with one) in the stands near the starting line; heads now appear from the apartments that overlook the Campo, and officials of the Comune look out from windows in the Palazzo Pubblico itself. The horses are cagey, as though they are aware of the crucial role they play in building suspense. Each time the judge asks the jockeys to take their assigned places, at least one horse will refuse to face in the right direction or respect the starting line. "*Gira*, Tartuca," turn around, Tortoise, the master of ceremonies continually pleads up to the instant when, visible only to those nearest the Costarella dei Barbieri, the race begins. The ten horses will finally have settled into starting positions after seemingly all the jostling and false starts, and a shot will ring out. We the uninitiated will ask, Did it start? And of course the answer is yes, for a swirl of manes and jockey caps—all one can see from the midst of the piazza—are careering around the Campo, making three circuits. Less than two minutes later, with another shot, a roar will go up as the crowd shouts the name of the winner, to be confirmed seconds later by the banner of the Selva above the finish line, which also happens to be the starting line. In the intervening two minutes, as I learn later, one jockey falls off (the horse finishes alone) and another careens into the wall that rounds the most tortuous curve of the Campo near Via del Porrione, where horses and jockeys have died, at least until the curve was padded two decades ago. But for now, all we know is that the neighborhood where we have rented an apartment for the summer has won. Suddenly the orange-and-green flag of the Selva that we bought the day before in a burst of patriotic spirit takes on new meaning, as its colors are waved excitedly throughout the Campo by those with far more claim to them.

And yet the pandemonium that sweeps the piazza lasts only a moment; it is quickly replaced by an extraordinary calm and the almost serene dispersion of so many people. We feel that in some small way we may have brought the *contrada* luck. While most of those present head home, resigned to the loss, savoring memories of another year's victory, we join the cluster of *selvaioli* who go with their jockey and horse to give thanks to the miraculous image of the Madonna in the church of Provenzano, to whom this July Palio is dedicated. This is the neighborhood where Sapia and her nephew once lived, tucked into the next valley after the Campo's. Unlike the jockey and his horse Fedora—one of the few mares in this largely masculine triumphal march—the horse's owner, the *capitano* of the Selva, and the families who live there whom I recognize from the bakery, or the fruit seller's shop, or the streets where early in the morning they are getting their newspapers, or their coffee, or their bread, we remain outside. This act of gratitude is not for strangers, and in any case by the time we arrive the church is far too crowded for us to get in. Days later I will learn from my friend Renata that she and many other *selvaioli* took the easy way out. Before the race started, they escorted their horse into the little oratory of San Sebastiano to be blessed. But rather than following the crowd into the Campo, and later going with their jockey and horse into the church of Provenzano for a different blessing after the race, they went to the communal hall down the street from Maurizio's apartment to watch the race on an enormous flat-screen television. Amid cheers, the prosecco was uncorked, and in the closed camaraderie of a space they and no others can call their own, they celebrated, glasses in hand.

I had entered the basilica of Provenzano once before. For all the other days of the year the church is quiet, the piazza virtually empty with its one restaurant—a wonderful pizzeria—drawing crowds, mostly locals, to its outdoor tables at night. There in the vacant nave of this late sixteenth-century church decorated with multicolored *bandiere*, banners—one for each *contrada*—and a reliquary designed to hold a miraculous shard of pottery with the Virgin's image, I came in part to understand what the Palio is about: vying to possess, for a brief time, the Madonna herself, to bring her home. This fierce if parochial act of patriotism in quest of a religious icon once attested, and perhaps still attests, to a belief in grace: to the willingness of the Madonna, implored by all, to choose on a particular day in a particular year this small cluster of houses and streets, this corner of the city, this segment of humanity, to receive favors that will carry them on to other *contrade*, to others' tables for others' food. In this ritual, members of the winning *contrada* assume the role of pilgrims—albeit victorious pilgrims—at the mercy of those who earlier in the day, or the month, had been their enemies: for several weeks after the Palio, the winning *contrada* dines at the expense of the neighborhoods who have lost. Banquets are spread to host the victors, and the sacred spaces of the losing *contrade*'s oratories are opened to them (and the casual visitor) as well. But the Mary who offers the victory of the *palio*, the fragile cloth bearing her image that waves high above the horses' heads, is the humble queen who insists on the *contradaioli*'s humility, their recognition that the victory is temporary, made possible only by her grace.

As the anonymous nineteenth-century author of the *Memorie della città di Siena* wrote, "Once in long-ago times, discord generated hatred, hostility, fighting, and a terrible administration of government. Now, with our system of the *contrade*, a more noble kind of discord produces the sustenance for our guilds, our prestige, and the decorum of our *patria*."

◆

In the Campo, a week after the Palio is over, a white flag with a strange emblem waves from the Palazzo Pubblico. What can it possibly mean? In 1577 the playwright, scholar, and man-about-town Scipione Bargagli wrote a 640-page treatise on the origins and meanings of emblems. He would also write about the parades, processions, and parties he took part in as a youth and rewrite a play by his deceased brother called, not insignificantly, *La pellegrina* (The female pilgrim), to be performed in Florence by Sienese actors for the wedding of a French princess and a Medici duke. Born in 1540, a generation before Francesco Vanni, straddling the last years of the republic and the first years of Medici takeover, he was an adolescent when the Sienese fell to Florence, a painful and impressionable fifteen. His *Trattenimenti* is a collection of short stories like Boccaccio's, but the crisis prompting the storytelling was not the Black Death but the "wretched, unpleasant" siege of Siena just when everyone there was living, as he puts it, in "such a happy, carefree way." He put his considerable energy into creating new kinds of communities to replace political ones. Perhaps he realized that culture alone could save Siena and identify it as unique, perhaps even making it superior to Florence. As it administered all of Tuscany and employed bureaucrats like Vasari to impose a once vibrant local identity onto a larger whole, Florence—so Bargagli thought—diffused and weakened what was truly its own while threatening to compromise the local cultures of the defeated. Siena, in the meantime, could preserve its own individuality without worrying about exporting it elsewhere, prey to the dangers that come with responsibility. No longer a middleman, Siena could at last set out to establish its real identity, even as the Florentines built the Fortezza on the outskirts of Porta Camollia and the Jews were forced into a ghetto over the protests of the Sienese. The communities to which Bargagli devoted his life and his pen were its Spedale (he served as rector or, in the grandiloquent rhetoric of the Medici regime, *ministro plenipotenziario del Granduca di Toscana*); its academies (namely the Academy of the Intronati, shut down by Cosimo in 1569 and reopened only in 1603 when Bargagli, by then an old man, gave the oration of his life); and its neighborhoods, which had begun to offer the horse races (then bull races) from which the Palio would emerge.

Yet what turned out to be most Sienese, according to Bargagli, was its language, a language he spent much of his life advocating, convinced that here resided not only the true dialect of his own people, but the true language of all Italians. The claim was not an idle one. Already in Bargagli's time foreigners were coming to Siena to learn "real Tuscan." Today's Università per Stranieri is an outgrowth of the city's commitment to teaching its native tongue.

And there's good reason for the draw. The first constitution in Europe to be translated into a vernacular was Siena's, in 1309, a document written in what were called *lettera grossa*, literally large letters, so it could be read by "poor people and all other people who don't know Latin" (*povare persone et altre persone che non sanno grammatica*). Chained to a block of stone in the courtyard of the new Palazzo Pubblico, the constitution could be consulted by all. The model for the vernacular constitution may have been the rules of the Spedale, turned into "Sanese" four years earlier. Possibly reflective of the same provincialism or *campanilismo* that many scholars have accused Bargagli of (he was seen as a slave to his own *campanile*, or bell tower, and in fact he rarely left Siena during his long life, only going on occasion to take the baths in Lucca for his rheumatism), this interest in translating the Latin of the priests, the doctors, and the Studio no doubt had something to do with the Sienese insistence on full political participation. It was the idea that people would be involved, would be informed, and would have an opinion, a contribution—preferably not the *superbi* or great ones of the city in accordance with the populist projects of Siena's Nove, the Nine, but the shopkeepers, the dyers, the butchers. Simone Martini wrote Mary's words in Italian a mere decade after the Costituto, bringing divine language down the steps from her throne to the elected officers standing before her. Surely he was inspired not only by Dante but by the accessibility of Siena's political language, its constitution available in the courtyard of the Palazzo Pubblico so that ordinary citizens could try to make sense of the myriad regulations that governed Sienese life: why one couldn't build a loggia over the narrow street, why a woman could be permitted to leave her husband—a revolutionary idea—and why hogs had to be kept out of the Campo. Yet that the rules were constantly being revised, even in minute ways, suggests they were not seen as immutable. Marginal notes exist in copies of the 1309 document. As with the ever-changing rules of the road, *Lo statuto*, here too historical layers have been preserved so one can note what was contested, and why.

The original manuscript of the vernacular constitution eventually made it into the archives of Bargagli's family, which numbered several famous lawyers and judges among its progeny. Scipione himself must have been fascinated by its existence as the earliest constitution in Europe not written in Latin, and he arguably took from it the rules for the ideal academies he set out in 1569. He was not immune from enlightening his fellow Sienese on subjects such as academies, or emblems, or the proper way to speak, and occasionally he falls into pedantry. His vast treatises, each longer than the last, admit to the same tenacity seen in the proud Provenzano, who "affixed himself" to the Campo. But one sees this trait in cultural projects too, which have preserved aspects of Sienese society for posterity. Members of the *contrada* of Valdimontone put together money to renovate their oratory, a baroque beauty dedicated to the Santissima Trinità, just behind Santa Maria dei Servi. The Biblioteca Comunale, Siena's gorgeous and recently renovated library—complete with an open courtyard where you can have a smoke and hallways lined with computers that descend belowground—was ardently promoted by Sallustio Antonio Bandini, the famous economist who invented the *cambiale*, or bill of exchange, and who proposed a radical plan to save the residents of the Maremma from malaria and poverty. (The recent crisis forced the Biblioteca to cancel its celebration of the two hundredth anniversary of its founding.) There was the project for Siena's first archaeological museum, and in 1904, the Italian version of a World's Fair to promote Sienese painting, an exhibition that led Bernard Berenson and others to begin reevaluating Sienese art. Both early twentieth-century projects were heavily promoted by Fabio Bargagli Petrucci, who had just finished his exhaustive study of the city's fountains and had yet to become Siena's first and only Fascist mayor. (Fortunately, another project of Bargagli Petrucci's, to build a highway across the valley where we look out at San Domenico, met with failure, as did his proposal to rebuild Siena's towers to their original medieval height. Mussolini refused to pay for the latter, and World War II intervened to prevent the former. Bargagli Petrucci's justification for his bridge was that there had been designs for such a viaduct back in 1365.)

Perhaps these cultural plans were inevitable substitutes for the failure of the republic, a channeling of energy into projects that come to matter more in the absence of political and economic power. In nearby Montalcino, where four hundred Sienese families were permitted to go into exile in 1555 under the flag of the French captain Blaise de Montluc, the imposing fort—now an *enoteca*, or wine bar, where one can pass several hours sampling the local wines—represented the last stronghold of Sienese liberty, as a plaque maintains. When the supportive French left after the Treaty of Cateau-Cambrésis on August 4, 1559, the representatives of the remaining Sienese, "dressed in mourning," surrendered to Cosimo's troops. A sign on the tower at Radicofani asserts instead that it was there that the last vestiges of the Sienese republic came to an end on August 19, 1559, when the Florentines demanded control of the mountain hideout that had once protected Sienese merchants from Siena itself. The energies of these dispersed collectives would return to a defeated Siena in the form of schools for the deaf, academies, convents, processions, Italian language classes, and the fuel-burning Palios of July and August, in the words of Corrado Forlin. Writing proudly about the origins of academies, Scipione Bargagli, ancestor of the Fascist mayor, presaged his town's future.

◆

The *contrade* gather their collectives in oratories, a legacy of the suppression of the convents under Leopold and then Napoleon; each has its *società* or headquarters where members share meals and plan their Palio, have an afternoon espresso, play cards. And they also have their fountains: seventeen of them, a testimony, along with the *bottini*, to their tenacity in creating and preserving community from among the would-be isolates on these hills. The fountains are now mostly decorative, and unlike the oratories, unguarded and public. Some have histories that began long before they were claimed by a particular *contrada*. Fontebranda, which our balcony overlooks, now abandoned save for the stray tourist, was once a pulsating city center surrounded by tanners, butchers, and washerwomen, as seen in an anonymous eighteenth-century painting. Palio may pose as *la vita*, but it is water that really is life. Here at the water's sources, communities were created long before the enforced sociability that is the *contrada*. Neighborhoods flourished, lured by the consoling, comfortable rhythm of water trickling into the basins, drawn in by the *bottini*. The painter probably does not exaggerate in depicting the life that teemed around the three basins: one for human consumption, one for animals, one for laundresses and dyers. Here too under Saint Anthony's watchful eye were the butchers, the leatherworkers, who needed copious salt and water to boil away the rank smell of cowhide, the hog sellers, and the travelers coming in from the roads that led to Volterra, Grosseto, the sea. And there was enough water left to power the mills just outside the city that ground flour and sent it back within the walls.

Other fountains similarly frame and diminish the commotion from on high. The Fonte d'Ovile, just outside Porta Pispina, is now in ruins, with two side arches, a column with grass tufts, a spout still pouring out water. If it were the nineteenth century this would inspire romantic drawings: outside the walls all is decadent, decayed. Above us the Bruco sing Palio songs. This was the fountain of the sheep, and herds passed through here during the *transumanza* or seasonal movement of livestock down from the Apennines, en route to more temperate climes. So this site below Siena's eastern slope served pilgrimages of a different kind, of animals and shepherds: as early as 1189 there are notices of a fountain that provided relief for the flocks and their herders. Now a single biker rinses out his sweaty T-shirt, while the Sardinian shepherds who still come to Tuscany in search of work stay to the west, among Volterra's great hills and plains.

On the other side of town the Fonte di Pescaia, so named because it once had pools full of fish, is a five-minute walk from the gate of the Fontegiusta. Now we find the occasionally open Museo dell'Acqua, staffed by

Fig. 29 ◆ *Veduta del piano di Fontebranda* (anonymous, eighteenth century). Oil on canvas. Photograph courtesy of Circolo degli Uniti, Siena.

volunteers from the Associazione La Diana, with multimedia exhibitions on its several levels. This area too was once a city in itself. Brick arches and the comfortable home of the medieval fountainkeeper tower over two pools that as recently as several decades ago were used for laundry (the western pool) and drinking water (the northern one); clotheslines once crowded the terraces that inch up toward the street. Photographs of the Fonte survive from the birth of the camera: a group of Sienese women pose, awkward and self-conscious, and one or two smile, their hands protectively gripping the garments they are washing, shyly acknowledging the camera. Those sitting at the other end of the basin don't deign to turn around. From dawn to dusk, this was the meeting place of women; the fields to the west and the city to the east were where men met. Beneath the fountain and the house built for the custodian of this sacred place, the *bottini* glide effortlessly, unnoticed, crossing from one *contrada* into another and erasing all distinctions between Pantera and Tartuca and between the city and its suburbs—the *sobborghi*.

These fountains outside the gates mark the limits of the *contrade*, legislated as being forever contained within the crenellated pink city walls. The inhabitants of the rural masses were excluded from the city's ruling organizations—reflecting the once dominant mentality that considered citizens superior to residents of the countryside, as Virgilio Grassi has observed, governed as they were by other customs and traditions. Outside Porta di Fontebranda, due west of the Fonte, you happen upon a cluster of apartments and gardens, a community that is part of no *contrada*. The little bar Il Chicco is at the center of this lively neighborhood on the edge of two parking lots—one where you have to pay, the other free (if you can find a space). Here, you think, you've discovered the community of a century or so ago that characterized the now lonely fountain just above. Among these aging buildings, with winding streets that take you into courtyards and around to gardens, neighbors sit at a picnic table in the parking lot with dogs underfoot or gather during the day on Il Chicco's terrace, with its four or five plastic tables, watching the cars jockey for a space. From here the campanile seems a toy, its striped turrets making you think of the sandcastles you once built at the seashore. It peeks above the trees, a small, insignificant thing: *trascurabile*, the Italians would say, easily missed, and the small golden cap of the cathedral sits casually alongside it, even more insignificant. This is not the Duomo that covers all of Tuscany with its shadow, as Alberti wrote of Brunelleschi's great cupola in Florence. From here, where Il Chicco's Neapolitan owner and his wife fly a flag of the Bruco rather than that of nearby Oca, it is all child's play.

The Campo exists outside and beyond the *contrade*, with its communal palace and its comforting bricked basin and its Fonte Gaia, or Gay Fountain. Even today the fountain is where women tend to sit, in a sun that fades too quickly, to complain about how confusing all the television channels are these days and to recommend a medicine that years

Fig. 30 ◆ Men in Costarella dei Barbieri (2010), Siena. Photograph: Alex Klein.

ago cured a sick child, while their grandsons play with the water that pours out of the tap, an endless source of fascination. The old men may find benches at the widest entrance to the Campo, the Costarella dei Barbieri where the horses line up for the Palio, guarding who goes in, who goes out. But the women sit in the Campo's midst, its heart, where water spews from a lion's mouth and toddlers stagger uncertainly up to the pigeons and make them scatter, all together.

SAINTS

5   The Pinacoteca, devoted almost exclusively to Sienese art, is in a spacious old palace with a pseudomedieval facade and wonderful views to the east from the second floor. Outside, as in front of the Spedale, there are benches for the weary, and–unlike the Spedale—a bar immediately across the way with excellent coffee. The Pinacoteca is a comfortable and unassuming space. There are lockers on the entry level for your things, and for an extra euro you can take photos. There had been talk about moving the collection to the Spedale; traffic might increase, even though the gallery is only around the corner from Via di Città and the Quattro Cantoni, where a video of the latest Palio is always playing in a store window. In the wake of the crisis, such talk has disappeared, and in the meantime the paintings seem to survive despite the lack of temperature controls and the occasional damaging shaft of sunlight from an unshaded window. You can make out masterpieces on walls that seem overcrowded: in the first few rooms, packed with renderings of the Madonna and child, there are standout works by Lorenzetti, Guido of Siena, and Duccio.

But by the time you get to the third room, the sources

become more varied. Until recently, the painting with pride of place was an altarpiece by Simone Martini. Commissioned by the friars of the church of Sant'Agostino just down the street from the Pinacoteca, it was dedicated to Agostino Novello, "the new Augustine," as contemporary a holy man as it was possible to paint; he died in 1309, and Simone might well have known him. Agostino was a Sicilian from a well-off family who studied in Bologna, eventually making his way to Siena and the Augustinian convent of San Leonardo al Lago on a hill to the city's northwest. As a learned and pious man, he was sought out both by his order—he became general of the Augustinians—and by a pope, to whom he became, apparently with reluctance, chief confessor. He came to Siena in search of a holy place and found it, and there he lived out his days. He was once called "Matteo of Termini," and the town of Termini in Sicily reclaimed his body after he was beatified in the 1700s, but Siena keeps Simone's altarpiece.

Learned or not, Agostino's most impressive powers seem to have come after his death, and these are the ones Simone decided to paint. The center of the altarpiece is dominated by a tall, gaunt man in black, concentrating fiercely as an angel whispers in his ear. The artist jumped the gun in giving Agostino a halo, and around him he has arranged four scenes, three of them distinctly urban. In one Agostino descends from behind towers to rescue a boy whose head has been mangled by a black dog that may be a wolf. In another a child falls from a balcony, and Agostino swoops down from a cloud to catch the wood that's broken off the poorly built wall. The mother screams from above, even as we also see her doppelgänger below, standing by two neighbors who gaze up at the offending structure. In a third scene a nurse has been rocking a baby a little too vigorously; the child flies out of the cradle and breaks her skull—made whole by Agostino's intervention. The odd thing about these little scenes is that we never actually see the act of salvation. We are meant to infer it, as the falling child in a smock with bright red-and-gray stripes heading to certain death is almost comically doubled by a child standing upright in the same dress, his relieved mother at his side. The mere presence of the man in black on his magic carpet cloud suggests we needn't waste time moaning in despair: the dog will die, the child will come back to life.

Fig. 31. ◆ Simone Martini, *The Blessed Agostino Novello: Miracle of the Baby Falling from the Balcony* (after 1309). Panel. Pinacoteca Nazionale, Siena. Photograph: Scala/Art Resource, New York.

These are intensely urban scenes, unfolding in narrow streets of Siena not unlike Via di San Pietro itself, where a little farther down from the Pinacoteca our former fruit seller has taken over her father's shop. Beyond that is Sant'Agostino, where the altarpiece hung above Agostino's wooden sarcophagus, and the Orto Botanico and Porta dei Tufi. In death Agostino is confined to his adopted hometown, flying in to save children from tragedy. He is thus not unlike other Sienese holy men from the late Middle Ages. Andrea Gallerani founded the Misericordia and lived the last part of his life within its walls; Joachim Piccolomini performed his miracles in a monastery outside the city, where his occasional seizures—seen as messages from God—prepared him to be invoked by victims of epilepsy (down the hall from Simone's altarpiece, a sculpture from a monks' choir loft shows an entire table with its plates and glasses upset by Piccolomini's seizure); Pier Pettinaio, a humble comb seller mentioned by Dante in the *Purgatorio*, selflessly prayed for souls, like the envious Sapia, who didn't quite make it to heaven; Giovanni Colombini gave away everything he had despite his wife's protests and begged for alms in the Campo so he could found a new order, the Gesuati. Their actions are confined to the city, their interactions confined to other Sienese—some of them from magnate families, for whom holiness became the path to becoming part of a world from which they were excluded. Simone Martini depicts that world in his vivid portrayal of Siena's narrow streets. The upper-level porches project out over the passageways, blocking the light as the wolf slinks into the city to prey on a small child and Agostino emerges—like Superman, as Timothy Hyman cleverly puts it—between two buildings to right all wrongs.

Like Agostino, the painter Simone Martini had a long and prodigious career. Unlike Agostino, he died far from Siena, in Avignon, where popes ruled and Petrarch wrote poems to Laura. Several years after his death, a woman was born who refused to settle for the local scope of Agostino's miracles. Catherine Benincasa's ambitious agenda took her to Avignon in the course of her brief life, before and after she traveled to other Tuscan towns—Lucca, Pisa, Florence, the holdings of Siena's combative Salimbeni family in the Val d'Orcia—and finally to Rome. She represents a new kind of saint for the city: an itinerant one, even as Tommaso Caffarini, her earliest hagiographer, defended her from attack by claiming she was not a *girovaga*, a wanderer. But in fact for her entire life she was bent on leaving Siena. So we can imagine her as a six-year-old pining to go out while she stood at the now long-gone Porta di Sant'Ansano (in the mid-1300s it was carved into a wall near what is now the Selva's oratory of San Sebastiano so the inhabitants of Via Vallepiatta could have easy access to Fontebranda). Or as little more than a teenager, traveling to Montepulciano to visit Tuscany's then best-known female saint, dead for several decades: Saint Agnes, who miraculously kicks Catherine in the face, determining her fate forever. Or going off to make peace between two warring factions of the Salimbeni family in the Val d'Orcia, or heading like Simone to Avignon to urge the pope to come back to Rome, or traveling to Florence to persuade the Florentines to give in to the pope when he finally did return to Rome. Like the parents of the young Tobiolo, Catherine's mother is in anguish about her daughter's travels and her refusal to stay home in Siena. Even though Catherine gave Christ a mantle outside the church of San Domenico and ministered to the sick in the Spedale, she would not use up her life in such small works of charity. She demanded a larger stage, and once she occupied it, she never left.

Prowling her neighborhood, now marked with signs calling attention to this *itinerario cateriniano*, one might wonder why she wanted to go at all. There was the bustle of the dyers and butchers and washerwomen at Fontebranda, now calm; the comfortable shop of her dyer father, now the oratory of the Oca, where a wooden statue of Catherine is wreathed in the bright blue-and-yellow colors of an Oca scarf; the house where she lived until her brothers were forced to relinquish it during the battles of the Riformatori in 1371, now the sanctuary where visitors flock to see the tiny cell where she tried to escape the turmoil of adolescence; the Costone di Sant'Antonio that falls sharply from our street of Vallepiatta into the basin of Fontebranda and affords the best view of the sunset in Siena. It was here that Catherine saw something else: a Christ rising above the church of San Domenico on the hill opposite, commanding her to demand more from life than this sight of the declining sun. I have a nineteenth-century engraving of the scene, bought from the same bookseller in Siena who sold me Faluschi's guidebook, and it shows her in the head scarf of a peasant, eyeing celestial beings while a small boy next to her plays with his dog.

But it was not just Christ who influenced her to leave her room. The Dominicans themselves, whose hulking church overshadowed the neighborhood where Catherine grew up among the dyers, were always leaving Siena. It's no accident that their church is on the city's westernmost ridge, close to a gate, paralleling the Franciscans' church on the eastern side of town in its proximity to easy getaways as well as to the urban poor. Saint Dominic was from Spain, and he made his way to Italy—stopping in 1216 in Siena, where he is said to have so impressed a local member of the powerful noble family of the Malavolti that he ceded part of his land on the ridge called Camporeggio to this new, restless order of preaching friars to build the first Dominican church in Tuscany. Once in Siena, the friars did not stay in one place: abjuring home and its comforts, they left through the gate of Fontebranda to head to Asciano or San Quirico—villages where Catherine's cousin Tommaso della Fonte preached for Lent and sent letters back to a young Catherine still landlocked in Siena.

Yet, at least in a manner of speaking, Catherine is back in the church that looms behind her home. And one wonders if the Sienese noticed she'd ever left. San Domenico is quiet and cool in the afternoons. It's open all day, unlike most churches in Siena, and at its entrance a sign proudly attests to the 1980 visit of Pope John Paul II, who came here as a *pellegrino* on the six hundredth anniversary of Catherine's death, shortly after his ascension to the papacy. Victim of fire, of lightning strikes, of earthquake, of military installations and siege—the Spaniards occupied the church for four years in the 1540s and 1550s while building the *fortezza* that the Sienese would destroy in two nights—San Domenico is a somber shell of its former self. On its benches you can sit for as long as you like, especially around the front altar, where you can sneak a photo of Guido da Siena's thirteenth-century Madonna with her long, stylized Byzantine hands. Also in the transept is a fragment of a fresco by Simone Martini, Jesus and Mary before a ragged John and a knight who is off to a crusade, or so it seems. The Mary is so bewitchingly beautiful that she takes the young crusader's breath away, and he is afraid to look up at the luminous presence before him, both human and divine.

But San Domenico's main attraction is in a side chapel. For a town

Fig. 32 ◆ San Domenico and surrounding neighborhood. Photograph: Andrea Fontana.

that has traditionally put little faith in relics, this is a place where a relic, if it can be called that, is famously preserved: the upright, shriveled head of its best-known citizen, who since being canonized in the fifteenth century, has been known simply by her first name. Raymond of Capua, Catherine's often beleaguered confessor, had the head solemnly transported to Siena in 1383, three years after her death. The rest of her body is interred in Rome under the main altar of Santa Maria sopra Minerva, the Dominican heart of the Holy City almost wholly designed by Florentines: Michelangelo, Fra Lippo Lippi, and Donatello, whose marble relief of Catherine's celestial incoronation once graced her tomb.

Thus much of Catherine stays outside Siena. But here in her native town she remains extraordinarily alive, the authenticity of her head attested by prominent signs in Italian and English. Her thumb is there too, in an easily overlooked glass case to the chapel's right, accompanied by the small chain she once grasped to inflict pain on her virgin body, and the stone she carried with her to serve as the site for movable masses wherever she went, a special privilege granted by the pope. By portraying her "local" miracles—saving the soul of a young man from Perugia condemned to death for treachery in Siena's "Campo della Giustizia" behind the Palazzo Pubblico; liberating a girl from a demon; giving her cloak to Christ, who she thought was a beggar—the Renaissance men who painted this chapel, Francesco Vanni among them, turned her into an Agostino Novello, confining her miracles to her own town. The stairs in the back of the church that take you up to a raised platform further confirm this Sienese desire to bring back the woman whose willfulness took her elsewhere. Here in this *cappella delle volte*—the chapel of the vaults—Catherine and the other Dominican women who kept her company attended Mass, standing behind a wall that prevented them from seeing—if not hearing—the service. A nineteenth-century sign informs us, in Latin, of the many miraculous things that happened to Catherine here. This is where she saw Christ; this is where he promised to be her husband; this is where a communion host once miraculously flew from a priest's hands after he'd forgotten—or refused—to give it to Catherine, the only food she supposedly ate each day. A painting by a man who may have been Francesco Vanni's ancestor, Andrea, hangs here too. It is the earliest known depiction of Catherine, in the act of blessing the lips of a girl who kneels before her, dressed in a colorful orange outfit and wearing the smart cap of a well-to-do young lady. Like a mitered bishop who extends his ring for the faithful to kiss, Catherine stands armed with a lily, her hand lightly grazing the woman's lips in this chapel where the real Catherine once stood straining to hear the Mass. The Cappella has been much restored; once it was accessible only by a narrow ramp to the left, but now the dividing wall is gone and wide stairs bring you up to see Andrea Vanni's depiction of the saint. Last time I was there the entire back wall of the church was covered with scaffolding, and you couldn't go up the steps at all.

What Catherine would not have seen were the flags draped around the church in honor of Siena's seventeen neighborhoods, lighting up this dark space (the local Drago and Oca flags are closest to the altar), or the tourists taking pictures of her head even though signs and the one guard severely discourage it, or the several paintings that depict various Dominicans saving cities. Ambrogio Sansedoni, who is buried here, intervened with a pope to ensure that the Sienese weren't cut off from their lucrative business as papal bankers, as we know from the bird's-eye view of Siena dedicated to Sansedoni by Francesco Vanni. Vanni has a painting in San Domenico too, featuring a little-known Polish saint, Hyacinth, who had just been canonized in 1594. Here too there is a cityscape, though of Kiev, not Siena, here besieged by the Huns as Hyacinth flees with a statue of Mary that glows an eerie white in the darkness. Was the mapmaker Vanni thinking of Siena? Of fires in the city, of the siege by Cosimo and the Spanish in the decade before he was born? Hyacinth's fellow friars, less resolute, lie prostrate in fear. In the shaft of January sun that for fifteen minutes rests deliciously on the painting, two ducks swimming happily in the stream below Hyacinth are brought to light, while behind them soldiers lay waste to the city and apocalyptic fire lights up Hyacinth's escape route. Ducks swim around the perimeter of the marble pavement across the nave too, in the chapel made holy by Catherine's head, an odd celebration of nature and movement in this place otherwise dedicated to Catherine's works. Water laps about them in the marvelous fantasy by the anonymous artist. The scene they rim is of Orpheus or some other mysterious and ancient pagan figure who gazes in a mirror while the fantastic creatures—eagle, tiger, lamb, lion, unicorn—gather about him and below Catherine. Her sightless gaze above them all is fixed directly ahead: facing east across Siena toward Jerusalem, where she had once hoped to lead a crusade.

A winding path alongside San Domenico and past some restaurants that keep their outdoor gardens warmed in the winter with space heaters and ovens takes you through a tunnel (above a little room, probably added on in the early twentieth century, that looks like and no doubt is a *gabinetto*—a toilet) and to the sloping street where Catherine's now-oversized house sits, complete with a portico from the Fascist era when she was made patron saint of Italy.

This now open, mostly useless space that welcomed Pope Pius XII for several minutes in 1939 was once the lively center of the church dedicated to Saint Anthony, patron saint of the Misericordia as well as of the animals who drank the waters of nearby Fontebranda. Unlike the hulking San Domenico, this was the neighborhood's parish church where the woolworkers and dyers, Catherine's father among them, would have worshiped. So a site rich with memories was destroyed to create a terrace with no function other than to announce that we are about to be ushered into a prominent place and to provide a toilet for tourists (at a charge of fifty cents). There are other memories left, though. The bedroom below contains a little cell, perpetually grated, full of flowers, medals, and photos the faithful have left in thanks, though one must ignore the lavishly decorated Rossetti-inspired frescoes of a young girl who floats up stairs and cuts off her hair so she can't be married. The large upstairs room is called the kitchen, featuring a hearth and a fifteenth-century tile floor, surrounded with late sixteenth-century paintings of public scenes of Catherine's life: meeting with popes, asking God to forgive two men condemned to death, accompanying Gregory XI from Avignon to Rome (a fantasy; she may have persuaded him to abandon the French Riviera for Italy, but she shrank from such public entourages).

But the most authentic aspect of the complex, small despite its prepossessing foyer, is in the dark chapel across from the kitchen, once the site of the Benincasa's orchard. It is a primitive crucifix from the early thirteenth century showing an adolescent Jesus, fragile as the wood he's painted on. He sports a light reddish beard and blinks in what seems to be mild surprise at finding himself here, of all places, nailed to a cross.

Brought to Siena in 1565—according to one account, a clever Sienese archbishop stole it—this is the crucifix Catherine was praying before in a chapel near the Arno in Pisa when this youth called out and invited her to share in his stigmata. Arms patiently extended to receive the nails that summon a trickle of blood the same color as his beard, this Pisan Christ behaved like other talking images found in Siena. But unlike Simone Martini's *Maestà*, who addresses the *consiglieri* in Dantesque rhyme inscribed on the painting's steps, this crucified Christ actually spoke, a conversation that led to Catherine's wearing on her body the same wounds that an unknown artist from Pisa painted on a piece of pine. Of all the scenes from her life, this is the one represented most frequently, even though Catherine reputedly told Christ not to transmit the signs of his suffering in any visible way: she was unworthy.

Perhaps the early sixteenth-century painter Domenico Beccafumi has the most moving version of this unexpected conversation and its staggering outcome. Downstairs from the Simone altarpiece in the Pinacoteca, the painting has pride of place in an appropriately darkened room. We see Catherine in profile as she extends her hand into the arch of light that rises behind her, while Beccafumi has curiously left the crucifix in the shade. Her gesture draws our attention to the almost Flemish landscape behind her: behind the mist rising over the Arno, a wooden bridge, embankments, bushes, a house, and a meandering dirt road. The river curves lazily, as it will do in Pisa, but then it vanishes into the horizon beneath the arch where Catherine is dramatically framed. This is a crowded scene, but no one else notices what is going on—and indeed, distracted by the outdoors beyond her, we may not notice either: a nun sleeps, Saint Jerome reads, Saint Benedict gestures idly toward her but does not turn his head. She's all in white, her gray mantle cast off by her side. This is a Catherine who is going places—out beyond the small, dark chapel to a world of light, even as her hand outstretched to Jesus seems to stop time, if only for a second. Yet it all happens as naturally as anything she might have imagined. There is no drama here, only calm, the soft, suffusing light of a northern dawn.

This painting captures something essential about Catherine. As an ascetic, she can hardly have been attracted by the elegant rug at the feet of Coppo's Mary in his painting in Santa Maria dei Servi. Still, her father

Fig. 33 ◆ Domenico Beccafumi, *Saint Catherine of Siena Receiving the Stigmata* (1513–15). Oil. Pinacoteca Nazionale, Siena. Photograph: Scala/Ministero per i Beni e le Attività Culturali/Art Resource, New York.

was a dyer, coloring the cloth that came in from the foreign fairs. Like Saint Francis, she was familiar with the ambiance of the well-run, well-off *comune* with its bustling merchants and bankers and feisty, entrepreneurial artisans. Her brothers were fined so heavily after the uprising of the woolworkers against the wool masters in 1371 that they went bankrupt and lost their house. She counted among her acquaintances the banking families of the Tolomei and Salimbeni. But simplicity drove her, the forcefulness of her vision of changing the Christian world as it was then known. The factionalism within Siena—which led to her brothers' troubles—led her to think that all of Europe was suffering from the same dysfunction, and indeed it was; Siena was a tiny and not inaccurate model of the world, particularly in those terrible years after the Black Death, when the building of the Duomo Nuovo came to a halt and the relatively stable government of the Nove that had commissioned Simone's *Maestà* and Lorenzetti's *Buon Governo* was in its own death throes. Emperor Charles IV marched into Siena in March 1355, rallying behind him the aristocrats and *popolo minuto*, or lower-class artisans, who had been excluded from the oligarchy of *mercanti, banchieri, la meça gente*: merchants, businessmen, the middle class. Chaos and a series of temporary governments followed. Catherine reasoned that if a single cause could unite the Sienese in particular and Christians in general, such infighting could be directed outward, one reason she championed a new crusade against what seemed to be a common enemy: Islam. This is why the pope had to come back to the Christian center of Rome from that peripheral town Avignon, and perhaps Catherine's only successful venture on the international scale was to influence Gregory XI to leave lovely Provence for the swamps of the Eternal City. But none of her other missions—a new crusade, making peace among the warring factions of Italy, rejecting the "antipope" elected by French cardinals stung by the return of the papacy to Rome—succeeded, and she died, despondent, at age thirty-three.

Still, one thing is clear. Had she not been tempted beyond the city she would have made a fine local saint, but we would have missed her letters. It is no accident that she is the first great epistolarist in the Italian language, writing just as Petrarch, true *Homo viator*, or traveling man, closes his brilliant career as a composer of Latin letters. Her often poetic language sings of movement—possibly because she is said to have walked around the room at a frenzied pace, firing off three epistles consecutively to a team of scribes (at least until, as she claims, she learned how to write). Almost four hundred letters survive (no doubt many more have been lost), emblematic of her constant movement out of her natal city. Catherine's letters constantly exhort to the chase, to persevering in one's path, to moving forward and never looking back. The worst sin is to be lazy. Her poor confessor Raymond suffers from her sharp tongue when he's slow persuading the pope to leave Avignon, and a hermit from Lecceto, not far from Agostino's convent at San Leonardo al Lago, is fiercely berated for not coming to Rome to join his colleagues in a time of crisis, choosing to stay in the calm pine forest a stone's throw from Siena. For Catherine the choice would have been simple: "When it's time to leave the woods and go into public places because God's honor demands it, his true servants go, just like Saint Anthony." References to Siena and its changing political climate pepper some of the epistles to her closest associates; to Andrea Vanni, who painted her portrait in San Domenico and who for a time was Siena's *capitano del popolo*, she says "Keep an eye on the poor"—alluding to Jesus in the manger and his simple needs. Her concern for her city, her family, her fellow citizens never wavered. But the road that led pilgrims to Lucca, where she spent several months, and to Rome, where she died, took her away forever.

◆

Catherine set the standard for Siena's holy men and women to come: for two in particular, both of whom had deep connections to the other side of town and to San Francesco, the other massive basilica built in honor of medieval mendicants. One was Pius II, the man who like Catherine was a great writer of letters. Patriotic Sienese that he was, he ensured that Catherine was finally canonized after she'd been passed over for eighty years. One of the paintings in the Libreria Piccolomini in the Duomo shows Pius presiding over Catherine's canonization, her head miraculously reunited with her body as she lies intact before him and his cardinals in Rome. In the summer he would climb the hill east of San Francesco to the little hermitage of the "Osservanza," the site where the other religious figure influenced by Catherine, and certainly a more saintly one, made his home while the future Pius II, Aeneas Sylvius Piccolomini, was seducing women in Basel. This was Bernardino of Siena, who sup-posedly influenced the young Aeneas while he was a student in Siena in 1425 to give up everything for the simple life of the Franciscan friars, although his friends dissuaded him. Aeneas Piccolomini didn't have the stuff of the "poor preachers," the holy rusticity of Francis. Although he could, one might add in hindsight, become a pope.

Our own walk up to the Osservanza—no longer a hermitage but a late fifteenth-century church probably designed by Francesco di Giorgio Martini—started on the main road, which seemed too dangerous for walking as it curved at a dizzying pace; by sheer chance we found a shortcut through a field and then up a hill, winding, but beautiful and safe. There at the top a wider path cut through orchards and arrived alongside the Osservanza, now emptied of most of its Franciscans to provide space for a school, like so many Italian churches. Parents stand outside in the parking lot talking on cell phones as they wait for their children to emerge at 3:00. We ring the bell and are rewarded when a Filipino caretaker swings open the big door to the church and turns on the lights. The church was bombed heavily in World War II and has been rebuilt, but the paintings are still recessed deep into the side walls where it is difficult to see them. A side room contains much of Bernardino's library: a treatise on usury, a breviary, Eugene's bull confirming Bernardino's orthodoxy, and sermons—others' as well as his own, written by hand on *carta pechorina* or goatskin. And there's also a death mask that suggests a thin face. But this is all you'll find here of the figure who for a time was the most popular man in Siena, if not in Tuscany or Italy, and its most formidable preacher. Unlike Catherine's, his body was left intact in L'Aquila, where he died in 1444. He was found lying peacefully on the ground in his travel cloak, exhausted after two decades of roaming Italy with the monogram that graces many a Sienese building, the mysterious IHS of Jesus's name. In his bag were a hat, two pairs of stockings, two pairs of eyeglasses, an hourglass, and a few books. His tomb was shattered by the earthquake that destroyed half of L'Aquila in 2009.

Bernardino Albizzeschi was born in the little town of Massa Marittima in the Maremma in 1380, the year of Catherine's death. Orphaned at three, he was raised by aunts, and by the time he was a teenager he was in Siena, volunteering in the Spedale, where at twenty he was made rector during an epidemic of bubonic plague. He too became gravely ill, battling death for four months in the hospital, patient where he had been nurse. Healed, he retired to an aunt's home near Porta dei Tufi, where he made a little oratory out of a single room and put a crucifix there, perhaps hoping it would speak to him as the painted crucifix in Pisa had spoken to Catherine. His first real vision, though, happened when he was asleep. He dreamed he was just outside another gate, Porta Ovile on the town's eastern side, near where sheep grazed during the seasonal crossings, when he saw a sumptuous palace devoured by flames. Only one room remained untouched, where a Franciscan friar called to him from a window. Bernardino determined that God meant for him to join the Franciscan order, so he signed up, leaving a Siena that he called *lenis, laetus, hilaris et jucundus*—"lovely, luxurious, fun-loving, laughing"—to go into his own version of a Franciscan countryside, first on the slopes of Mount Amiata, then to the gentler hill called Capriola, site of the future Osservanza, given to Bernardino by the new rector of the Spedale. His goal was to recreate the primitive, simple church and to make Christ a thing of joy. This is why he chose as his symbol a sun with dazzling rays: a sun granted pride of place on the facade of the Palazzo Pubblico, painted in 1425 when Bernardino was still alive and still there today, with the letters IHS and a cross in its center.

Yet the death mask at the Osservanza does not have the features of a particularly joyful man. Vecchietta, the painter of the Spedale and Bernardino's contemporary, carved a life-size wooden statue of the preacher now in Florence's Bargello, gaunt and gray, tassel hanging down the front of his robe. He holds out to us his monogram, the new logo he designed for a battered Siena in the hope of sparking unity among these people who were not quite his own. If Catherine had championed a crusade as a means of healing divisiveness, he championed Christ. His face is wizened, cheeks pinched, toothless, as he was indeed in life; heads of cherubs are immobilized beneath his sandaled feet, not unlike the real feet that took him on the road, relentlessly visiting houses of the Sienese citizens and sermonizing in Pisa, Florence, and Rome. Yet his cheeks are ruddy despite his asceticism, and you feel this is how Vecchietta saw him in life, sap bursting within a worn-out tree. The artist left his own proud statement of authorship on the base: SENENSIS: a work of Siena.

Catherine is constantly depicted in different settings, especially in her "house": writing, preaching, healing, exchanging hearts with Christ, choosing the habit of the Dominican order, graciously welcoming the pope to Rome. But Bernardino is almost always frozen in the same pose, sometimes holding awkwardly before him the variously sized, variously shaped letters IHS, Jesus, as on a painted pillar in the Sala del Mappamondo, also by Vecchietta. Only in two small panels in the Museo dell'Opera del Duomo do we see him actually doing what he supposedly did best: preaching, vigorously. He speaks from a pulpit set up outside the Campo in one, in front of San Francesco in the other, women decorously separated from the men. He lashed out against faction, against sodomists, against women who painted their faces, often using clever little fables that must have been riveting, or at least memorable, since many listeners recorded the best parts. In particular he attacked the rich. The Monte dei Paschi, created in 1472 as the Monte di Pietà, was founded partly because of his attacks on usurious practices of Sienese Christians and Jews alike. Thus from a sermon against usury, given not in Siena—although it could have been—but in Florence in 1424:

> They say that in the Arno there was once a little boat with five men inside, one to guide the ship, the others who worked with their feet or their hands. And just imagine what happens when heavy waves and heavy winds arise: the boat pitches and rolls over. The one who was guiding it sees immediately what's happening, and arriving in the prow completely unhurt, just a little wet, he dries himself off and he's fine. Another one, thrown into the water, starts to swim, all worn out, but he tears off a piece of wood and with great energy and anxiety is saved. A third man goes up and down in the water, the waves tossing him here and there, and finally he grabs the branch of an overhanging tree and escapes. The fourth goes down into the water and gets all beat up in the surf, but at the end, exhausted, he survives. And the fifth gets thrown into the water, drowns, and dies. What's the moral of this story? If you realize you're in the wrong, you can get out of it!

Siena could not keep him. Felice Alessio writes that "the fifteenth century is full of San Bernardino," and the many images of him on the second floor of the Pinacoteca make you think that the twenty-first century is full of him too. Yet all told he spent little time here after he climbed down the hill from the Osservanza. His travels took him to Alessandria, Piedmont, Milan, Perugia, Lucca, Rome. Siena was a constant touchstone but rarely a place of rest, save for his great Lenten sermons of 1427-28. By 1430, from the pulpit and in public enemies were accusing him of heresy, censuring his new devotion to the name of Jesus. His preaching was marked by the zeal of future reformers such as Luther who urged abandoning the rituals and hierarchy of the Catholic Church for a more direct and immediate experience of Christ. But Pope Martin V came to Bernardino's rescue, and the next pope, Eugene IV, sent a bull from Rome that defended Bernardino and praised his "honest discourse and his praiseworthy religious life." For his "integrity, his worthy sermons on God's word, and for the beneficial fruits of his works," he was absolved, in aeternum, of the "odious imputations" by those who were no doubt jealous of his fame and intent on bringing scandal. After his death the town said to be most affected was Siena; there were processions through the city and into the Campo, days of mourning, the (unheeded) demand that his body be returned to where it belonged. All that came back were the several objects we saw at the Osservanza—eyeglasses, an hourglass, and stockings—along with the donkey who used to transport Bernardino and his books to his next appointment. But he became a saint quickly enough, just six years later, celebrated by fireworks, bells, and trumpets. A chronicler of the mid-fifteenth century wryly remarks that the festivities a decade later for Saint Catherine, Siena's truly homegrown saint, were no greater.

Vecchietta puts the two in an interesting relation to one another in his *arliqueria* or reliquary, the large wooden case he made to hold the Spedale's sacred relics shortly after he painted his little fragment of Tobias. It was moved from the sacristy in the sixteenth century and is now in the Pinacoteca. It's a well-made cabinet with sturdy hinges and a lock, which it needed: it once contained a nail and fragments of the wood of the cross, a piece of the sponge dipped in vinegar to quench Christ's thirst, a strand of hair from his beard—the relics bought at a huge price by the Spedale after the Black Death. When the cabinet's doors are closed, as they are in the Pinacoteca, they reveal what Van Os calls "a kind of anthology" of recent local holy people, almost none of them officially recognized as saints at the time. Vecchietta went to work on it in the 1440s, before either Catherine or Bernardino was canonized. There they are, among other Sienese, some of them mythical, like Sorore, the founder of the Spedale, or Sant'Ansano. Agostino Novello, Pier Pettinaio, and Ambrogio Sansedoni are there too. Each inhabits a little panel, as though Vecchietta was thinking of the covers he had painted for the *Biccherna*. Indeed, this too is a cover, a painted gateway that conceals treasures. Vecchietta places Catherine—the only woman—in the bottom row as she kneels in prayer before her Pisan crucifix, while above her, to the right, Bernardino holds his mystical symbol of Jesus's name and gazes downward. He appears to be looking at Catherine, and Catherine, though in fact gazing at the crucifix, could be looking at him. Besides the crucifix and the sacred name of Christ, only one other form interposes itself into this silent dialogue: the Sienese *balzana*, its white-and-black crest exactly halfway between the two in the frame that divides them, reminding us that these far-flung saints-to-be are anchored here in the city, or more precisely in the Spedale, where they prayed, and preached, and tended to the needs of those who lacked a way to find God on their own.

If Siena's new saints were itinerant ones, Siena's artists tried to immobilize them, as Vecchietta does here in this touchingly artisanal work, a wooden cabinet. Beccafumi holds Catherine back as well, granting her a moment of suspension as she ponders Christ's image in the early morning light. And even though the life of Pius II is all about movement in the paintings by Pintoricchio in the Duomo—he is depicted in Basel, in Rome, in Ancona where he died, having also failed to launch a new crusade—the weighty body of the dying pope, like the mummified Catherine he canonized, clings to this space, *in urbem*, where he is buried. So does Siena reclaim these wild people. With the city's mercantile influence in decline, it trusted to spiritual capital instead, reclaiming for itself the saints and popes who left to go elsewhere.

◆

Through the first half of the fifteenth century San Francesco remained the only major church in Siena still outside the walls. The fourteenth-century circuit closed in just a few dozen meters from the imposing facade of Francis's church, arriving at the "arch of the minor friars," where Via dei Rossi ends. As Ilaria Bichi Ruspoli suggests, this was the "Achilles' heel of the city": not only one of the city's poorest areas—hence the presence of the ministering Franciscans, dedicated since Francis to tending the urban poor—but its sketchiest. Given the absence of controls normally exercised inside gates, here people could congregate as they wished, eluding control and conducting shady affairs. It's in this region of the city, the easternmost part that juts out on a ridge where now an escalator takes you down, that prostitutes once lingered—as is still evident from (ironic) street names like Via delle Vergini, now in the *contrada* of the Giraffe. This neighborhood was home to the lowliest of the city's artisans, its silk workers, and the *contrada* of the Bruco or Caterpillar may be so named because this is where Siena's never very robust textile trade was concentrated. (The Bruco's symbol may also relate to sheep having grazed in the area immediately outside Porta Ovile; *brucare* is the Italian word for grazing.) The Caterpillar is the oldest symbol of a Sienese neighborhood, going back to at least 1371, when those very silk workers revolted against their masters, including Catherine's brothers. In retaliation, the artisans' rickety wooden houses were burned down and their tools confiscated. The neighborhood still clings to its populist roots: the Bruco Museum is regularly open to visitors rather than sealed behind locked doors, and when we were there for a party—a band played in their spacious yard out back—we met an excited young woman from California who had recently been baptized into their *contrada*, "simply because I'd made friends who were Brucaioli!"

Bernardino, who took his vows in San Francesco in 1402, encouraged the city to build walls around his favorite area just below the Osservanza, even though the absence of a gate meant easy access up the hill to the mother house. But it was Pius II, whose parents were buried in the 1450s in the left transept of the church, who forced the issue: and so the walls went up, despite Pius's increasing difficulties with the Comune. Thus was San Francesco, along with the city's southernmost water source, the Fonte di Follonica, finally brought into Siena. At the same time, Porta Ovile—once the place for *la vita maladetta* or sinister nightlife—was built up, complete with a guard who would control customs and protect against fraud. A call went out in 1462 for "foreigners who had skills as bricklayers, brickmakers, welders, and stone-cutters to build the walls of Follonica," guaranteeing them the chance to become citizens once the work was done. The area thus was gentrified so as to honor, if nothing else, the deceased parents of a pope.

Situated so precariously on the edge of the city—seen from the back or from above, it seems it is about to slip off its ridge—San Francesco has become, through chance or purpose, a place of doors. Immediately inside, above the entryway, are the remains of the paintings that were once found, in far better condition, on Porta Romana and the nearby Porta dei Pispini: a Coronation of the Virgin by Sassetta, in which you can make out a celestial sky and four or five angels at the far lower left—the Virgin herself is long gone—and, in even worse condition, a Nativity by Sodoma. We see a splash of red, a flitting angel in one of the rare moments when the perpetually dark basilica is lit up by a fleeting ray of morning sunlight. At right angles to the Sassetta a massive, beautiful marble frame dwarfs a small painting of the newest Franciscan saint, Padre Pio. This, in fact, used to be the main entryway into San Francesco, carved by Francesco di Giorgio Martini, who was also hired to raise the roof of the basilica in 1469 when he was still a young man. Asked to return eleven years later to do more in the church—he was offered a thousand florins, plus the gift of the Fonte Follonica and absolution of *ogni pena*, or all his sins—he declined, so the Fonte was given to the friars of nearby Santo Spirito, while the work in the church went to lesser-known engineers. The church's subsequent fate over the years—emptied out to be used as an arsenal by the Spanish, damaged by the earthquake of 1798, bombed in World War II along with the Osservanza on the hill above—has rendered it a shell of its former self. But even before the war, the facade was deemed too dangerous, Francesco's imposing door too heavy, as though it threatened to pull the church down the hill. It was removed along with the lower facade's white-and-black stripes, seen in the panel where San Bernardino is preaching, and moved inside in the early 1900s. It was replaced by a poor imitation of a Gothic entrance, derided by the Sienese ever since.

On the seventeenth of each month the normally empty basilica becomes home to a small crowd of local retirees for a series of masses in a side chapel—to the right as you walk in during the winter, to the left in the summer—to celebrate the miracle of the sacred *particole*, 223 Communion wafers that were stolen in 1730, the year the princess Violante of Bavaria laid down the boundaries of Siena's *contrade*. The hosts were discovered in the nearby church of Provenzano several days later, untouched by decay. They remain uncorrupted—and uneaten—to this day, despite a second theft in 1971. In honor of the day they were stolen (to wit, the seventeenth), twelve times a year their reliquary is brought out, the chapel lit, and a service said. A woman's cell phone goes off in the middle of the Mass I attend one January 17. She leaves to stand just outside the doors, and you can hear her talking to her husband's doctor—not urgent, he hasn't been eating, a low fever, but still he needs attention. The minute the service is over the priest heads out for a cigarette, the last verse of the hymn barely done. The next circle of the faithful clusters outside, ready for the 11:00 Mass, and a few visitors strain to make out the blood-red background of Lorenzetti's *Crucifixion* in the other transept: angels calmly surround Christ's head in this feverish setting of a sky turned violent, while a cluster of weeping women huddle to the left, the disciples to the right. But the febrile light makes all inspection difficult even on this chilly, brilliant January morning—though it's not too cold for brightly colored laundry to be draped on clotheslines, stiff as leather, flapping in the breeze that comes in from the west: Catherine's side, the other side of town from San Francesco.

Though Bernardino took his vows here, his memory is best preserved in the oratory in the building next to the church, alongside the cloisters, where now the faculty of mathematics of the University of Siena has its offices and students gather in the courtyard between classes to smoke and drink coffee. Rarely visited, the stunning rooms of the chapter house contain some of Beccafumi's most memorable frescoes, all of Mary's life. Here is Christ's tormented hand reaching out to us from his agonizing painting of the Crucifixion, or Mary's lithe, slender body as she accepts Joseph's ring, or the blur of women tending to an older, dying Mary. Viewers are struck by the orange marmalade-shaded robes of the elderly man staring vacantly outward—his back is to Jesus, who is flying down from the heavens to take his mother back with him—"and make her queen," a father who like us is visiting the oratory patiently explains to his daughter. "Queen of what?" asks the little girl, who can be no more than seven. "Of heaven." "But why?" And so, unlike us, he knows nothing of this miracle of the Assumption to come. Bernardino himself presides over Beccafumi's painting of the Annunciation. Between the angel and the annunciate, all human history unfolds, while Bernardino watches, the back of his toothless head to us while he offers his monogram to Jesus and Mary, whose fingers lightly graze his balding scalp.

Just as in his painting of Catherine's stigmata, Beccafumi is intrigued here by the lure of worlds beyond. In the scene of Mary's *sposalizio* or wedding day, she's dressed in white with a simple necklace and yellow embroidery around the collar. Her eager husband reaches out to touch her hand, and behind him stand a toga-clad Roman and soldiers. There are ancient reliefs on the doorframe, with frolicking putti, and we're reminded that this marriage was celebrated in the midst of Rome's golden century, the era of Augustus and Ovid and Virgil, whose Aeneas gave the name to Pius II's secular self.

But there is no more poignant image of productive suspension and tension between worlds than an archway Beccafumi painted in what was once a chapel in the Spedale. As in his later painting in the Oratory of San Bernardino, he brings together two worlds, in this case the aged parents of Mary at the "scene at the golden gate." Joachim is from the world of shepherds, rustic, outside the city; Anne is from the town, with her waiting women, maidservants in elegant clothing, patient and officious. The spouses, no longer young, grasp each other's hands, having decided to end their celibate lives after he has a dream commanding him to leave his pastoral retreat outside the walls. From their union in old age, Mary, salvation of a people, patroness of Siena, will come forth. It is not clear who is coming, who is going. To the left Beccafumi gives us a cave, dogs, sheep, and a peasant somewhat more gnarled than his master. To the right the city woman Anne has her beautiful young servant beside her as though to ensure that the embrace remains chaste between her mistress and the aging shepherd. The bright goldenrod tones of Joachim's tunic match those of Anne's servant, drawing him into the urban space.

If anything is reminiscent of Florentine painting, it is this work. You

Fig. 34 ◆ Domenico Beccafumi, *The Meeting of Joachim and Anne at the Golden Gate* (1512). Fresco. Ospedale di Santa Maria della Scala, Siena. Photograph: Scala/Art Resource, New York.

think of Jacopo da Pontormo's grand and faded cycle in the Certosa just outside Florence, where once vibrant blues and oranges now shimmer suggestively against the yellowed walls, and ghostly figures emerge from the nebulous background. But more than Pontormo's influence, it is really a shared patrimony in the early years of the sixteenth century, when Siena was still hopeful about its independence and, for a moment, less mistrustful of Florence. Leonardo's technique of sfumato pervades these works, and Enzo Carli speaks of Beccafumi's painting in the Spedale as exemplifying "the way that form is undone by light." But perhaps even more than the influence of Florence or Pontormo or Leonardo, it is the

bright colors of the Sienese Middle Ages, now known in their glory because of the wonders preserved in the crypt, that enabled Beccafumi to
restore brightness to Sienese life after the somber experiments of the fifteenth century: gorgeous reds, yellows, and ambers, shockingly vibrant
azure. Beccafumi made the "golden gate" the arch of the chapel itself,
designed with flowers and curious faces from pagan antiquity, studded
with stars in a blue sky, next to the entrance of what was a first aid station and then a *clinica oculista* or eye clinic—the sign, carved into the
stone, is still there. One can barely imagine what this dark little corner
looked like when it still hosted the relics for which Vecchietta painted
his colorful wooden cabinet, when Beccafumi's *Resurrection of Lazarus*—
destroyed by the 1798 earthquake—was still on the opposite wall. What
was it like before Domenico di Bartolo's painting of the Madonna del
Manto was sawed apart and shoved into the new sacristy, before tastes
changed and the growth of the hospital demanded this site be put to more
practical use? Given all the human traffic that has crossed this space in
the five centuries since Beccafumi painted, that the colors remain at all is
almost as miraculous as the host that flew across San Domenico to Catherine's mouth.

Unlike Simone Martini, or Catherine, or Bernardino, Beccafumi spent
most of his life in Siena. Only rarely did he take up commissions outside
the city, returning as soon as he could to his native town. In his *Lives of
the Artists*, Giorgio Vasari reports that when he went to visit Beccafumi
in Pisa, the Sienese painter told him that unless he was in the *aria di Siena*, the air of Siena, he couldn't work, and Vasari admits that the Pisans
were disappointed by what they commissioned from him. But when he
was in Siena's air he was a workhorse, and what he did is spectacular.
Far from being only a painter, Beccafumi designed the last great mosaics
for the Duomo's floors, regrettably covered over for most of the year but
visible as sketches in the Pinacoteca: Moses kneeling on the mountain
to claim the Ten Commandments while the Hebrews worship a golden
calf below; Elisha open-mouthed while the chariot of his master Elijah,
inspirer of the Carmelites, ascends to heaven. These are also works about
the meetings of worlds—in these cases, heaven and earth. The more quotidian paintings of Mary's espousal to Joseph and her elderly parents'
charming reunion affirm another kind of meeting, exemplified by the

prominence of the gate, a coming together of country and city, rustic and elegant urbanite, simple Christian legacy and alluring Roman and classical past.

There is something more personal at work here too. Domenico Beccafumi's parents were peasants, and his last name is not his father's but that of one Lorenzo Beccafumi, the wealthy man on whose estate his father worked. Vasari tells this story too: Beccafumi recognized the boy's talents and sent him to Siena. The artist's successes brought him enough money to purchase a house in town as well as a vineyard a mile from Porta Camollia, where according to Vasari he spent much of his time alone. When he died he asked to be buried in the Duomo, "and he was carried to his grave"—an unmarked one—"by all the artists of Siena." His final works were eight angels for the cathedral in bronze, a medium that literally killed him. He spent twenty-four-hour days by the furnaces tending to the work and took sick. Along with Vecchietta's ciborium from the Spedale, the angels now protect the high altar. Once they also stood before Beccafumi's paintings in the apse of the Madonna's assumption into the realm of God and the glory of the angels, scenes that must have been in the stirring colors that were his favorites: violet, lemon yellow, metallic greens, intense reds, and especially pink. They too were virtually obliterated in the 1798 earthquake, then restored— badly—in the nineteenth century.

◆

A mile outside Porta Camollia, Beccafumi could still linger in Siena's air, having struck that delicate balance between worlds that is a compositional motif in his paintings and for which the gate is a powerful metaphor. He is hardly alone in being fascinated by gates. They are ubiquitous throughout the Pinacoteca and elsewhere in Siena: in paintings of the Annunciation and of the Nativity (a Francesco di Giorgio Martini in the often-closed Sant'Agostino; I have seen it only in art books, an enormous cracked classical gate that looks out to a white-and-black land of plenty, with hills, trees, and a little castle). Gates appear in the meeting of Elizabeth and Mary in the Spedale's Pellegrinaio; in Lorenzetti's *Buon Governo*; and in Duccio's panel of Jesus disguised as a pilgrim on the road to Emmaus. Surely these artists were inspired by Siena's actual gates, each with its own personality, which let you in as well as out. Catherine had some thirty-six of them to linger longingly beside and eventually to pass through, Pius II and Bernardino had fewer. At some point they went out one of Siena's gates for the last time, probably not knowing they were leaving the city forever.

Gates are one way, perhaps the most obvious, to keep track of Siena's complicated geography. Many have long been walled over—*tamponate*—like one of the Due Porte at Stalloreggi. Or destroyed, like the original gate of Camollia, once protected by a defensive tower badly damaged during the siege. For fifty years, to its left, a provisional and unassuming entrance marked as "P. Camullia" by Vanni on his map let the Sienese in, before the tower was knocked down and replaced by the ornate gate there today. The once imposing thirteenth-century Porta di Pescaia, near the church of Santa Maria at Fontegiusta, is near a fountain that probably dried up when the Bottino Maestro was built. An image of Mary and child, since removed, was kept in a little closet on the gate. To find these ghostly gates is the walk of a pleasant afternoon or morning, depending on the heat. Also worth tracking down are "arches," once entrances into the city, now passageways from one street or neighborhood into another. Thus Porta San Giuseppe, at the top of the precipitous Via Giovanni Duprè, was the gate you once would take to get to Sant'Agostino, outside the city until the last ring of walls—excepting the section behind San Francesco—went up in 1326. (See figure 26 in chapter 4.)

As for the existing seven gates that now connect Siena to the world beyond, letting in people and the occasional car, start with the uninspiring seventeenth-century replacement for the once grand Porta Camollia on the north side, with the inscription—no doubt thought up by a Florentine—designed to welcome Ferdinando I de' Medici to the city in the early seventeenth century, "Cor Magis Tibi Sena Pandit": Siena's heart expands to let you in. You curve around to Porta Ovile and then to the imposing Porta dei Pispini on the southeastern side, flanked by the tower of Baldassarre Peruzzi, in remarkably good condition, even if you can only lament that this last bastion of civic defense constructed in the late 1520s failed to keep out either the Spanish or the Florentines. (*Pispino* is Sienese for the Italian *zampillo*, a jet or spray of water; a fountain was discovered at this gate in the 1530s, when it was still called Porta San Viene, the place where Sant'Ansano's body reentered the city in 1259 after a skirmish with the Aretines, who had kept it for a millennium after Ansano's martyrdom. Out the same gate went the Sienese a year later for their triumphant battle with the Florentines at Monteaperti. Those were good years.) Continuing westward, the last segment of Via Roma that leads to Porta Romana, once called Porta Nuova, is straight (uncharacteristic for a Sienese street), offering the departing traveler a view from high up of countryside and a grand arch that is displaced at the last minute by a swerve to the right and a view of the real arch, and an even grander view of two doors opening into the world beyond Siena. The walls of San Niccolò, the psychiatric hospital just to the right of the gate, suddenly glow brilliant rose in the afternoon sun, but by the time the camera's out, they've become a bleached pink, fading into oblivion like the imposing building itself, abandoned even by the mad. Now, twenty years later, it houses a university too poor to maintain it, so the building's been sold and the university rents it from the buyer.

And then there are the gates of the dead. To the west of Porta Romana and Santa Maria dei Servi was once Porta di Giustizia: the gate of justice. The condemned held in the bowels of the Palazzo Pubblico were led down Via dei Malcontenti and out Porta di Giustizia, a door impossible to open from the outside. There they were hanged or decapitated or quartered, depending on the crime, and their bodies were tossed into the valley below. You can see the stretch of land they would have crossed on their final walk when you stand in the Mercato Vecchio behind the Palazzo Pubblico, center for a thriving food market as late as the 1970s, now deserted except for the third Sunday each month, when antiquarians gather to sell their wares. Cosimo de' Medici had a theater constructed above these old prisons in the Palazzo Pubblico. He converted what had been the "great room of the *consiglieri*," used on those occasions when hundreds of Sienese men had to debate the problems of the republic and the room with Lorenzetti's *Mappamondo* was too small. Restored and reopened in 2009 for the seven hundredth anniversary of Siena's constitution, it is among the oldest theaters in Italy, with five hundred seats and a central glass chandelier shaped like a bell that was once raised by a hand-cranked rope at the start of a performance.

The Spedale built a cemetery on lands it owned outside Porta dei

Tufi, when the area around the hospital became too crowded with the dead. Via Mattioli, a straight shot from the Pinacoteca, travels past the botanical garden and through a part of the city given over to the university and parking lots: enormous decaying convents and monasteries, vast spaces, remnants of lives and habits that can no longer be maintained. But the Spedale's cemetery, along with that of Monte Oliveto, the monastic order in the Crete that built another monastery closer to town, has given way to a different city of the dead, to which my friend from the Misericordia takes me one hot July afternoon. The rising heat shimmers around Mount Amiata, making it seem farther than it is, and the clouds and the heaving dry winds from Africa bring no rain. When Napoleonic reforms swept what was then called the kingdom of Etruria, the monastery was razed. The Misericordia took it over, turning it into not just a public cemetery but a museum, thanks to the powerful sculptures of Tito Sarrocchi. In the late nineteenth century Sarrocchi built mausoleums and tombstones for Siena's aristocrats, the wealthy who could afford his works: the Chigi, the Saracini, the Brandi, the Piccolomini, and the Tolomei. They are here side by side, rivalries set aside at last. Sarrocchi's statues convey an unbelievable verisimilitude—the buttons bursting on a boy's shirt as he bends to put flowers on his father's grave, the delicate embroidery on the sleeve of a dead young girl whose father stands melancholy behind her, his jacket waving ever so slightly in an imagined wind. This is very different from the Etruscan images to the dead that the basement of the Spedale is full of. There, atop urn after urn, the dead all turn to face the living, wives raising their hands to husbands in leave-taking before they enter the door and disappear forever. The wise Etruscan sculptors captured them there on the threshold, offering solace to those who stayed behind, as though their last thoughts had been about them alone.

Here just outside Porta dei Tufi the dead are beyond such thoughts, gone off to a place where they can't be recaptured, despite all the Christian theology of resurrection that surrounds them. But the community tries. There are modest plaques here too, such as one to a Misericordia volunteer who died helping a family out of a burning car. The family survived, but the car rolled on him and he was killed. My friend pays his silent respects, as he says he has done every week since that fateful day in 1976.

♦

Bound up with these definitive departures is the sense of estrangement you feel on coming back after having stayed away too long. Both Catherine and Simone Martini (if not Bernardino, who was inimitable) had their twentieth-century avatars, figures who looked to them and their adventures as they too left their city. One was the writer Federigo Tozzi, whose haunting final novel *Il podere* [The farm] projects what could have been his own return to the countryside outside Siena after his departure for Rome and his father's death in 1915. A son comes back to the family farm for his father's funeral and, realizing he is now the master, tries to run things. But he does so badly, antagonizing his father's mistress and the peasants, and he is ultimately murdered by the most outspoken of his peasants: the book ends with an ax slicing into his brain. There is no Blessed Agostino Novello here to make things right.

Tozzi was fascinated by Catherine, anthologizing some of her letters in 1918. He died in Rome at age thirty-seven, around the corner from the place where she died, in Via del Gesù. As Roberto Barzanti has remarked, this winding part of the city near Santa Maria sopra Minerva makes you think of Siena itself with every step—the narrow streets, the piazza you suddenly come upon, the reentry into the labyrinth. Tozzi spent his last few years in an apartment on the third floor of this building, possibly struck, as Barzanti hypothesized, by a *misticismo disperato*, or desperate mysticism, his febrile religiosity leading him, perhaps, to compile the anthology dedicated to Catherine. "Something in her," Tozzi writes, "helps us break free from all those obstacles that prevent us from reaching what is most profound within ourselves." Was it her breaking free from Siena and going to Rome that provided such a model for his own release? "I come back only very rarely to Tuscany, and always for just a few days. So when I'm with a few friends and without my bicycle, I try to breathe in the fresh air and I don't let myself get caught up in the goings-on of the city."

Tozzi was born in Via dei Rossi, the road that takes you east from Banchi di Sopra to the church of San Francesco. His father ran the little tavern called Il Sasso, which is still there, modernized and enlarged as an expensive, sprawling restaurant with a few tables outside and many more inside. Tozzi's other great, despairing novel, *Con gli occhi chiusi* [With closed eyes], is a thinly veiled autobiography that opens in an inn; the young protagonist is a sensitive sort who grows up there, and the travelers who come and go make fun of him. This place of hospitality, the tavern, turns against the main character as irrevocably as the peasants turned against the antihero of *Il podere*. From these travelers who were always on the road and had the liberty both of movement and of what may have seemed to the fragile boy an ironic detachment from small-town affairs and concerns, Tozzi must have gotten his hankering to work for the Italian train system as a way of leaving home. Catherine too may have instilled in him a sense that Rome was the best place to discover causes greater than provincial Siena and himself: the postwar Continental realist novel, written in the style of Dostoyevsky and Turgenev. Yet the quest to leave took him repeatedly back to his youth and to imagined returns to his city, where his character in *Il podere* finds only death—and in *Con gli occhi chiusi*, disappointment.

More recently there was Mario Luzi, often mentioned as Italy's next Nobel laureate for poetry, who lived as a boy next to the church of Santa Maria in Provenzano into which members of the winning *contrada* of the July Palio parade with their horse. A large plaque proudly proclaims that this handsome white house was the home in adolescence of the poet, who died only recently at almost one hundred. I stand in the hot piazza one late April day with students who, in Luzi's honor, read aloud some of his poems, much influenced by Eugenio Montale and other hermeticists, even as he developed his own style as a modern mystic. Luzi left Siena after high school and wrote a brief few pages on his own attempts to return over the years, titled "Ritorno a Siena." After evoking the solidness of Siena's squat houses and the yellow fields outside its gates, the dependability of its *contadini* and the reserved ways of its citizens, he declares that you cannot go back and live in Siena once you have left it: "This is a city in which it's impossible to live as a stranger." Still, in a long poem published not long before his death, he takes on the voice of the painter Simone Martini, who influenced the young Luzi profoundly, inspiring

him to "learn something about our ancestors through their images . . .
they are the means of entering into the Sienese mind and its ambitions,
which remain at heart an isolated thing, isolated and incomparable." In
this magnificent work called *The Earthly and Heavenly Journey of Simone Martini*, Luzi envisions the dying painter, still in Avignon, deciding
to return to Siena in a caravan, accompanied by his wife and a young
scholar. Siena is the true protagonist of this final epic poem of Luzi's, the
city that shimmers in the distance and offers Simone his only chance to
understand his origins as an artist. Even though he spent much of his life
teaching French at the University of Florence, Luzi wrote these lines in
the midst of this celestial journey, used as the epigraph for the introduction to this book:

> Ah, Florence, Florence. Dazed, the wayfarers
> doze off during their stop.
> Better set off again,
> take the road to Siena, right away.

Dazed though he was by Florence, Luzi nonetheless remained there,
where in the 1990s he assisted in a campaign against animal rights activ-
ists, Franco Zeffirelli and Brigitte Bardot among them, who were calling
for an end to the Palio on the grounds that the horses were mistreated.
Stefano Bisi, editor of the *Corriere di Siena*, wrote of the moment:

> They launched a veritable crusade against the Palio, and
> I remember that there was a strong response. The news-
> paper the *Corriere di Siena* responded in turn with a call to
> defend the game. The first person who signed the petition
> was the poet Mario Luzi. I remember that I went to find
> him in Florence, at his house in Bellariva, and he didn't
> hesitate to launch a manifesto to safeguard the festivi-
> ties he had known as a young boy when he attended Li-
> ceo (high school) Aeneas Silvius Piccolomini in the Piazza
> Sant'Agostino. After Luzi signed on, scientists, actors,
> politicians, industrialists expressed their support too,
> and the crusaders shut up. They waited for a dead horse.

No horses died, and Oca won, *contrada* of Saint Catherine. They threw a party for their *barbero*, Mississippi, who was draped in the year's three-color *palio* for the photos.

For Tozzi and Luzi, modern Sienese, the return to their native city is a phantom image, with threat as well as promise. Luzi's own epigraph to a book his editors called *Parole pellegrine*—"pilgrim words"—are these four enigmatic lines, addressed, one can only imagine, not simply to the "world" in general but to the world of Siena that was once his:

> Mondo, in che parte
> di me o di te ero?
> A cosa ero d'un colpo
> fatto complice e straniero?

> [World, in what part
> of myself or you was I?
> To what was I at once
> both accomplice and stranger?]

He was an accomplice to things Sienese, helping to save the Palio, re-membering it as the city for which the dazed traveler should leave Florence. But Luzi himself stayed away, estranged in Florence as Simone was in Avignon, dreaming of the caravan that would take him back to his city on the hill, and dying outside Siena.

◆

There are caravans in one final painting to consider, as well as a miracle. In a work painted several decades after Simone Martini's death, Bartolo di Fredi depicts the Magi in the act of discovering Christ, just outside a city's walls, beneath a star. Bartolo was the first painter to feature the coming of the Magi in a major altarpiece, depicting the kings in gold leaf and resplendent colors in the company of an extensive equipage. It is in the same room in the Pinacoteca as Simone's altarpiece of Agostino Novello of fifty years earlier, and since early 2013 it has been in a solid glass case right in the middle of the room. Clearly no costs were spared for its preservation, just as the Magi spared no costs to seek out and honor this child for whom they traveled from the exotic East. They find him with

Fig. 35 ◆ Bartolo di Fredi, *Adoration of the Magi* (ca. 1375). Oil on wood. Pinacoteca Nazionale, Siena. Photograph: Scala/Ministero per i Beni e le Attività Culturali/Art Resource, New York.

Mary on a comfortable throne—no baby in a manger, but a palatial scene worthy of visiting royalty. All three kings—one old, one middle-aged, one a mere youth—gaze at mother and child while Joseph scrutinizes the first gift and two servants delicately hold the Magi's tall hats in their hands, signs of their easternness; a horse, rather indiscreetly, turns his backside to us. A dog crouches beneath his feet, while one swarthy attendant suggests by his gestures that he cares more for the horses than for the Christ.

Bartolo painted his masterpiece in the 1380s for the Dominicans on the great hill, and the theme of the Magi, itinerants like Saint Dominic and Bartolo's contemporary Saint Catherine, would quickly come to dominate Italian painting. But what marks Bartolo's painting as Sienese is the city of Jerusalem in the painting's upper left corner, diagonally from Mary's head. It is Bartolo's town in miniature, the cathedral's dome and the comforting dark stripes of its bell tower rising unmistakably from within the pink walls. In this first pilgrimage under the Christian dispensation, the Magi undertake an arduous itinerary, one that takes them across what look like shifting gray tectonic plates susceptible to earthquakes, as Bartolo depicts the caravan no fewer than four times. They first wind their way to a village or hill town in the painting's upper right corner—possibly the nearby San Gimignano, where Bartolo received his first commissions—then enter the Jerusalem that doubles as Siena for a hurried meeting with Herod, anxious to have news of the child. They next leave by the southern gate to reemerge below, full-sized, where Jesus awaits them, alert and preternaturally old; Mary calmly focuses on the elderly king kneeling before her as he kisses the little toes peeking out from beneath the blanket. Atop the elegant outdoor chapel where Mary sits hovers a tiny star, like a firecracker that has just started to sizzle.

The promised city of Jerusalem thus has become the threatening city of Herod, a Herod who will soon order the massacre of the innocents, a theme so ubiquitous in Sienese art. What would become the goal of pilgrims is still the cursed city of a wicked tyrant. Such are my thoughts. The guard in the Pinacoteca notes that I'm standing before the Bartolo for a long time. He ambles over, and I tell him I'd seen the painting in New York only six months earlier, its first trip abroad, in this indestructible glass case. He tells me that before the trip there was no glass case, but that the *americani* paid for it and let the Sienese keep it as a gift. I tell him about all the people who came to see Bartolo in New York when it was the centerpiece of a little exhibition at the Museum of Biblical Art, and he laments that here no one comes to see it. I am indeed the only visitor in the museum at this hour—a chilly Saturday afternoon in January, where outside it has just begun to snow. We lapse into silence to study the scene, and he points out not only San Gimignano but two more hill towns tucked into the upper right corner of the painting that I'd missed before: tiny outposts on hillocks that rise above the uneven gray plates that could easily catch the hind hoof of a camel or horse. Then he suggests that the little chapel that shelters Mary and Jesus from the desert rain or snow is the chapel outside the Palazzo Pubblico, built just after the Black Death to thank Mary for saving half—though only half—of Siena's townspeople from the plague. This is a curious detail, and intriguing. It means that Bartolo had the Magi leave the walled city of Siena only to come, improbably, into the Campo. In effect, we as spectators gather in the Campo to see the Magi line up to grace Jesus with their visit, as foreign ambassadors would have done when coming to the city. We are both within Siena and outside it, glimpsing it from below—as indeed, one does when in the Campo, looking up to see the Palazzo's tower directly above us, and, to our right, the stripes of the campanile. Is this Bartolo's way of saying that the miracle he was looking for in Siena after the plague, after the political battles that had burned down half the Campo in his lifetime, should be looked for right there in the city's heart? Which Tobias saved the family: the one who went out, or the one who stayed?

The night before I leave for the summer, I think Bartolo may have gotten it right, as I stand at the edges of the crowded Campo while they draw lots in the Palazzo Pubblico for who will be in the August Palio. Trumpets sound with the announcement of each of the winning *contrade*. The surging cries, the relief, the joy: "Let me live for another Palio." One thinks that, bank failures or not, the miracle happens here. The Selva isn't chosen; my friends smile their understanding, knowing smiles as if they'd already sensed that they wouldn't be a part of this race. They'll have their dinner on their lovely terrace overlooking San Domenico nonetheless,

will review the footage of the winning Palio from 2010, and will hope
to find in each other and in their neighborhood a sense of purpose even
if the town can no longer offer them work: the prefect who spoke at the
Selva dinner a few nights before about Saint Francis's return to the city
after eight hundred years has recently been told to take early retirement
from his job at the Monte dei Paschi.

And then my own departure. One way to leave is the bus to Pisa air-
port, and Maurizio takes me to the bus stop just off Via Federigo Tozzi in
his little red car at 7:00 a.m. as the sun is already pouring light into the
town, a few days after the July Palio, a few weeks after the longest day
of the year. It is an improbably long and complex route—to go less than
a mile we travel five or six, down, around, up hills I now know after my
walks and car rides out of the city to go to the sea, to the Val d'Orcia, to the
baths of Petrolio where an emperor died. My suitcase is stowed beneath
the bus, among its contents a bottle of wine with the green and orange
Selva colors, a present from our fruit seller, or *fruttivendolo*, Alberto. I
wave to Maurizio in his white linen suit, ready to face the day with a *caffé
corretto* and friends. The bus heads out through sunflower fields to Poggibonsi, past rolls and coils of hay in the fields near Gambassi Terme, and
then we're on the straight, flat road to Pisa and the sea. Hence out of the
province Siena once ruled and into Florence's domain, the world Cosimo
made his own, the world Siena had hoped to control, or at least compete
with. Perhaps it has finished by becoming a world unto itself.

Afterwords

Back in Siena for a week, I dropped in, as always, to the Spedale, where the dark halls of the Etruscan museum held an exhibition of the works of Steve McCurry, a photographer best known for his searing image of a young Afghan girl that appeared twenty years ago on the cover of *National Geographic*. His photos were taken all over the world using some of the last rolls of Kodachrome ever made. Over two hundred of his shots filled the mysterious, cavernous rooms in the Spedale's bowels. Husbands and wives forever entwined in each other's arms look out from their stone couches onto these bright colors of the twenty-first century as they immortalize (or not: How long will these colors survive?) the tragic and joyful moments McCurry encountered in his wanderings around the globe: 9/11, seen from his apartment window in Tribeca; the Arab Spring; war-torn Pakistan where a boy, his nose running, holds a gun to his own head—in play or in jest. Such scenes are interspersed with other moments: fire hydrants opened for grateful kids in the steaming streets of a Chicago summer, Times Square in the snow, bazaars in Egypt, an Indonesian dawn, and fishermen hauling up nets heavy with fish from the Indian Ocean.

As Gabriella Piccinni suggests, the Spedale once was a kind of El-
lis Island, a receptacle for all who came to Siena's shores. Many of the
pilgrims and passersby left vital bits of information about themselves,
either in confession or to reclaim goods they'd left for safekeeping. Abandoned children also frequently arrived with tags: half a torn heart, a
fragment of clothing, or a single shoe, so that a parent returning months,
years later—economic circumstances having changed—might take back
a son or daughter given up for lost. There is no scene of such a reunion
in the paintings in the Pellegrinaio, and I suspect they were rare. Still,
the variegated worlds and social classes that found a gathering place at
the Spedale, as evinced by these testaments—heartbreaking in so many
cases, quotidian in others—suggest that McCurry's international ram-
blings and the mass of humanity he photographed to assemble here, under the watchful eyes of the Etruscans unearthed from the *terra* outside
Siena, is fitting for the Spedale as it seeks to redefine itself after a thousand years of activities have ceased.

The Duomo was more crowded than I've ever seen it, and the Spedale
was too, the McCurry exhibition drawing those who otherwise wouldn't
have gone in. This seemed like a good sign for the decision, which was
soon to come, on whether Siena would make the short list of five or six
cities vying to be the next "capital of European culture." Earlier in the
year my landlord Maurizio invited some friends to a gathering at his
apartment in the Contrada della Selva, in the old street where servants
once unloaded the heavy trunks of their masters who had come to see
Siena on the Grand Tour, where nuns were walled up in little rooms, and
where the powerful family of the Berardenghi had its castle. We talked
mostly about Siena's chances of winning the title. There were twelve
Sienese and thirteen opinions, and the events regarding the Monte dei
Paschi and a resigned mayor and the university were still too fresh to
have been fully digested; indeed, things are still unfolding. Siena isn't
open enough to the outside, it's too open to the outside; it's not cutting-
edge, it's tried too hard to be avant-garde; the intense bonding of the
contrade is good for the city as a whole, the secrecy of the *contrade* in-
terferes with attempts to give the city a single identity. Maurizio had
invited Roberto Barzanti, mayor of Siena during the turbulent 1960s and
1970s, but he couldn't come, and over the summer I caught an article by

Barzanti in the *Corriere della Sera*. Pisa had just entered the race, another Tuscan town throwing its hat into a ring already crowded with Siena, Naples, Bari, Venice, Lecce, Ravenna. Did he think Siena could still pull it off? In his always elegant prose, Barzanti wrote, "The cities that have attracted attention haven't been those that are just symbols but places that are moving toward economic revival, thanks to innovative and creative managing of their environmental resources and their historic vocations." Culture is, after all, rooted in *cultus*, which is rooted in the land. Banishing cars from the center of the city established Siena's own commitment to both respecting its historical vocation and controlling fumes and traffic within the city walls. The Green movement in Italy praises Siena as an example of "sustained community." Can the European Union find in the city a model for an uncertain future, as a vacant hospital embraces a new life, as McCurry's photos of the homeless and the marginalized remind us of the damaged lives that found refuge here, pausing in the midst of their itineraries?

Those with a disposition to being pilgrims or tourists leave familiar places to immerse themselves in the unknown, even as globalization makes it increasingly difficult to find places that are thoroughly unfamiliar; they walk a tightrope between the common and exotic, as McCurry does in his exhibition. Coming back to Siena over the years has made this city less unknown to me, and it is reassuring to see faces I recognize. In a reversal from the medieval pilgrimage, or the heady plunge into banking, or a search for sanctity beyond the walls, it's our daily lives that have suddenly become wrenchingly unpredictable. Siena instead had taken on the contours of the unchanging, welcome because it seemed no different than the last time we were here. What lies ahead now that its foundations have been threatened, now that the slogan for a new party has become "Siena cambia"? Or could that eternal sameness be an illusion—a projection of our own desire for stability somewhere in the world, along with similarly understandable desires on the part of the Sienese? On which *mappamondo* does Siena belong?

Acknowledgments

This book has been a long labor of love, first suggested by Randy Petilos when he saw how bereft I was after finishing my book on Catherine of Siena. The past few years have thus seen me back in Siena for more sustained visits, with the delightful outcome of introducing me to many Sienese and non-Siense alike who have opened their hearts and often their doors. My warmest thanks to Monica Banti, Roberto Barzanti, Elena Brizio, the family Cervini, Vincenzo Coli, Rosanna de Benedictis, Stefano Carrai, Mario de Gregorio, Anna di Castro, Alessandro Falassi, Marcello Flores, Machtelt Israëls, Giada Mattarucco, Gordan Moran, Michele Pellegrini, Gabriella Piccinni, Marzia Pieri, Patrizia Pizzorno, Eugenio Rifredi, Anna Scattigno, Antonio Tizzani, and Enrico Toti.

Special thanks go to Maurizio De Ricco, who has been the most generous of landlords, introducing us to his wide circle of friends and ensuring that his little rental apartment nestled into the hill overlooking San Domenico was as comfortable as it could possibly be. Debora Barbagli was many times over a gracious guide to the institution that is at the center of these reflections, the Spedale della Scala, and special thanks go to her for helping procure the photograph of Tobias as she was preparing for the opening of the new permanent exhibit on Siena's history from its origins through the Middle Ages. Andrea Fontana shared his love and knowledge of Siena as well as his stunning photographs, one of which I am proud to reproduce in chapter 5. The volunteers of the Associazione La Diana were enormously helpful in taking us on tours at the Museo dell'Acqua, at the Spedale, and through *bottini*. My students at the Scuola Normale Superiore di Pisa and at New York University's Villa La Pietra helped pose—and answer—fascinating questions about the city during our several field trips to Siena in the spring of 2012. Joseph Connors first introduced me to Francesco Vanni's map of Siena during a long conversation about the city at Villa I Tatti. The librarians and staff at the Biblioteca Comunale di Siena were immensely patient with my repeated requests for help, and I'm also grateful to staff at the Biblioteca Laurenziana in Florence. Finally, Penny Marcus, in whom I have found a kindred spirit and fellow lover of Siena, was a wonderful dinner companion on numerous occasions when we found ourselves together in the city.

None of this work could have been done were we not sustained in ways other than intellectual. At his *alimentari* on Via Franciosa, Alberto gave us the best fruit the Contrada della Selva had to offer and wonderful wines with the Selva seal. I am also grateful to the baristas at the Caffè Diaccetto and the patient women in the Pasticceria Magnifico, with its excellent riccioli and sustaining breads. And we had many a good iced coffee sitting on the little patio of Il Chicco d'Oro just outside the Porta Fontebranda.

On this side of the Atlantic, Susan Spano provided the gift of a reporter's notebook and sent encouraging comments when I had doubts. Colleagues at the Humanities Initiative at New York University provided helpful comments when I read a draft of chapter 3 in spring 2013; special thanks to Martin Scherzinger for information about banking practices. I'm also grateful to Albert Ascoli, Victoria Kahn, and other colleagues at the University of California-Berkeley for feedback on a talk on the Pellegrinaio paintings in fall 2013. Julie Salamon, Deborah Pellegrino, Roberto Barzanti, Gwynneth Malin, and Alex Klein all read chapters and gave helpful advice; Julie's fabulous book, *Hospital*, has been an inspiration from the start. Nicola Lucchi stepped in at the last minute to help me figure out how to choose and obtain images. Liz Mercuri was indispensable at Art Resource. Carl Strehlke, Konrad Eisenbichler, and Fabrizio Nevola shared their extensive knowledge of Siena with me in conversations and e-mails. Above all, my colleagues and students in the Department of Italian Studies have been wonderful interlocutors in conversations about this book as it unfolded. I enjoyed visiting Siena with Stefano Albertini and our students over several summer sessions, and I have gained a great deal from exchanges with Maria Luisa Ardizzone, Virginia Cox, John Freccero, and Ara Merjian, whose thoughtful gift of *Siena, Florence, and Padova* has come in handy.

In addition to Randy Petilos, Alan Thomas at the University of Chicago Press has been supportive of this book project since its inception. I thank him along with Alice Bennett, whose painstaking and careful editing has made this a far better book. June Sawyer assisted with the index.

I am fortunate to have had my sons, Alex and Nathan Klein, and my husband, William Klein, as partners in this enterprise. They took photographs, went on long walks, commented on paintings and city streets, and suggested jaunts to the corners of Siena's rich province: Mount Amiata, Bagno Vignoni, Radicofani, Talamone, Montalcino. My mother, who had fond memories of her trip to Siena in 2001, and especially of the visit to the Spedale, gently insisted that the hospital and its fascinating history should occupy the center of this book. I dedicate these pages to her.

◆

In chapter 1, I reproduce several paragraphs from my essay "Mapping Siena," in *Renaissance Studies in Honor of Joseph Connors*, edited by Machtelt Israëls and Louis A. Waldman (Florence: Villa I Tatti, 2013). I am grateful to Harvard University Library, the artist Antonio Possenti, the Circolo degli Uniti, the Associazione La Diana, the Comune di Siena, and a private collection in Venice for permission to use photographs. I also want to thank NYU's Faculty of Arts and Science for the generous research funding that allowed me to travel to Siena and the Humanities Initiative at NYU for assistance with procuring permissions.

Notes

For general background on the history of Siena, there are no better places to start than Judith Hook's *Siena: A City and Its History* and William Bowsky's *A Medieval Italian Commune: Siena under the Nine*. For medieval and Renaissance art history, Timothy Hyman's lively *Sienese Painting* is a terrific introduction. *Painting in Renaissance Siena, 1420–1500*, by Keith Christiansen, Laurence Kanter, and Carl Brandon Strehlke, is a more technical introduction but well worth reading and with beautiful illustrations. Michael Kucher's thoughtful *The Water Supply System of Siena, Italy: The Medieval Roots of the Modern Networked City* is both an excellent guide to underground Siena and its geological idiosyncrasies and a valuable discussion of the city's urban politics over the centuries. Most guidebooks to Tuscany give Siena short shrift, but Alta MacAdam's *Blue Guide* is more detailed than most and written in MacAdam's characteristically engaging style. And Kate Simon's *Italy: The Places in Between* opens with a substantial section devoted to Siena and its environs.

Readers of Italian may want to start with Giuliano Catoni and Gabriella Piccinni's *Storia illustrata di Siena*, while Paolo Cammarosano provides a wonderful guide to the city's topography and history in *Il medioevo nelle città italiane*. Iltesorodi siena.net is a valuable online resource for all things Sienese, with ongoing blogs and additions to the site. Sienalibri.it, called "Il portale della cultura senese" really is a portal onto Siena's lively cultural events as well as a great place to check out (and buy) books about Siena, many of them in English. You can also subscribe free online to one of Siena's local papers—*La Nazione*. The journal dedicated to Sienese history, *Bullettino Senese di Storia Patria* (*BSSP*), has articles on all aspects of Siena's culture, many of them available online.

There are still too few translations into English of excellent work on Siena in Italian. The notes below refer to English texts whenever possible.

INTRODUCTION

Giovacchino Faluschi's *Breve relazione delle cose notabili della Città di Siena* is available in a modernized edition, but the one I used was published by Francesco Rossi, in Siena, in 1784. His comments on the Palazzo Pubblico and Lorenzetti are on pages 110–11. For discussions of the *mappamondo*, see most recently Marcia Kupfer's article "The Lost Wheel Map of Ambrogio Lorenzetti." Chiara Frugoni has an elegant presentation of the Sala del Mappamondo and Lorenzetti's work more generally in her *Pietro e Ambrogio Lorenzetti* (with English translation).

While most histories of Siena concern themselves with the Middle Ages, Antonio Cardini's *Storia di Siena* is a good introduction to modern history since the Risorgimento. Events at the Monte dei Paschi continue to unfold, but Michele Taddei's *Scandalosa Siena* makes for interesting reading as it follows the author's blogs over the tumultuous year of 2012–13. Articles in the business section of the *New York Times* and *Financial Times* periodically provide updates, not to mention Italian papers such as *Corriere della Sera*.

Bird's-eye views of the city may not say it all, but Luca Betti and Vincenzo Coli's *Il cielo sopra le terre di Siena* (with English translation) contains gorgeous aerial views of Siena and its territory.

For learning about the origins of the names of Siena's roads, the best book, hands down, is Roberto Cresti and Maura Martellucci's *Stradario/StraNario*—my guide over the past three years as I walked around the city. Alberto Fiorini's exhaustive *Strade di Siena* (Pisa, 2014) appeared too late to be of use. On Francesco di Giorgio's house, see Fabrizio Nevola's essay, available online, "Lots of Napkins and a Few Surprises," in *Annali di Archittetura*, and Petra Pertici, *La città magnificata*.

The list of Sienese "firsts" is taken in part from the appendix to Gabriella Piccinni's pamphlet—and manifesto—on why Siena should be chosen as the next cultural capital of Europe, *Città murata, città globale*. Architects interested in Siena as a place for sustainability include Spiro Kostof, *The City Shaped*, and

Thomas Harvey, whose essay "Siena/Sustainability" is available online. The citation of Corrado Forlin's poem and his quotation about gasoline (along with the 1937 painting) are in Gabriele Borghini, "Splendore simultaneo del Palio di Siena." Books on the Palio come out all the time, the most recent being *Siena: Le stagioni del Palio*, written by Massimo Biliorsi, a member of the Contrada del Drago. One of the virtues of the book is its insistence that the Palio is not just a horse race but is a way of organizing Sienese life. For a more scholarly work see *La Terra in Piazza* by Alan Dundes and Alessandro Falassi, also available in English. A website with considerable information in English about the Palio and approved by the Sienese committee that oversees the race is available at http://www.ilpalio.org/index_english.htm.

On the Spedale and the Pellegrinaio, the work of Gabriella Piccinni is fundamental; there is a good general discussion of the paintings themselves in Mariella Carlotti's *Ante gradus*. A number of Vecchietta's paintings are discussed in *Painting in Renaissance Siena* and in Diana Norman's *Painting in Late Medieval and Late Renaissance Siena*. The Catholic Geneva Bible contains the apocryphal books, including the Book of Tobias.

CHAPTER ONE

For the 1798 earthquake, see the 1798 book by Ambrogio Soldani, *Relazione del terremoto accaduto in Siena il di 26 maggio*. A conference held in Rome in 2007, "Cos'è successo a Siena il 26 maggio 1798?" focused on the 1798 earthquake and what could be learned from it for future planning, online at http://www2.ogs.trieste.it/gngts/gngts/convegniprecedenti/2007/presentazioni/2_23/2_23_13_Albarello_1798_def.pdf.

Fabrizio Nevola writes about the experience of Siena's "curtained" streets in his excellent study *Siena: Constructing the Renaissance City*. Federigo Tozzi's phrase about suicidal streets is from his *Bestie*, his collection of sixty beast fables, which contains hallucinating descriptions of the city. They have not yet been translated (sadly, for a man who translated a great deal of literature written in English, including Kenneth Grahame's children's book *The Wind in the Willows*). But a recent edition of *Bestie* was published with illustrations by the well-known Italian artist Antonio Possenti, and they capture the morbidness and electricity of Tozzi's febrile imagination—as is clear from the one example reproduced in this book (figure 4). For a map of the expansion of Siena's walls over several centuries, see Norman's *Siena, Florence and Padua* (2:11). The eighteenth-century intellectual Girolamo Gigli devotes a number of pages to the walls in his *Diario senese*. Also see Pellegrini, *Fortificare con arte*.

The Vanni and Bonsignori maps are available at Harvard's website. Letizia Galli's comment on Vanni can be found in her entry for Vanni's map from *Siena e Roma*, page 88. Vanni's own comment on the "strange hills" is found in his letter to the Medici administrator, in Luciano Banchi and Scipione Borghesi's *Nuovi documenti*, page 613.

The archaeological evidence on Siena's origins is still somewhat sparse, but Debora Barbagli and Giuseppina Carlotta Cianferoni's *Siena, Santa Maria della Scala: Guida al Museo archeologico* has nice background on individual objects found in and around Siena. Current scholars working on the land beneath the Spedale include Federico Cantini of the University of Pisa and Silvia Pallecchi from the University of Siena. A collection of documents on the work related to recent excavations was published in 2011, Fabio Gabrielli's *Ospedale di Santa Maria della Scala: Ricerche storiche, archeologiche e storico-artistiche*. The story of Senio and Aschio is ubiquitous in Sienese lore from the fifteenth century onward. The introduction to Timothy Smith and Judith Steinhoff's *Art as Politics in Late Medieval and Renaissance Siena* is a lively and succinct overview of Siena's history from the thirteenth century through the sixteenth.

Michael Kucher's fascinating *Water Supply System of Siena* covers mainly the story of the *bottini*, but he also delves into the city's geological formation. Dante's quip about Sienese vanity and the search for the Diana is in *Purgatorio*, canto 13, the terrace of envy. Extensive work has been done on the "Diana" and the *bottini* by the volunteer Associazione La Diana, which offers guides to the *bottini* and runs the society's museum in Fonte Pescaia. The Associazione La Diana's *A ritrovar La Diana* is a good start, and for children there's the comic book our guide to the *bottino* gave us after our tour, called *L'Acqua di Siena*. The CD/DVD *Siena Città dell'acqua* recreates the journey through Siena's major *bottino*. Finally, Patrizia Turrini has several examples of legal dealings with the *bottini* in her *Per honore et utile de la città di Siena*.

Toscani's essay on geology can be found in the epochal *Siena e il suo territorio*, available in a modern reprint and with excellent foldout inserts of individual buildings as well as maps. There are fewer better sources on the history of the Fonte Gaia than the exhibition itself in the Spedale, with extensive commentary and comparisons that can be directly made between Tito Sarrocchi's nineteenth-century sculptures (for which plaster casts are present) and Jacopo della Quercia's worn originals. The quotation about the soft marble of the *montagnola senese* is from one of the exhibition's signs.

Hayden Maginnis's *The World of the Early Sienese Painter* mentions paintings as "doorways to heaven" on page 121, where he also talks about a tradition in

Siena of pictures that could speak. Mary McCarthy's *Stones of Florence* remains one of the best introductions to Siena's most enduring rival.

The Fisiocritici's museum can be found in Via dei Tufi, and quotations are from the extensive exhibition. On the use of minium in medieval illumination as well as other minerals, see the ever-useful *The Materials and Techniques of Medieval Painting* by Daniel V. Thompson.

Machtelt Israëls has several seminal essays on fifteenth-century outdoor painting and processions in Siena, in which she talks about Mary's apotropaic function, including her essay in Philippa Jackson and Fabrizio Nevola's *Beyond the Palio*. For a good description of Simone's *Maestà*, see Diana Norman, *Siena and the Virgin*. C. Jean Campbell has a wonderful analysis of Simone's role as painter and "writer" in *The Commonwealth of Nature*.

Pietro Clemente and Paolo De Simonis's *Visibili tracce* has some of the best photographs I know of the contemporary life of the Sienese *contado*—in addition to powerful images of the country in the city, such as the one alluded to on pages 12–13, simply titled "Un orto in Valle di Porta Giustizia." The now-closed psychiatric hospital of San Niccolò, which opened in 1818 and closed in the 1980s, was the subject of an exhibition at the former hospital in 2009, called "Arte, Genio, Follia."

CHAPTER TWO

Studies of medieval pilgrimage are legion, especially in the wake of the new millennium, but Gerhardt Ladner's "Homo Viator" from 1967 remains the best account of its origins and persistence. New books abound on the Via Francigena, as much European Union money has gone to reclaim the old roads that defined medieval Europe; Renato Stopani's *La Via Francigena nel Senese* contains a number of essays, including Franco Cardini's. For those interested in pursuing the trail in Tuscany, see Letizia Galli's *In viaggio nel Quattrocento: Guida al Rinascimento nelle terre di Siena*. Mario Bezzini's *Storia della Via Francigena: Dai Longobardi ai Giubilei* offers some particularly good details about the Via Francigena as it passed just outside and through Siena and has been extremely useful for the opening of this chapter.

Italo Moretti's quotation is from his essay "La Via Francigena: Una strada per Roma," in Bruno Santi and Claudio Strinati's *Siena e Roma*. For Lucca, see the little guidebook by Giovanni Macchia, *Il pellegrinaggio medievale a Lucca*. Ernesto Sestan's classic essay on Siena, "Siena avanti Montaperti," which deserves to be translated into English, is still viable after fifty years; it's cited in almost everything you run into on the medieval town. It was published in a classic volume of Siena's homegrown journal *Bulletino Senese di Storia e Patria* (*BSSP*) in 1961, along with Giuseppe Martini's equally classic essay on Sienese history until the fall of the Nine, "Siena da Montaperti alla caduta dei Nove."

For a brilliant reading of the Lorenzetti fresco of *Buon Governo*, see Randolph Starn's slender *Ambrogio Lorenzetti* as well as his longer study with Loren Partridge, *Arts of Power*. Quentin Skinner has a reading of the fresco heavily influenced by his study of medieval political theory ("Ambrogio Lorenzetti's *Buon Governo* Frescoes"). The statute of Siena's roads is available in a modern edition by Thomas Szabò and Donatella Ciampoli, *Viabilità e legislazione di uno stato cittadino del Duecento*. Boccaccio and Dante refer to Ghido in, respectively, the *Decameron* 10.2, where the ruthless thief is cast as a *buono brigante*, or good brigand, and in *Purgatorio* 6. The book on mercenaries is that of William Caferro, *Mercenary Companies and the Decline of Siena*, while Catherine's words to Hawkwood are from Suzanne Noffke's excellent edition and translation of her letters, 1:79–81 (letter T140). Hawkwood's life and times are colorfully evoked by Frances Saunders in *The Devil's Broker*.

For the French influence on Siena, see Moretti's essay along with Fabio Gabrielli's "Architetture di strada," in Santi and Strinati's *Siena e Roma*. Dante's citation from *Purgatorio* 8 is from the Mandelbaum edition. Machtelt Israëls mentions Sano's altarpiece in Sant'Andrea in her article on processions cited above. The *New York Times* article on Siena ("36 hours in Siena") appeared on October 11, 2012. Euro Gazzei's *Da Trombicche . . . una sera di giovedì* has quotations from pages 14 and 101 (on Siena's legendary hospitality).

Faluschi refers to the Via dei Borsajoli on page 92 of his *Breve relazione*. The anonymous chronicler who talks about the boon that pilgrims bring to the city is cited in Piccinni's essay in *Siena e Roma*, page 235. Another work of Piccinni's, *Storia illustrata*, contains the Alfieri quotation on page 160. As always, Cresti's *Stradario/StraNario* is helpful in not only talking about the origins of Vicolo degli Orefici, but explaining how to find it.

The best book on medieval notions of purgatory is Jacques Le Goff's *The Birth of Purgatory*. Not much has been written on the faded purgatorial frescoes in Santa Maria dei Servi; Joseph Polzer's essay in *Art Bulletin* is a comprehensive study of purgatorial scenes throughout Italy in the Middle Ages. (Among the many projects funded by Agostino Chigi's final descendant, Guido Saracini-Chigi, was the restoration of the church in the early twentieth century.)

On Catherine's life and her giving her father's cloak to a beggar, see the hagiography by her confessor Raymond of Capua, book 1, chapter 10. Andrea

Gallerani's painting is in the Pinacoteca, while Duccio's *Maestà* is in the Museo dell'Opera del Duomo. The painting has been extensively written about, most recently on the occasion of its seven hundredth anniversary; see, for example, the essay by Diana Norman in volume 2 of her *Siena, Florence, and Padua*. Mariella Carlotti has a helpful guide to the panels, *Il cuore di Siena*, and Cesare Brandi's *Duccio*, first published in 1951, was the first monograph in Italian dedicated to the Sienese painter; it has recently been reprinted. As always, Timothy Hyman's book on painting in Siena is a terse and accessible tour de force. My thanks to Susan Klein for some penetrating insights about the panel of Jesus on the road to Emmaus.

Zbigniew Herbert has a magnificent, brooding essay on Siena from the 1960s, translated in his *Barbarian in the Garden*, from which came the citation on the sky as the Duomo Nuovo's roof; see "Siena" in his *Collected Prose*, page 64. On the Facciatone and the aborted project of the new cathedral, see Enzo Carli's work on the Duomo, *Il Duomo di Siena e il Museo dell'Opera*.

The history of the Spedale della Scala is graphically illustrated in the recent work of Beatrice Sordini, *Dentro l'antico Ospedale*. Gabriella Piccinni and Michele Pellegrini are also excellent guides. Petra Pertici's *Siena Quattrocentesca: Gli anni del Pellegrinaio* offers some interesting historical background to the paintings of the Pellegrinaio. The food patients ate is described in Maddalena Belli's recent *La cucina di un ospedale del Trecento*. The figures of the annual intake of *figli* to the Spedale are from Carlo Falletti-Fossati's *Costumi senesi nella seconda metà del secolo XIV*. Giovanni Macchi's illustration, now in Siena's Archivio di Stato, has been widely disseminated; Roberto Barzanti, Alberto Cornice, and Ettore Pelligrini's *Iconografia di Siena* has a particularly good reproduction.

On Vecchietta, see the few pages dedicated to him in Christiansen, Kanter, and Strehlke's *Painting in Renaissance Siena, 1420–1500*; Diana Norman has an essay on him in Smith and Steinhoff's recent *Art as Politics in Late Medieval and Renaissance Siena*. Friedrich Ohly's *Sensus spiritualis* has a careful description of the cathedral, and he cites the Vasari quotation as well. For beautiful images of the *pavimento*, see Robert Cust's *The Pavement Masters of Siena*. For "wide-eyed Madonna," see Norman, *Siena and the Virgin*, chapter 2.

For the life of Alberto Aringhieri, see T. B. Smith's recent dissertation, "Alberto Aringhieri and the Chapel of St. John the Baptist." T. S. Eliot's "Love Song of J. Alfred Prufrock" has the catchy lines, "the women come and go / Talking of Michelangelo." On the crypt—still unphotographed for the most part—see Roberto Guerrini's *Sotto il Duomo di Siena*. Michele Bacci's *Iconografia evangelica a Siena* is the source of the quotation about the musical goings-on beneath the church (page 90). Sura 19 in the Qur'an contains verses about Mary praying for a miracle from the date tree when she goes "off into the east."

CHAPTER THREE

Two very different works on the life of Agostino Chigi are Felix Gilbert's *The Pope, His Banker, and Venice*, and Ingrid Rowland's essay in *Renaissance Quarterly*. The story about "Pochointesta Petrucci" is cited in Patrizia Turrini's *La comunità ebraica di Siena*, page 17.

Ludovico Zdekauer wrote a series of essays on the Sienese merchant, most notably his talk at the Accademia dei Rozzi called "Il mercante senese nel Dugento." His *La vita privata e pubblica dei senesi nel Dugento* is also illuminating on merchants' lives. On early transactions of businesses, see Edward English's *Enterprise and Liability in Sienese Banking*, which is fundamental for understanding the "commercial revolution" of the thirteenth century. The citation about Sienese merchants' "exquisite artistic sense" is from Romolo Caggese, *La repubblica di Siena e il suo contado nel secolo decimoterzo*, page 8.

Randolph Starn's books again deserve mention for magnificent studies of the Lorenzetti frescoes. On the Loggia della Mercanzia and the Croce del Travaglio, see Nevola's *Siena*. The citation about "merchants and other honorable citizens" is from Faluschi's *Breve relazione*.

On the Salimbeni, see Franco Salimei's and Alessandra Carniani's books. And for the Tolomei, see Roberta Mucciarelli's *I Tolomei banchieri di Siena*, very helpful in general on the "magnate" families and their battles with one another. Saint Francis comes to Siena in 1212, as recounted in *The Little Flowers of Saint Francis*, chapter 11. Dante cites Pia Tolomei in *Purgatorio 5*, in the Mandelbaum translation. For the history of the Monte dei Paschi, at least up until the current crisis, see Francesco Gurrieri, *La sede storica del Monte dei Paschi di Siena*, which includes the Vanni drawings and painting of Joseph.

The quotation from the letter of David Reubeni is also from Turrini's *La comunità ebraica di Siena*, from the introduction by Anna del Castro (page vii). The *Stradario/StraNario* mentions the varying origins of the mysterious word *Salicotto*, pages 39–40. *La comunità ebraica* goes into great detail about the ghetto and the eighteenth-century riot, less so on World War II. The phrase *Aemuli Iudeorum* is from Michele Pellegrini's excellent study of relationships between usurers and Christians in Siena, in volume 2 of Piccinni's *Fedeltà ghibellina, affari guelfi*.

The *biccherne* are the subject of a large coffee-table book, as well as of a smaller guide available for purchase at the Archive (tours at 9:30, 10:30, and

11:30 every morning but Sunday). For the legend of San Galgano, see Eugenio Susi's *San Galgano e l'eremita cortese*.

See the recent edition of Giovanni Antonio Pecci's *Lo Stato di Siena antico, e moderno*; the quotation on Siena's territory forming an "imperfect oval" is on page 11. William Bowsky recounts the difficulties of Siena's countryside in *A Medieval Italian Comune*. For the fascinating system of the granaries, there is no better guide than the Museo della Grancia in Serre di Rapolano, Rapolano Terme. For teaching purposes, they've produced, among other things, large (11" × 17") diagrams of the various rooms and occupations of the *grancia*, called simply "Grancia delle Serre," demonstrating the "network of the grance" as well as the olive press, the courtyards, and "the road." The work is produced by the Centro di Documentazione sulle Antiche Grance del Santa Maria della Scala. There's a separate book on Cuna, Giuseppina Coscarella's *La grancia di Cuna in Val d'Arbia: Un esempio di fattoria fortificata medievale*. On Ristoro Menghi di Giunta, see Michele's Pellegrini's essay cited above. For an elegant study of Siena's relation to the countryside in the fourteenth through sixteenth centuries, see Odile Redon, *L'espace d'une cité: Sienne et le pays siennois*.

Koichi Toyama writes about Giovanni di Paolo and the possibility that he knew Taccola's treatise on engineering; also see Kucher's chapter on Francesco di Giorgio Martini and Taccola in *The Water Supply of Siena*. Pius II has been the subject of numerous works; a recent volume (2006) of the *Bullettino Senese di Storia e Patria* was dedicated to him, in which the editors refer to him as *un uomo difficile*—a difficult man (page 376). Margaret Meserve and Marcello Simonetta have recently edited and translated his *Commentaries* for the I Tatti Renaissance Library. Pius is one of the very few Sienese mentioned (and discussed at some length) in Jacob Burckhardt's *Civilization of the Renaissance in Italy*. For Pienza, see Piero Torriti's *Pienza* and the work of Fabio Pellegrini on Pienza's "dream of humanism." The exhibition on Count Silvio Piccolomini was at last notice still open on the ground floor of the Palazzo Piccolomini in Pienza, with an impressive amount of background information on this family and its decline. Rowland's comment on Chigi's "economic machinations" is from her *Renaissance Quarterly* article, page 693.

Colombini, founder of the Gesuati, left a number of letters, as did Saint Catherine; her quotation is from her *Dialogue*, chapter 165, based on an event she read about in *The lives of the Fathers*. There is a fascinating life of Colombini by the fifteenth-century Florentine writer Feo Belcari, *I primi compagni del B. Giovanni Colombini*.

Our guidebook to the Crete was available at the tourist office in Siena, in the

Campo. Dickens's quotation is from *Pictures of Italy*, chapter 9: "As bare and desolate as any Scottish moors . . . as barren, as stormy, and as wild, as Cornwall in
England," written in 1846 (this quotation follows immediately after he suggests
that Siena "is like a bit of Venice, without the water"). Gigli's *Diario senese* provides the quotation on the Crete. Iris Origo's beautiful account of life in the Crete
before and during World War II, *War in the Val d'Orcia*, is a moving document for
capturing this area in the years right before the feudal system of sharecropping
(*mezzadria*) came to an end. For Talamone and its history, see Beatrice Sordini's
Il porto della "Gente vana." In his *Iconografia di Siena*, Roberto Barzanti mentions
the procession of Palm Sunday that would have concluded at Porta Salaria in order to greet "il Cristo ingrediente" (page xi).

CHAPTER FOUR

The epigraph is from Niccolò Tommaseo's nineteenth-century dictionary of
Italian words. (Tommaseo himself was a big fan of Saint Catherine, and there
are many Sienese dialectal variants in his dictionary, even though he adapted
Florence—Settignano, more precisely—as his home.) The source of the proverb
is unknown.

The princess's 1730 *bando* is often reproduced in modern editions of works
about the Palio; see, for example, Dundes and Falassi's *Terra in Piazza*. One can
purchase maps in Siena with the *contrade*'s territories marked, usually in different colors. Barzanti's quotation is from his preface to a famous book by Antonio Francesco Bandini from the eighteenth century, often reprinted on the
contrade, page ix. *La magna e trionfante festa et chiaccia che si fece nel inclita città
di Siena nellanno MCCCCCVI adi XV d'Agosto* was published in Siena in 1506 by
the first publisher who was a Sienese native, called Il Rosso; a loyal Sienese, he
debuted with the *Sconficta di Monte Aperto* in 1502. For Castelvecchio, Benvoglienti's *Trattato* goes on to delineate three gates into the area (pages 3–6). Roberto Cresti's comments are on pages 59–61; he also cites Count Bernardo's rental
document.

For Saint Anthony and the altarpiece (probably by Sano di Pietro, although
others maintain the "Maestro dell'Osservanza" is still unknown), see Machtelt
Israëls's work on Sano. Saint Jerome's story of Saint Anthony is in his *Life*, translated into Italian by the Dominican Domenico Cavalca in the fourteenth century
and known by many Sienese. For the dispute between the hermits, Cavalca has
it like this: "Paul alleged that Anthony should be the first to break that bread,

since he was the guest, and a pilgrim, while Anthony said that Paul should in fact be first, since he was older, and more saintly" (Cavalca, *Vite di santi padri*). For a history of the Misericordia, see *La Misericordia di Siena attraverso i secoli*, especially Paolo Nardi's "Origini e sviluppo della Casa della Misericordia." Maureen Dowd's comments were in her Christmas 2012 column in the *New York Times*, titled "Why, God?" She attributed the phrase to an unnamed theologian.

Piccinni uses the term *genio collettivo* in *Città murata, città globale*. The Intronati's most famous play, *Gli ingannati*, has been translated since the sixteenth century as *The Deceived*. The Rozzi plays await translation, but the recent modern Italian edition, well annotated by Pietro Trifone and his colleagues, is bringing some of them to the attention of a modern audience, and Marzia Pieri's edition of the plays of "Lo Strascino" (the lame man) is an equally welcome addition; Strascino was a Sienese playwright and actor who performed before the Congrega dei Rozzi was formed. The Rozzi are the object of a classic study by Carlo Mazzi, *La Congrega dei Rozzi*. For a study of Pandolfo Petrucci, "Il Magnifico," see Maurizio Gattoni's *Pandolfo Petrucci e la politica estera della repubblica di Siena*. The quotation by Machiavelli is found in *The Prince*, chapter 22 ("On Servants"); the letter is from 1498 and found in *The Historical, Political, and Diplomatic Writings*, volume 3.

Mario Ascheri talks about the "anachronistic luxury of full political participation" in his introduction to *La città del Costituto*. Saint Catherine's "vice" of *superbia* is addressed in great detail by Raymond of Capua in his *Life of Catherine of Siena*, in the final chapter of the third book. For Dante's discussion of Sienese purgatorial penitents, see Sapia on the terrace of envy (*Purgatorio* 13), and Provenzano (*Purgatorio* 11). The citation from thirteenth-century chroniclers on Provenzano is in Charles Singleton's edition of the *Divine Comedy*.

The case against the Oca was finally resolved in 2012. Pope John XXII's quotation about the Palio is in the little museum of the Palio in the Spedale. Giuliano Catoni's recent book on Bargagli Petrucci's life alludes to the controversy about Forlin. His poem and Farfa's are excerpted in Borghini, "Splendore simultaneo."

On the construction of the Torre del Mangia, as well as the Palazzo Pubblico more generally, see "Design of Town Halls" by Colin Cunningham, in Diana Norman, *Siena, Florence, and Padua*. The controversy about the Muslim nuances of the 2010 palio was widely reported on in the Sienese papers; see, for example, issues of *Corriere di Siena* for June 2010. For the race itself and the processions proceeding and following it, see Dundes and Falassi and Massimo Biliorsi, *Siena: Le stagioni del Palio*. Lis Harris's *New Yorker* essay is an engaging account of her experience of the Palio in the 1980s. Gerald Parsons's study, *Siena, Civil Religion and the Sienese*, is a careful and elegant assessment of the role the Palio—and the Virgin—have played in Sienese life for eight centuries.

Scipione Bargagli is surely one of the more fascinating Renaissance Sienese. His dialogue titled *Turramino* is a blistering attack on the Accademia della Crusca, the Florentine academy that was attempting to legislate the use of Italian in the seventeenth century. The oration he gave on Italian academies is in Siena's Biblioteca Comunale. The quotation from his short-story collection *I Trattenimenti* is from the opening frame to the tales themselves. The end of the republic, which Bargagli witnessed, is written about in vivid early twentieth-century English prose by Edwin and Evangeline Blashfield in *Italian Cities*, as they quote extensively from the diaries of the French general Blaise de Montluc; see the appropriate chapters in Douglas's lively *History of Siena* as well.

The constitution was celebrated to much fanfare on its seven hundredth anniversary in 2009. Recent discussions of the Sienese constitution are in books by Mario Ascheri and Duccio Balestracci. The most recent edition of the vernacular constitution was published in 2002 by Mahmoud Salem Elsheikh, in four volumes.

A beautiful new book on the Oratory of the Contrada of Valdimontone was published in the summer of 2012, *Una gemma preziosa*. When I attended a celebration of the book and a tour of the restored oratory on the eve of the July Palio, there was discussion about focusing efforts on a "baroque tour" of Siena concentrated in their *contrada*. The 1904 exhibit of Sienese art prompted an anniversary catalog, but the original catalog edited by Corrado Ricci is much better (*Mostra dell'arte antica senese*). Giuliano Catoni's book on Bargagli Petrucci mentions the plans to redo Siena's roads.

Faluschi discusses the vibrant life of Fontebranda in his *Breve relazione*, page 223. For the fountains, Fabio Bargagli Petrucci's work (*Le fonti di Siena e i loro acquedotti*) remains valuable, but also see the Associazione La Diana's works (with fascinating nineteenth- and twentieth-century photos). The Museo dell'Acqua at Fonte di Pescaia has a lively interactive exhibit showing what some of the fountains looked like. For a while there were efforts to have "speaking fountains" at Fontebranda, with catchy phrases and reminiscences from "medieval" people; the attempt has been discontinued.

Leon Battista Alberti mentions Brunelleschi's Duomo in the preface of *On Painting*.

CHAPTER FIVE

For the Pinacoteca, see the handy guide *Pinacoteca Nazionale: Itinerari*, and Timothy Hyman's *Sienese Painting*. Both have detailed descriptions of the Martini altarpiece of Sant'Agostino. Pier Pettinaio is mentioned in *Purgatorio* in connection with Sapia, while Colombini's story is told in the little tale by the fifteenth-century Florentine dramatist and writer Feo Belcari. Hyman's quotation on Superman is on page 59.

On Catherine of Siena's life, see Noffke's introduction to the *Letters*, as well as the life by Raymond of Capua. My *Reclaiming Catherine* talks about her as a writer of lucid and inventive Italian prose. A Florentine archbishop, Antonio Pierozzi, encouraged the creation of the tomb in Santa Maria sopra Minerva; he wrote his own short life of Catherine in 1461, when she was canonized. On the Casa di Santa Caterina, see Roberto Sabelli, *Il santuario-casa di Santa Caterina*. The competing stories about the crucifix being brought to Siena as a result of theft—or not—are alluded to in Faluschi, *Breve relazione*. For Catherine's letters, see Noffke's translation; the allusion to Saint Anthony leaving the woods is Letter T328, in volume 4, pages 78–79. Her letters to Andrea Vanni are T358, T363, and T366, all in volume 4.

Bernardino da Siena's life has been captured in lively prose by Maria Sticco. She records, among many other things, the objects found on his body when he died in L'Aquila; she also refers to his sign of Christ as a symbol of "youth, fecundity, and love." Bernadette Paton, *Preaching Friars and the Civic Ethos*, and Cynthia Polecritti, *Preaching Peace in Renaissance Italy*, have both written excellent books on the role of Bernardino's preaching and of the Franciscans more generally in fifteenth-century Italy. A recent monograph by Franco Mormando, *The Preacher's Demons*, focuses on his attacks on usurers, sodomites, and heretics. The sermon on usury is taken from his 1425 sermons in Florence. There is regrettably no good English translation of his sermons; a nineteenth-century translation (using "thou" and "thee") is available online. Felice Alessio's quotation is from *Storia di San Bernardino*; he also cites Eugene's papal bull. For Vecchietta's *arliqueria*, see Henk Van Os, *Vecchietta and the Sacristy of the Siena Hospital Church*.

For the area around San Francesco, see Ilaria Bichi Ruspoli's essay in *Fortificare con arte*, as well as the *Stradario* for street names. The call for workers for Fonte di Follonica is found on page 127 of the Ruspoli. For Francesco di Giorgio's contracts with the church of San Francesco and the proposals to bring him back, as well as other useful details about his life, see Giustina Scaglia, *Francesco di Giorgio: Checklist and History of Manuscripts and Drawings in Autographs and Copies.* The story of San Francesco and its mistreatment in the twentieth century is alluded to in most guidebooks; see Piero Torriti, *Tutta Siena*, as one example.

Beccafumi has been the subject of a number of monographs, starting with Giorgio Vasari's account of his life in his *Lives of the Artists.* Enzo Carli has a comprehensive essay on him in his *Pittori senesi*, which the quotation about light comes from. For the city's gates, see Ettore Pellegrini's *Fortificare con arte.* The Teatro dei Rinnovati, whose reopening was celebrated in 2009, is the subject of a stupendous coffee-table book, *Storia e restauri del Teatro dei Rinnovati di Siena*; my thanks to Antonio Tizzani for the splendid tour of the theater as well as for a copy of the book.

Tozzi's two great novels are still awaiting an English translator. His citations on Catherine are from his anthology of Catherine's letters (online), while references to his Roman sojourn are from Barzanti's essay in Santi and Strinati's *Siena e Roma.* Mario Luzi's poetry, on the other hand, has been translated into English, although by no means all of it. His poems on Siena, along with his essay, are collected in the 1990 volume titled *Siena e dintorni* (Siena and surroundings); his lines from the *Earthly and Heavenly Journey of Simone Martini* (in the translation of Luigi Bonaffini) are on page 251. Stefano Bisi's musings on Luzi's defense of the Palio can be found online at his website: http://www.stefanobisi.it/?p=4437. Luzi's *Parole pellegrine* contains his questions about being both accomplice and stranger, on the opening page.

The Bartolo di Fredi altarpiece came to New York accompanied by a catalog as well as a very helpful brochure. There it was reunited with the predella for the first time in several hundred years. That the women in the panel are Dominicans is of some interest, given the Dominicans' itinerancy; one would like to imagine that one of the unidentified Dominican women in Bartolo's panels is Catherine herself, lifting her hands for the stigmata. On the reconstruction of the altarpiece, see the work of Bruce Boucher and Francesca Fiorani, the two curators for the exhibition *Bartoli di Fredi.*

AFTERWORDS

The Steve McCurry exhibition was in the Spedale from April through October 2013. For the things that pilgrims left, see Piccinni's essay in *Siena e Roma*, titled "Ritratti di pellegrini diretti a Roma nell'Ospedale di Santa Maria della Scala di Siena nel tardo medioevo." For orphans and their identifying marks, see *Gettatelli e Pellegrini* by Alessandro Orlandini.

Barzanti's article appeared in the *Corriere della Sera* on June 26, 2013. The architects and architectural historians who find Siena interesting as a space for civic responsiveness include Spiro Kostof (*The City Shaped*) and Peter Rowe (*Civic Realism*).

As it turned out, two months after my visit in September 2013, Siena did make the cut. November 2014, however, saw the honor of the next Italian city to become a European Capital of Culture going to Macerata. That same month, three former administrators of the Monte dei Paschi were sentenced to jail terms and the bank's deficit grew to five billion euros. The bank itself is formally up for sale. There will be no easy fixes for Siena. But given all that it has confronted over the centuries, it will surely discover new ways to adapt.

Bibliography

Alberti, Leon Battista. *On Painting*. Translated by John R. Spencer. New Haven, CT: Yale University Press, 1956.

Alessio, Felice. *Storia di San Bernardino e del suo tempo*. Mondovì: Graziano, 1899.

Alighieri, Dante. *The Divine Comedy*. Translated by Alan Mandelbaum. Berkeley: University of California Press, 1980–82.

———. *The Divine Comedy*. Translated and annotated by Charles S. Singleton. Princeton, NJ: Princeton University Press, 1970–75.

Ascani, Valerio. *Pinacoteca Nazionale, Siena: Itinerari*. Rome: Istituto Poligrafico e Zecca dello Stato, 1997.

Ascheri, Mario. *Lo spazio storico di Siena*. Siena: Fondazione Monte dei Paschi di Siena, 2002.

Ascheri, Mario, and Donatella Ciampoli. *Siena e il suo territorio nel Rinascimento*. Siena: Il Leccio, 1986.

Associazione La Diana. *L'acqua di Siena: Dai bottini medievali all'acquedotto del Vivo*. Illustrations by Alessandro Andreucetti. Sociville: Ticci, 2005.

———. *A ritrovar La Diana*. Siena: Alsaba, 2001.

Bacci, Michele, ed. *Iconografia evangelica a Siena dalle origini al Concilio di Trento*. Siena: Monte dei Paschi, 2009.

Bagatti, Corinna, and Marta Brignali. *Guida del pellegrino in terra di Siena: Sei itinerari*. Siena: Alsaba, 1999.

Balestracci, Duccio. *Il potere e la parola: Guida al Costituto Volgarizzato di Siena*. Siena: Protagon, 2011.

Banchi, Luciano, and Scipione Borghesi. *Nuovi documenti per la storia dell'arte senese*. Siena: Torrini, 1898.

Banchieri e mercanti di Siena. Preface by Carlo Maria Cipolla. Texts by Franco Cardini et al. Siena: Monte dei Paschi di Siena, 1987.

Bandini, Antonio Francesco. *Notizie sulle Contrade e sul Palio*. 1838. Preface by Roberto Barzanti. Reprinted, Siena: Contrada della Tartuca, 2009.

Barbagli, Debora, and Giuseppina Carlotta Cianferoni. *Siena, Santa Maria della Scala: Guida al Museo Archeologico*. Milan: Silvana, 2008.

Bargagli, Scipione. *Delle lodi dell'accademie: Orazione di Scipione Bargagli da lui recitata nell'Accademia degli Accesi in Siena*. Florence: Bonetto, 1589.

———. *I Trattenimenti*. Rome: Salerno, 1991.

———. *Il Turamino: Ovvero del parlare e dello scrivere sanese*. Siena, 1602.

Bargagli Petrucci, Fabio. *Le fonti di Siena e i loro acquedotti*. Siena: Olschki, 1906.

Barzanti, Roberto. "Appunti per un itinerario romano. Lo scrittore e la santa." In *Siena e Roma*, edited by Bruno Santi and Claudio Strinati, 454-64. Siena: Protagon, 2008.

Barzanti, Roberto, Alberto Cornice, and Ettore Pellegrini. *Iconografia di Siena: Rappresentazione della città dal XIII al XIX secolo*. Siena: Monte dei Paschi di Siena, 2006.

Belcari, Feo. *I primi compagni del B. Giovanni Colombini*. Bari: Paoline, n.d.

Belli, Maddalena, et al. *La cucina di un ospedale del Trecento*. Pisa: Pacini, 2004.

Bellosi, Luciano. *L'oro di Siena: Il tesoro di Santa Maria della Scala*. Milan: Skira, 1996.

———. *Francesco di Giorgio e il Rinascimento a Siena, 1450–1500*. Milan: Electa, 1993.

Benvoglienti, Bartolomeo. *Trattato de l'origine et accrescimento della città di Siena*. Translated by Fabio Benvoglienti. Rome: G. degli Angeli, 1571.

Bernardino da Siena. *Prediche volgare sul Campo di Siena, 1427*. Edited by Carlo Delcorno. 2 vols. Milan: Rusconi, 1989.

Betti, Luca, and Vincenzo Coli. *Il cielo sopra le terre di Siena: 158 fotografie aeree raccontano la storia e l'ambiente./The Sky above Siena and Its Territory: History and Environment in 158 Photographs*. Siena: Betti, n.d.

Bezzini, Mario. *Storia della via Francigena: Dai Longobardi ai Giubilei*. Siena: Il Leccio, 1998.

Biliorsi, Massimo. *Siena: Le stagioni del Palio*. Siena: Il Leccio, 2013.

Blashfield, Edwin H., and Evangeline W. Blashfield. *Italian Cities*. New York: Scribner's, 1912.

Borghini, Gabriele. "Splendore simultaneo del Palio di Siena." *Accademia dei Rozzi* 16 (2009): 69–73.

Boucher, Bruce, and Francesca Fiorani. *Bartoli di Fredi*. "*The Adoration of the Magi*": *A Masterpiece Reconstructed*. Charlottesville: University of Virginia Art Museum, 2012.

Bowsky, William M. "The Impact of the Black Death upon Sienese Government and Society." *Speculum* 39 (1964): 1–34.

———. *A Medieval Italian Commune: Siena under the Nine, 1287–1355*. Berkeley: University of California Press, 1981.

Brandi, Cesare. *Duccio*. Edited by Mauro Civai. Siena: Protagon, 2007.

———. *Pittura a Siena nel Trecento*. Turin: Einaudi, 1991.

Brilli, Attillio. *Viaggiatori stranieri in terra di Siena*. Siena, 1986.

Burckhardt, Jacob. *The Civilization of the Renaissance in Italy*. New York: Harper, 1958.

Burckhardt, Titus. *Siena Città della Vergine*. Milan: Archè, 1977.

Cacciorgna, Marilena, and Roberto Guerrini. *Il pavimento del Duomo di Siena: L'arte della tarsia marmorea dal XIV al XIX secolo*. Milan: Silvana, 2004.

Caferro, William. *Mercenary Companies and the Decline of Siena*. Baltimore: Johns Hopkins University Press, 1998.

Caggese, Romolo. *La repubblica di Siena e il suo contado nel secolo decimoterzo*. Sala Bolognese: Forni, 1983.

Cambi, Carlo. *Una gemma preziosa: L'Oratorio della Santissima Trinità*. Poggibonsi: Tap Grafiche, 2012.

Cammarosano, Paolo. *Siena: Il medioevo nelle città italiane*. Spoleto: Centro Italiano di Studi Sull'Alto Medioevo, 2009.

Campbell, C. Jean. *The Commonwealth of Nature: Art and Poetic Community in the Age of Dante*. University Park: Pennsylvania State University Press, 2008.

Canestrelli, Antonio, and Italo Moretti. *L'architettura medieval a Siena e il suo antico territorio*. Florence: Libreria Chiari, 2004.

Cantini, Federico. *Archeologia urbana a Siena: L'area dell'Ospedale di Santa Maria della Scala prima dell'Ospedale*. Siena: Università di Siena, 2005.

Cardini, Antonio. *Storia di Siena dal Risorgimento al miracolo economico*. Florence: Nerbini, 2009.

Carli, Enzo. *Il Duomo di Siena e il Museo dell'Opera*. Florence: Scala, 1976.

———. *I pittori senesi*. Milan: Electa, 1971.

Carlotti, Mariella. *Ante gradus: Quando la certezza diventa creativa. Gli affreschi del Pellegrinaio di Santa Maria della Scala a Siena*. Florence: Società Editrice Fiorentina, 2011.

———. *Il cuore di Siena: La "Maestà" di Duccio di Buoninsegna*. Florence: Società Editrice Fiorentina, 2007.

Carniani, Alessandra. *I Salimbeni quasi una signoria*. Siena: Protagon, 1995.

La Misericordia di Siena attraverso i secoli. Edited by Mario Ascheri and Patrizia Turrini. Siena: Protagon, 2004.

Catherine of Siena. *The Dialogue*. Translated by Suzanne Noffke. Mahwah, NJ: Paulist Press, 1980.

———. *Letters*. Translated by Suzanne Noffke. 4 vols. Tempe, AZ: Medieval and Renaissance Texts, 2001-11.

Catoni, Giuliano. *Il fiero podestà: Fabio Bargagli-Petrucci e il patrimonio di Siena*. Siena: Protagon, 2010.

Catoni, Giuliano, and Gabriella Piccinni. *Storia illustrata di Siena*. Pisa: Pacini, 2007.

Cavalca, Domenico. *Vite di santi padri*. 1342. Reprinted, Trieste: Lloyd Austriaco, 1858.

Ceppari Ridolfi, Maria A., Cecilia Papi, and Patrizia Turrini. *La città del Costituto: Siena 1309-10; Il testo e la storia*. Introduction by Mario Ascheri. Siena: Pascal, 2010.

Christiansen, Keith, Laurence Kanter, and Carl Brandon Strehlke. *Painting in Renaissance Siena, 1420-1500*. New York: Abrams, 1988.

Civai, Mauro, and Enrico Toti. *Siena, il "sogno gotico": Nuova guida alla città*. Siena: Alsaba, 1992.

Clemente, Pietro, and Paolo De Simonis. *Visibili tracce: Civiltà della terra in Toscana nei 150 anni*. Photographs by Giovanni Santi. Rome: Effigi, 2011.

Cohn, Samuel. *Death and Property in Siena, 1205-1800*. Baltimore: Johns Hopkins University Press, 1988.

Coscarella, Giuseppina. *La grancia di Cuna in Val d'Arbia: Un esempio di fattoria fortificata medievale*. Florence: Salimbeni, 1983.

Il Costituto del Comune di Siena volgarizzato nel MCCCIX-MCCCX. Edited by Mahmoud Salem Elsheikh. 4 vols. Siena: Fondazione Monte dei Paschi di Siena, 2002.

Cresti, Roberto, and Maura Martellucci. *Stradario/StraNario: Storia, curiosità e stranezze nei toponimi di Siena*. Siena: Betti, 2007.

Cust, Robert H. Hobart. *The Pavement Masters of Siena (1369-1562)*. London: George Bell, 1901.

D'Ascia, Luca, and Enzo Meccaci, eds. *Conferenze su Pio II nel sesto centenario della nascita di Enea Silvio Piccolomini*. Siena: Accademia Senese degli Intronati, 2006.

Dickens, Charles. *Pictures from Italy*. Edited by Kate Flint. London: Penguin, 1998.

Dini, Giulietta Chelazzi, Alessandro Angelini, and Bernardina Sani. *Pittura senese*. Milan: Motta, 1997.

Douglas, Robert Langton. *A History of Siena*. London, 1902.

Dundes, Alan, and Alessandro Falassi. *La Terra in Piazza: An Interpretation of the Palio of Siena*. Berkeley: University of California Press, 1975.

Eisenbichler, Konrad. *The Sword and the Pen: Women, Politics, and Poetry in Sixteenth-Century Siena*. Notre Dame, IN: University of Notre Dame Press, 2012.

English, Edward D. *Enterprise and Liability in Sienese Banking, 1230–1350*. Cambridge, MA: Medieval Academy of America, 1988.

Falassi, Alessandro, and Giuliano Catoni. *Palio*. Siena: Monte dei Paschi di Siena, 1982.

Falletti-Fossati, Carlo. *Costumi senesi nella seconda metà del secolo XIV*. Siena: Bargellini, 1881.

Faluschi, Giovacchino. *Breve relazione delle cose notabili della Città di Siena*. Siena: Francesco Rossi, 1784.

Frugoni, Chiara, ed. *Pietro e Ambrogio Lorenzetti*. Firenze: Le Lettere, n.d.

Gabrielli, Fabio. *Ospedale di Santa Maria della Scala: Ricerche storiche, archeologiche e storico-artistiche*. Siena: Protagon, 2011.

———. "Architetture di strada." In *Siena e Roma: Raffaello, Caravaggio e i protagonisti di un legame antico*, edited by Bruno Santi and Claudio Strinati, 226–33. Siena: Protagon, 2008.

Galli, Letizia. *In viaggio nel Quattrocento: Guida al Rinascimento nelle terre di Siena*. Milan: Silvana, 2010.

Gattoni, Maurizio. *Pandolfo Petrucci e la politica estera della repubblica di Siena (1487–1512)*. Siena: Cantagalli, 1997.

Gazzei, Euro. *Da Trombicche. . . . una sera di giovedì*. Siena: Il Leccio, 1996.

Gigli, Girolamo. *Diario senese*. 2 vols. Siena, 1854.

Gilbert, Felix. *The Pope, His Banker, and Venice*. Cambridge, MA: Harvard University Press, 1980.

Grassi, Virgilio. *Le contrade di Siena e le loro feste: Il Palio attuale*. 5th ed. Siena: Periccioli, 1987.

Guerrini, Roberto. *Sotto il Duomo di Siena: Scoperte archeologiche, architettoniche e figurative*. Milan: Silvana, 2003.

Gurrieri, Francesco. *La sede storica del Monte dei Paschi di Siena*. Siena: Le Monnier, 1988.

Harris, Lis. "Annals of Intrigue: The Palio." *New Yorker*, June 5, 1989, 83–104.

Harvey, Thomas. "Siena/Sustainability: The Quintessential Hilltown." http://www.terrain.org/articles/20/harvey.htm.

Herbert, Zbigniew. "Siena." In *The Collected Prose, 1948–1998*, edited by Alissa Valles, 46–75. New York: Ecco, 2010.

Hook, Judith. *Siena: A City and Its History*. London: Scolar Press, 1980.

Hyman, Timothy. *Sienese Painting*. London: Thames and Hudson, 2003.

Israëls, Machtelt. "Altars on the Street: The Arte della Lana, the Carmelites and the Feast of Corpus Domini in Siena 1356–1456." In *Beyond the Palio*, edited by Philippa Jackson and Fabrizio Nevola. Special issue of *Renaissance Studies* 20, no. 2 (April 2006).

———. "New Documents for Sassetta and Sano di Pietro at the Porta Romana, Siena." *Burlington Magazine* 140, no. 1144 (July 1998): 435–44.

Jackson, Philippa, and Fabrizio Nevola, eds. *Beyond the Palio: Urbanism and Ritual in Renaissance Siena*. Special issue of *Renaissance Studies* 20, no. 2 (April 2006).

Kostof, Spiro. *The City Shaped*. Boston: Little, Brown, 1991.

Kucher, Michael. *The Water Supply System of Siena: The Medieval Roots of the Modern Networked City*. London: Routledge, 2005.

Kupfer, Marcia. "The Lost Wheel Map of Ambrogio Lorenzetti." *Art Bulletin* 78, no. 2 (1996): 286–310.

Ladner, Gerhardt. "Homo Viator." *Speculum* 42 (1967): 233–59.

Le Goff, Jacques. *The Birth of Purgatory*. Translated by Arthur Goldhammer. Chicago: University of Chicago Press, 1984.

The Little Flowers of Saint Francis. Edited by Beverly Brown. New York: Doubleday, 1958.

Luzi, Mario. *Earthly and Heavenly Journey of Simone Martini*. Translated by Luigi Bonaffini. Copenhagen: Green Integer, 2003.

———. *Parole pellegrine*. Naples: Pironti, 1991.

———. *Siena e dintorni: Poesie e prose*. Edited by Carlo Fini. Siena: Il Leccio, 1996.

MacAdam, Alta. *Blue Guide: Tuscany*. London: Somerset, 2009.

Macchia, Giovanni. *Il pellegrinaggio medievale a Lucca*. Pisa: Pacini, 2009.

Maginnis, Hayden. *The World of the Early Sienese Painter*. University Park: Pennsylvania State University Press, 2001.

La Magna e Trionfante Festa et Chiaccia che si fece nel inclita città di Siena nel-lanno MCCCCCVI adi XV d'Agosto. Siena, 1506.

Malavolti, Orlando. *Dell'historia di Siena.* Venice, 1599.

Martini, Giuseppe. "Siena da Montaperti alla caduta dei Nove." *Bulletino Senese di Storia e Patria* 68 (1961): 75–128.

Mazzi, Carlo. *La Congrega dei Rozzi.* 2 vols. Florence: Le Monnier, 1882.

McCarthy, Mary. *The Stones of Florence.* New York: Harcourt, Brace, 1959.

Meiss, Millard. *Painting in Florence and Siena after the Black Death.* Princeton, NJ: Princeton University Press, 1951.

La memoria dell'acqua: I bottini di Siena. Edited by Roberta Ferri. Siena: Comune di Siena, 2006.

Ministero per i beni culturali e ambientali. *Le biccherne: Tavole dipinte delle magistrature senesi.* Rome, 1984.

Minucci, Giovanni, and Leo Kosuta. *Lo studio di Siena nei secoli XIV–XVI.* Milan: Giuffré, 1989.

Moretti, Italo. "La Via Francigena: Una strada per Roma." In *Siena e Roma: Raffaello, Caravaggio e i protagonisti di un legame antico,* edited by Bruno Santi and Claudio Strinati, 218–33. Siena: Protagon, 2008.

Mormando, Franco. *The Preacher's Demons: Bernardino of Siena and the Social Underworld of Early Renaissance Italy.* Chicago: University of Chicago Press, 1999.

Mucciarelli, Roberta. *I Tolomei banchieri di Siena.* Siena: Protagon, 1995.

Nardi, Paolo. "Origini e sviluppo della Casa della Misericordia." In *La Misericordia di Siena attraverso i secoli: Dalla Domus Misericordiae all'Arciconfraternità di Misericordia,* edited by Mario Ascheri and Patrizia Turrini. Siena: Protagon, 2004.

Nevola, Fabrizio. *Siena: Constructing the Renaissance City.* New Haven, CT: Yale University Press, 2007.

———. "Lots of Napkins and a Few Surprises: Francesco di Giorgio Martini's House, Goods, and Social Standing in Late Fifteenth-Century Siena." *Annali di Archittetura* 18–19 (2006–7): 71–82.

Norman, Diana. *Painting in Late Medieval and Renaissance Siena.* New Haven, CT: Yale University Press, 2003.

———. "*Santi Cittadini*: Vecchietta and the Civic Pantheon in Mid-Fifteenth-Century Siena." In *Art as Politics in Late Medieval and Renaissance Siena,* edited by Timothy B. Smith and Judith Steinhoff, 115–40. London: Ashgate, 2012.

————. *Siena and the Virgin: Art and Politics in a Late Medieval City-State*. New Haven, CT: Yale University Press, 1999.

————, ed. *Siena, Florence, and Padua: Art, Society, and Religion, 1280–1400*. 2 vols. New Haven, CT: Yale University Press, 1995.

Ohly, Friedrich. *Sensus Spiritualis: Studies in Medieval Significs and the Philology of Culture*. Translated by Kenneth J. Northcott. Chicago: University of Chicago Press, 2005.

Origo, Iris. *War in the Val d'Orcia 1943–4: A Diary*. Boston: Godine, 1984.

Orlandini, Alessandro. *Gettatelli e pellegrini: Gli affreschi nella sala del Pellegrinaio dell'Ospedale di Santa Maria della Scala di Siena*. Siena: Nuova Immagine, 1997.

————. *Piccola storia di Siena*. Siena: Salvietti e Barabuffi, 2011.

Parsons, Gerald. *Siena, Civil Religion and the Sienese*. London: Ashgate, 2004.

Paton, Bernadette. *Preaching Friars and the Civic Ethos*. London: Centre for Medieval Studies, 1992.

Pecci, Giovanni Antonio. *Lo stato di Siena antico e moderno*. Edited by Mario de Gregorio and Doriano Mazzini. Siena: Accademia Senese degli Intronati, 2008.

Pellegrini, Ettore. *Fortificare con arte: Mura, porte, e fortezze di Siena nella storia*. Siena: Betti, 2012.

Pellegrini, Fabio. *Pienza: Il sogno dell'umanista*. Arezzo: L'Etruria, 1995.

Pellegrini, Michele. "Attorno all''economia della salvezza': Note su restituzione d'usura, pratica pastorale, ed esercizio della carità in una vicenda senese." In *Fedeltà ghibellina, affari guelfi*, edited by Gabriella Piccinni,2:395–446. Pisa: Pacini, 2008.

————. *La comunità ospedaliera di Santa Maria della Scala e il suo più antico statuto*. Pisa: Pacini, 2005.

Pertici, Petra. *La città magnificata: Interventi edilizi a Siena nel rinascimento*. Siena: Il Leccio, 1995.

————. *Siena Quattrocentesca: Gli anni del Pellegrinaio nell'Ospedale di Santa Maria della Scala*. Siena: Protagon, 2012.

Pesciolini, Giulio Venerosi. "La strada francigena nel contado di Siena nei secoli XIII-XIV." *La Diana* 8 (1933): 116–56.

Petrarch, Francesco. *Petrarch's Lyric Poems: The Rime Sparse and Other Lyrics*. Translated by Robert Durling. Cambridge, MA: Harvard University Press, 1976.

Pianta della Città di Firenze, eseguita da Don Stefano Bonsignori, Monteolivetano, nel 1584. Florence, 1584.

Piccinni, Gabriella. *Il Banco dell'Ospedale di Santa Maria della Scala e il mercato del denaro nella Siena del Trecento*. Siena: Pacini, 2012.

———. *Città murata, città globale*. Siena: Salvietti e Barabuffi, 2011.

———. *Fedeltà ghibellina, affari guelfi*. 2 vols. Pisa: Pacini, 2008.

———. "Ritratti di Pellegrini diretti a Roma nell'ospedale di Santa Maria della Scala di Siena nel tardo medioevo." In *Siena e Roma: Raffaello, Caravaggio e i protagonisti di un legame antico*, edited by Bruno Santi and Claudio Strinati, 235–45. Siena: Protagon, 2008.

Piccini, Gabriella, and Lucia Travaini. *Il libro del Pellegrino (Siena 1382–1440)*. Naples: Liguori, 2003.

Pieri, Marzia. *Lo Strascino da Siena e la sua opera poetica e teatrale*. Florence: ETS, 2009.

Pius II. *Commentaries*. Edited and translated by Margaret Meserve and Marcello Simonetta. 2 vols. Cambridge, MA: Harvard University Press, 2009.

Polecritti, Cynthia. *Preaching Peace in Renaissance Italy: Bernardino of Siena and His Audience*. Washington, DC: Catholic University Press of America, 2000.

Polzer, Joseph. "Andrea di Bonaiuto's Via Veritatis and Dominican Thought in Late Medieval Italy." *Art Bulletin* 77 (1995): 262–89.

Raymond of Capua. *The Life of Catherine of Siena*. Wilmington, DE: Glazier, 1980.

Redon, Odile. *L'espace d'une cité: Sienne et le pays siennois*. Rome: École Française de Rome, 1994.

Ricci, Corrado, ed. *Mostra dell'antica arte senese. Aprile–agosto 1904. Catalogo generale illustrato*. Siena: Istituto dei Sordo-muti di L. Lazzeri, 1904.

Rowe, Peter. *Civic Realism*. Cambridge, MA: MIT Press, 1997.

Rowland, Ingrid. "'Render unto Caesar the Things Which Are Caesar's': Humanism and the Arts in the Patronage of Agostino Chigi." *Renaissance Quarterly* 39 (1986): 673–740.

Ruspoli, Ilaria Bichi. "Da Porta Ovile a Santo Spirito." In *Fortificare con arte*, edited by Ettore Pellegrini, 120–27. Siena: Betti, 2012.

Sabelli, Roberto. *Il santuario-casa di Santa Caterina*. Florence: Alinea, 2002.

Salimei, Franco. *I Salimbeni di Siena*. Rome: Editalia, 1986.

Santi, Bruno, and Claudio Strinati. *Siena e Roma: Raffaello, Caravaggio e i protagonisti di un legame antico*. Siena: Protagon, 2008.

Saunders, Frances. *The Devil's Broker: Seeking Gold, God, and Glory in Fifteenth-Century Italy*. London: Faber and Faber, 2004.

Scaglia, Giustina. *Francesco di Giorgio: Checklist and History of Manuscripts and Drawings in Autographs and Copies*. Bethlehem, PA: Lehigh University Press, 1992.

La sede storica del Monte dei Paschi di Siena: Vicende costruttive e opere d'arte.
Siena: Monte dei Paschi di Siena, 1988.

Seidel, Max, et al. *Le arti a Siena nel primo Rinascimento: Da Jacopo della Quercia a Donatello.* Milan: Motta, 2010.

Serino, Vinicio. *Siena e l'acqua: Storia e immagini di una città e delle sue fonti.* Siena: Nuova Immagine, 1998.

Sestan, Ernesto. "Siena avanti Montaperti." *Bulletino Senese di Storia e Patria* 68 (1961): 151–92.

Siena Città dell'Acqua. CV/DVD. Siena: Comune di Siena and Banca Monte dei Paschi di Siena.

Siena e il suo territorio. Siena: Istituto dei Sordo-muti L. Lazzeri, 1862.

Skinner, Quentin. "Ambrogio Lorenzetti's *Buon Governo* Frescoes: Two Old Questions, Two New Answers." *Journal of the Warburg and Courtauld Institutes* 62 (1999): 1–28.

Smith, T. B. "Alberto Aringhieri and the Chapel of St. John the Baptist: Patronage, Politics, and the Cult of Relics in Renaissance Siena." PhD diss., Florida State University, 2002.

Smith, Timothy B., and Judith Steinhoff, eds. *Art as Politics in Late Medieval and Renaissance Siena.* London: Ashgate, 2012.

Soldani, Ambrogio. *Relazione del terremoto accaduto in Siena il di 26 maggio.* Siena, 1798.

Sordini, Beatrice. *Dentro l'antico Ospedale: Santa Maria della Scala, uomini, cose, e spazi di vita nella Siena medievale.* Siena: Protagon, 2010.

———. *Il porto della "Gente vana": Lo scalo di Talamone tra il secolo XIII e il secolo XV.* Siena: Protagon, 2000.

Starn, Randolph. *Ambrogio Lorenzetti: The Palazzo Pubblico.* New York: George Braziller, 1994.

Starn, Randolph, and Loren Partridge. *Arts of Power: Three Halls of State in Italy, 1300–1600.* Berkeley: University of California Press, 1992.

Sticco, Maria. *Pensiero e poesia in San Bernardino da Siena.* Milan: Vita e Pensiero, 1945.

Stopani, Renato. *La Via Francigena nel Senese: Storia e territorio.* Florence: Salimbeni, 1985.

Susi, Eugenio. *San Galgano e l'eremita cortese.* Spoleto: Centro Italiano di Studi sull'Alto Medioevo, 1993.

Syson, Luke, ed. *Renaissance Siena: Art for a City.* London: National Gallery, 2007.

Szabò, Thomas, and Donatella Ciampoli. *Viabilità e legislazione di uno stato cit-*

tadino del Duecento: Lo Statuto dei Viari di Siena (1290–99). Siena: Accademia Senese degli Intronati, 1992.

Taddei, Michele. *Scandalosa Siena: Dalla vicenda MPS alla crisi politica*. Siena: Cantagalli, 2013.

Thompson, Daniel V. *The Materials and Techniques of Medieval Painting*. New York: Dover, 1956.

Tommaseo, Niccolò, and Bernardo Bellini. *Dizionario della lingua italiana*. Turin: UTET, 1861–79.

Tornabuoni de' Medici, Lucrezia. *Sacred Narratives*. Translated by Jane Tylus. Chicago: University of Chicago Press, 2001.

Torriti, Piero. *Tutta Siena contrada per contrada*. Florence: Bonechi, 1954.

———. *Pienza: la città del Rinascimento italiano*. Genoa: Sagep, 1979.

Toyama, Koichi. "*La fuga in Egitto* di Giovanni di Paolo riesaminata: Luce, ombre portate." *Bulletino Senese di Storia e Patria* 103 (1996): 477–90.

Tozzi, Federigo. *Bestie*. With illustrations by Antonio Possenti. Siena: Università degli Studi di Siena, 2007.

Trifone, Pietro, ed. *Commedie rusticali senesi del Cinquecento*. Siena: Betti, 2004.

Turrini, Patrizia. *La comunità ebraica di Siena: I documenti dell'Archivio di Stato dal Medioevo alla Restaurazione*. Siena: Pascal, 2008.

———. *Per honore et utile de la città di Siena: Il Comune e l'edilizia nel Quattrocento*. Siena: Tipografia Senese, 1997.

Tylus, Jane. *Reclaiming Catherine of Siena: Literacy, Literature, and the Signs of Others*. Chicago: University of Chicago Press, 2009.

Van Os, Henk W. *Vecchietta and the Sacristy of the Siena Hospital Church*. New York: Schram, 1974.

Vasari, Giorgio. *Le vite dei più eccellenti pittori, sculturi, et architteturi*. Edited by Gaetano Milanesi. Florence: Sansoni, 1906.

Vigni, Laura, and Ettore Vio. *Storia e restauri del Teatro dei Rinnovati di Siena: Dal consiglio della Campana al salone delle commedie*. Siena: Pacini, 2010.

Violante di Baviera. *Bando per le contrade di Siena*. Siena, 1730.

Waley, Daniel. *Siena and the Sienese in the Thirteenth Century*. Cambridge: Cambridge University Press, 1991.

White, John. *Duccio: Tuscan Art and the Medieval Workshop*. London: Thames and Hudson, 1979.

Zdekauer, Lodovico. "Il mercante senese nel Dugento." Paper presented at the Accademia dei Rozzi. Siena: Lazzeri, 1925.

———. *La vita privata e pubblica dei senesi nel Dugento*. 1896. Reprinted, Siena: Arnoldo Forni, 2004.

Index

88–92, 94, 105, 108–10, 123–24, 128–29, 134–36, 139–41, 143–44, 146–47, 158–59, 162–64, 166, 170, 172–74, 176–78, 181–91, 193–95, 198, 208; as city of color, 40–42, 47; cloth in, 98; collective ingenuity in, 149–51; comings and goings, preoccupation of in, 110, 129; commercial societies in, 129; Comune, 32, 128, 133, 151, 158, 188; *condottieri*, 57; constitution in, 161–62; *contrade* of, 5, 131–35, 141, 148–49, 152–56, 159, 163–64, 166, 188, 190, 208; countryside, relations with, 116–21; Crete Senesi, 121–22, 126, 197; culinary innovations in, 60; disorientation in, feelings of, 18–20; earthquakes, 17–18, 21, 113, 194; emblems, 160; Etruscan encampments, 28; factionalism in, 181; Florence, enmity between, 104; Fortezza Medicea, 14, 48, 160; founding of, 29; fountains in, 18–19, 32, 34, 37–40, 62, 77, 143, 146, 163–67, 178, 188–89, gardens in, 47–49, 149, 172; gates of, 4, 28, 61–62, 66, 71, 104, 140–41, 173, 184, 188–89, 194–97; geology of, 19–20; goldsmiths (*orefici*), 66, 91; *grance* (granaries), systems of, 117–20, 223; green spaces of, 47; guilds of, 46, 151; highwaymen, 57; hills of, 27–29, 32; hospitality of, 63, 71, 78, 148; hospitals in, 9–11, 13–14, 19, 28, 40, 43, 49, 60, 71, 75–84, 86, 88, 90, 97, 99, 104, 107, 110, 117–20, 135–36, 140, 143–44, 148–49, 151, 161, 169, 173, 186–87, 191–94, 196–97, 207–8; idea of itself, 30; identity of, 160–61; Il Divo (restaurant), 23, 30;

importance of, 55–56; individuals, suspicion of in, 151; innovation in, 8; Itinera bookshop, 2; and Jesus, 112; Jewish ghettos in, 107, 109, 146, 160–61; Jewish population in, 33, 105, 108–10; Jews, banning of, 108; Jews, lynching of, 109; lands outside, as dependent on, 27; language of, 161; leprosy, 82; Loggia della Mercanzia, 101–2; Madonna del Voto, as protector of, 89; Il Magnifico Panificio, 6; maps of, 21–23, 25, 27; Mary, as patron and defender of, 42–46; Mercato Rionale, 61; Mercato Vecchio, 196; Misericordia, Archconfraternity of, 86, 144, 146–49, 172, 178, 197; moneylending in, 98–99, 109; money practices in, 101–2, 110, 113, 115, 125–26; Monte dei Paschi, 6, 102–6, 109–10, 115, 185, 205, 208; *murellos* (ancient walls), 139; museums in, 25, 28, 30, 41–42, 71–72, 76, 83, 86, 89, 112–15, 121, 144, 147, 155, 162, 164–65, 169–70, 179, 185–87, 193–94, 197, 201, 203; *notte bianca* ("white night"), 64; Nove (Nine), 150–51, 161, 181; as obligatory stopping place, 99; palaces in, 1–3, 7, 11, 27, 40, 43–47, 49, 68, 96, 101, 103–4, 111, 116–17, 119, 123–24, 126, 128–29, 140, 150, 155–58, 160–62, 184, 196, 204; Palio, 5–6, 8, 11, 14, 17, 27, 46, 86, 106, 111, 123, 132–37, 141, 143, 146, 149, 153–61, 163–64, 167, 169, 200–201, 204–5; *passeggiata* (evening stroll), 64; Pesciolini, Giulio Venerosi, 55–56; pilgrims in, 53, 55–56, 60–61, 63–66, 68, 71, 74–75, 79, 81–82, 91, 94, 99,

SIEN

Porta
Camollia

B

D

A

U

ISTRICE

LUPA

C

21

22

12

BRUCO

15 R

6

DRAGO

20

GIRAFFA

E

18

23

25

8

14

OCA

CIVETTA

Banchi di Sopra

26

11

Banchi di Sotto

LEOCORNO

G

9 Q

F

IL CAMPO

10

24

SELVA

19

5

N

27

H

2

P

O

13

7

TORRE

AQUILA

Via di Città

I

1

L

MONTON

4

PANTERA

ONDA

28

17

M

3

J

TARTUCA

CHIOCCIOLA

Porta
Tufi

K